DOUBLE HERITAGE

My Life in Two Worlds

Marie Fiat

Front cover art by Donna Cernak
Author photo by Olan Mills

Please direct all correspondence and book orders to:
Cupcake Valley Press
P. O. Box 634
Easthampton, MA 01027

Library of Congress Catalog Card Number 98-73600

Promotion by Diane Chilson

Published by

Printed in the United States of America

I Dedicate this book
with all my love to:

My Husband
Michel

All My
Daughters

Grandchildren
Great-Grandchildren
to come.

The publication of my book, I have both feared and welcomed.
Feared because everyone will realize my families past.
Welcomed as it brings together experiences and memories that can bring tears, laughter, and joy to my readers!

The photographs occupy a prominent place in my home and memories in my mind.

Contents

Acknowlegements

To my Birth Siblings who let me into their lives
present and past so I may understand what it was
like for each of them growing up.

Thanks to my husband for it isn't easy to live
with someone who is having an affair with a
book in progress.

My children and grandchildren who treasure and
believe in me were instrumental in the creation
of my book.

Thanks to the LaBarge family for including me and
my new husband in all their family gatherings.

Acknowledgment to all host families special people
who opened their homes to many French students.

Thanks to all my friends, some who read
portions of my manuscript in its evolution
encouraging me to put my life in writing.

Many thanks goes to Ann Henry my adoption search
buddy guiding me in the right direction.

Book doctor's Ed, U of M grad student Alex
for their patience with a fine tooth comb
along with Joy, Joannne, Diane and Donna
grateful for their questions which
helped shape my manuscript.

Sincere thanks to my editor Bill Strange
for not altering the meaning or
intent of my writing.

Many thanks to Ann Hughes
my adoption and doula friend
for guiding me through the intricacies
of book production that proudly represents
the years of effort and love
spent preparing the material.

DOUBLE HERITAGE

Me

Everybody's life is a story filled with facts, feelings and issues. Mine is a double heritage. Born to one set of parents, given up for adoption in 1947 to be raised by a widow. For that reason alone, I think about things that non-adopted people do not. It has affected my birth parents, my adoptive parent, and my entire life.

My children call me the pack-rat. I collect everything from old diaries, newspaper clippings, letters, photographs, cards, scrapbooks, baby books, wedding albums, year books, report cards, awards, birth & marriage & death certificates, funeral booklets, religious records, family Bibles to wills and mortgages. They all fill in important pieces of my life.

My birthmother's depression did not go away. She eventually was forced to give up my siblings and me. A neighbor noticed that we seemed to be left home alone much of the time and often wandered around the streets looking shabby and undernourished. In addition, my siblings fell asleep in class; so the courts intervened and removed us from our birth parents home.

I, Marie Eunice Westcott, am a twin. Mary Unite Westcott died at birth. I am left-handed, easy-going, cheerful, a pleaser with a talkative manner, an easy smile, and the spitting image of Shirley Temple. So folks said. I was child number thirteen of fifteen. During my fourth year, in 1943, I was in four different homes. With my birthmother in Boston, Mrs. Shields in Wakefield, Mrs. Farley in Medford, and Mrs. Pratt in Easthampton, where I spent the rest of my childhood. Talk about bonding. My memories go back to Chapman Avenue, Easthampton, where I was brought at age four.

My birthbrother Roger (who was nine at the time) remembered our trip to Western Massachusetts when he was dropped off at a foster farm for boys in Amherst. He said to me, "All you did for the long ride to my new foster home was cry and cry." At home with my birth family, I was a happy baby, singing all the time. According to the letters written in my file Roger said to me, "Everything will be fine, and started to sing my favorite songs." He thought

I might join in and sing with him for the long ride, but it did not work, I still cried.

The social worker and I pulled up to an eight unit apartment building, with front porches so filled with green trumpet vines, I was unable to see in. I could hardly tell where the door was, since it was windy and had rained like a tropical storm. We entered a large hallway that smelled muggy, with rugged flights of stairs that were dark, scary, and creaked as you walked up to the next floor. My social worker knocked and knocked then said, "They knew we were coming, they must be home."

I felt scared and wanted to run. Finally the door opened and a large-framed, strong looking women with hazel eyes, silver rimed glasses, and black hair frizzed by permanent, stood erect in the doorway. She wore a long housedress with an apron, heavy black laced shoes, and no smile. Behind her was another woman, with a smile on her face, stooped down and beckoned me to come. This same woman held my hand while I slept throughout the night in my fourth home in four years.

My social worker asked, "May we come in?" The woman opened the door wider, so we could enter and I saw two children standing at the very end of a long, dark hallway. I was told by the social worker to call this lady "Grandma".

Grandma, Lillian Bader was born in the year 1886 in Holyoke, Massachusetts. She always dressed and looked the same way. Her father, Casper Carl Bader, born in the year 1854 in Zella Mhehlis, Thuringia, Germany had died at age 74. Casper had been a skilled mechanic and a part-time farmer. Her mother Agusta Johanna Theinert was born in the year 1866 in Pittsfield, Massachusetts. She had died at age sixty in Easthampton. Agusta and Casper Bader had had eight children: Anna, Lillian, Clara, Mable, Edith, Edward, Charles, and George. Their second child Lillian, was my adopted mother. They had many grandchildren and great grandchildren. Both sets of grandparents were farmers from Germany.

Before I was born, my adopted mother, Lillian Bader, married Jessie Horatio Pratt on January 27, 1906. A widower with two children, Elizabeth and Nelson. Mother was twenty years old and Jessie was thirty-three, some thirteen years older. In 1910, they had Edith, and in 1914 a son, Raymond.

By the time I arrived in 1943, Elizabeth, Nelson, and Raymond were already out of the house. My aunts told me that my mother had a hard life. She buried her husband Jessie, on April 2, 1926 and her mother,

Agusta on April 28, 1926 the same month. I was told she slipped into a coma from the emotional shock of the deaths for a short period of time. She said to me, "I heard everything my horrible sisters and brothers said while I recuperated in my bedroom." Apparently what she thought she heard, she was unhappy with. She was a difficult person to understand. As a child hearing these kinds of conversations, I often felt sorry for my mother, as an adult I now understand why her family spoke like they did about her.

When her husband died, Edith was sixteen years old and Raymond was twelve. My mother was left a widow with two children. Edith never married and took care of my mother until her dying days. I know my mother and sister Edith loved me very much, even though they did not seem to show it.

In the early 1900's, social service agencies decided what became of us state wards. It all depended on what period of history we happened to be born in and how lucky we were. Families were large in those days. Maybe not as large as mine, but birth control methods did not exist for the poor and uneducated, and even if they had, few people wanted to use them. Agencies sent out investigators who looked into the character and finances of families who applied for us children. Later the investigators reported how hard we children worked, whether or not we were sent to church on Sunday, given enough food and clothing, and allowed to go to school. The status of children in these families was rather vague. My foster mother was told not to get attached to the foster children, as this might be temporary. We were not exactly servants, but we were not full-fledged members of the family either. The family could discharge us children at any time they found us useless or otherwise unsatisfactory. We children were free to leave - if we did not like the way things were going, if we knew who to speak to and if they believed us.

The first state to pass a law that permitted legal adoption was Massachusetts, with several restrictions, most of them broken in my case. My adopted mother was a widow (single parent adoption was unheard of in 1947), and of age 61 (grandmother age) and the adopted child was to be of the same religion as the adopted parents (which I was not.)

As you have read, there were many regulations not enforced. On the fourteenth day of October in the year one thousand nine hundred and forty-seven, appearing in the newspaper called, Daily Record of

Boston, Massachusetts, was as follows:
COMMONWEALTH   OF   MASSACHUSETTS   Hampshire,
ss.   Probate   Court.   To   all   persons
interested   in   a   petition,   for   adoption   of
MARIE   EUNICE   WESTCOTT,   (me)   of   7   Chapman
Avenue,   Easthampton,   Massachusetts   in   said
county of Hampshire, praying for leave to adopt
said Marie Eunice Westcott, a child of ALFRED
WESTCOTT, formerly of New York City, New York
and of Boston, Massachusetts and MARY HAMBLEN
WESTCOTT, his wife, and that the name of
said child be changed to MARIE SHIRLEY PRATT
(named after Shirley Temple.) If you desire to
object thereto, you or your attorney should file
a   written   appearance,   in   said   Court,   at
Northampton,   Massachusetts   in   said   County   of
Hampshire, before ten   o'clock in the forenoon,
on   the   eighteenth   day   of   November   1947,   the
return day of this citation. Witness, William
M. Welch, Esquire, Judge of said   Court. Frank
E. Tuit, II, Register o16 20 27.
    I saw my name in large print in this very
important newspaper.   Even though I did   not like
the smell of the print of this   newspaper, my little
red scissors cut this   article out. I cut only the
part where my name was in capital letters, not the
whole article.   My mother was furious with me.   She
grabbed my petite hand with her large hand and pulled
me as we walked briskly back to the newsstand to
purchase another Gazette. Tears flowed and my arms
hurt from her yanks as I walked apprehensively through
the town.
    A letter arrived from my social worker, Bertha
I. Berger, saying Mr. Sparrow, head of the adoption
agency, would do   everything he could to avoid having
my name for upcoming adoption posted in our local
newspapers.   He said, he felt he could put the
adoption through, without any publication whatsoever.
My adopted mother had requested that no one know
of my adoption, but at school, I had a name change.
    The   first   step   in   the   adoption   proceedings
was a letter to the Director. As soon as that was
approved by Miss Joyce, the information went to Mr.
Sparrow, who then drew up the petition, which was
sent to my foster mother to sign. Mr. Sparrow then
notified us   several days   before the case came up
in the Hampshire County Probate Court. He then put
the adoption through for us (free of charge) and
we received the decree a week later.
    Changing the birth record was a problem, because
as it stood, I was the legitimate child of married

parents and since my foster mother was a widow, no
father's name could appear, on the birth record
change. They suggested, we leave the certificate
as it was, and merely explain if questioned that
I was adopted by a relative.

I recall, "like it was yesterday," walking up
the many sandstone stairs to the first floor where
the porch with its brick arches entered the Hampshire
County Court House. Being age eight and all dressed
in my organdy puffed sleeve, white flared, dance
dress, I held hands, with my new mother on one side,
and my new sister Edith on the other. I was
intrigued by this Romanesque four story building
built in 1890 of gray granite with brown stone trim
and a large tower with a bell. This looked like a
scary, important building as I gazed up at the tower
towards the blue sky. This court house was surrounded
by a fence of granite posts three feet high, suspended
between were lengths of heavy iron chains. Inside,
all the files and large cases of books were seen
over the extremely high counter. Because I was
petite, that counter was in my way. I really did
not know what was going on. I was told by mother:
"This was a very important day for both of us."

"There goes THE BIRTHMOTHER," my adopted mother
said, and pointed to those many stairs again. "She
just signed all those important papers for me to
adopt you." Apparently the clerk at the desk had
given her this information. With a quick glance,
I saw for the first and last time the back of my
birth mother, an extremely stout woman (like a circus
lady) slowly walking away with her head down.

This must have been a difficult time for my
birthmother. I found out later that she had an
enormous sense of guilt as she relinquished me.
She was told I was being adopted by a rich family,
who loved me dearly. She thought it was best. My
birthsiblings, whom I did not remember, later said
that my birthmother spoke about me with tears and
wondered if I was all right. They also told me our
birthmother was never what you would call stout.

At this time, all the rights and responsibilities
of parenthood were turned over to Lillian Bader
Pratt, at 61 years of age. At the same time, the
rights and responsibilities were ended for my birth
parent, Mary Hamblen Westcott, 46, from Boston. From
then on in the eyes of the law, my adoptive parent
was my real and only parent. Now my adoption decree
read as follows:

COMMONWEALTH OF MASSACHUSETTS, Hampshire,
ss., Probate Court to Lillian Pratt of Easthampton,

Massachusetts, in said County. In accordance
with Chapter of the acts of the year, I certify,
that Marie Shirley Pratt of Easthampton, in the
County of Hampshire, a child born on the third
day of May 1939, was adopted by you, on the
twentieth day of November, in the year of
our Lord, one thousand nine hundred
forty-seven. Signed and sealed in gold, saying
Court of Probate, Hampshire County - Massachusetts.

Mother Pratt took in many state wards. Why
was I and not the rest, adopted? Because I was
cute, agreeable, they fell in love with me (hard
to believe) and most important of all I would be
a companion to my sister Edith, who was 29 years
older. I was expected never to marry and to support
my sister Edith until her dying days.

As of the day of my adoption I was to call my
foster Grandma, Mother, instead of grandma. Can you
imagine how hard that was for me to adjust to? I
received many a whack across the head with the back
of her large hand until I remembered, at age eight,
to call her Mother.

"You are disrespectful now calling me grandma
instead of mother, after I adopted you, she said."
Meanwhile, the other foster children still called
her Grandma.

Each time I was curious about my birthmother,
my adopted mother said, "If you really loved me,
you would not care about the other person," meaning
my birthmother. Another swat across the head with
the back of her hand, which hurt, came as she said,
"You are so, ungrateful."

I fantasized that Edith, a heavyset woman with
a stern look and quite unhappy at 37, was my
birthmother, and my adopted Mother was my real
grandmother. This made a lot of sense to me, as I
was adopted by a widow (unheard of in the forties)
of grandmother age. My birth certificate was never
changed. They did not want me to engage in a family
search. The same kind of abuse was never used on
me as was used on the state wards who lived with
us. They showed me their loving ways by telling me
how lucky I was to be an adopted child, instead of
a state ward.

Since I had no adopted father, I felt bad.
So on Mother's Day I bought a loving card for Mother
Pratt, but not for Edith Pratt who helped bring me
up. Then on Father's Day I bought Edith a card.
I crossed out Father's Day and wrote Sister's Day
on the front of the card. It had a picture of a blue
car on the front and I liked that, because Edith

had just bought a blue car and I knew she was fond
of it. Inside of the card was a loving message,
and I signed, "OOOO & XXXX (hugs & kisses) Marie."
They laughed, and laughed meanly at me. My tears
flowed, but I felt my heart was in the right place.
Other people who lived in this apartment house
complained to our landlord about the screaming noises
that came from our apartment. When we were evicted
my mother's brother, who was economically able to
help his sister, decided to buy her a home, where
she continued to take care of these state wards.
He bought a two-story eight room house on upper Main
Street.

"The best, the right side of the tracks," Mother
said. We were told again and again how lucky we were
to live at 341 Main Street. Our phone number was,
447r, instead of the ten digit numbers of today.
"My brother can afford the house and he should take
care of me," my ungrateful Mother said. He never
realized how she was taking care of us children.

I close my eyes today and see the interior rooms
of my childhood home clearly. Our four bedroom home
had a large sofa in the parlor. The blue cover
on the sofa was handmade by Mother, and the
intricate lace pattern she crocheted hung on the
back and arm rests. Mother sat by the window in
a large old fashioned reclining chair, where she
saw us, I swear, for the straight mile down Main
Street. In the corner of the parlor was a tall
mahogney grandfathers clock that struck in a deep
tone every quarter hour. On the wall above the sofa
hung two pictures of Jesus carrying the cross, which
had been worked in needlepoint by my sister Edith.

When we did the heavy house-cleaning, we were
told these must never be changed. "They must hang
where they hang," was what my mother said. We never
did find out why. Next to mother's recliner was
placed a Victorian-styled floor lamp with a metal
base and a hand made lace scalloped shade with braided
trim and fringe. When mother was not looking, I
snuck up onto the recliner, so I could be next to
the Victorian lamp, with the rays beaming towards
me. If I shuffled on the thick rug, with my index
finger pointed at the radiator, I enjoyed the thrill
of a tiny spark before touching.

At times our cats tore at the furniture, stropped
their front claws into mother's favorite chair.
This was their way of exercising and strengthening
their claws. They knew it was mother's chair. They
responded to her personal fragrance and added their
scent. These animals were kicked constantly with

mother's big black shoes, but continued to go back
again and again.

Our dining room table extended to eighty-four
inches with the pop-up inserted leaf. Eight armless
chairs had sculptured backs and two chairs had carved
arms. All had maroon silk cushioned seats. Only
mother and Edith could sit in those wonderful large
arm chairs. Covering the large table was a fully
hand crocheted 100 per cent cotton tablecloth, similar
to an Elizabeth Gray Collection. In the center of
this table was a porcelain soup terrain with a
huge ladle. Above the dining room table was a five
bulb ribbed glass chandelier, with a brass-plated
steel body that had a polished finish to it.

The china cabinet had a large glass door, with
a fancy grill and one large drawer where our mahogany
flatware chest, lined with anti-tarnish material
was kept. I polished all ninety-six pieces of silver
stored here several times in my childhood. However
we did not use these very often, as special occasions
did not come frequently in our household.

In the cabinet part, I saw through the glass
Versailles stemware of 14K gold, wine and goblet
glasses. These were never used to my knowledge,
as wine was not drunk in our household, but they
were pretty to gaze at. Our dishes, iridescent rose
colored depression glass, called Normandie Bouquet
and Lattice, was my favorite. When I held them up
to the light, I saw the flower bouquet and lattice
more clearly. The set of large plates were divided
in three parts and the serving dishes made for a
great family style dinner. This depression glass
did not chip or break easily, therefore it remained
as a complete set.

Those dishes were obtained by my mother, during
the depression, when she attended movies, one piece
each time. Depression glass dishware was one of
the few things I inherited. Because I did not see
everything their way, I was punished, even in my
adult life. Other items I treasured were already
gone as I had expected, given away so I did not
end up with what I wanted.

The buffet was extremely long with three drawers
in the center and cupboards on each side which
opened. Placed on top of the buffet was a huge
bowl, filled with imitation waxed fruits, and on
each side was placed brass candlesticks.

Whenever we children thought we heard someone
at the door we said: "Hold on, did you hear that?
Was it the door?" We were not allowed to go near
the door. If it was the door and someone entered,

my mother argued and insulted my relatives enough
so they did not come back for years at a time.

We had a very large kitchen with a big black
stove Mother polished weekly. Attached to the stove
was a large silver pipe which I climbed on a ladder
to shine each month.

One morning a very disturbing accident happened.
I was on the ladder shining away and the pipe detached
and fell on my mother's wrist. The cut was extremely
deep and mother bleed profusely. She did not allow
me to call the doctor. She said over and over, "You
did this on purpose so you would not have to clean
this pipe, and I now am going to bleed to death."

I was already scared to death but her words
scared me even more. I did not have it in me to harm
mother or anyone else. She whacked me and whacked
me on my head and back with the broom. Finally she
collapsed. I shook with fright while I called to
her, but she did not move. Mother was immobile on
the floor, as if she had taken a deep breath and
had not let it out.

Through my voice and tears of fear, I called
the doctor. The doctor said to stop crying and wrap
Mother's wrist tight and he would be right there.
I put a Kotex sanitary napkin on the cut, and wrapped
it tightly with a dish towel. Before the doctor
arrived, the smell of blood made me sick to my
stomach. It seemed like the doctor took a long time
to come. When he finally arrived, he gave Mother
some smelling salts, bandaged the top side of her
wrist where the wound was, and helped her into bed.
She fought him all the way. Mother said: "What
are you doing here, I am fine?"

The doctor ignored her, gave her a shot, hugged
me, and said to me: "Don't worry Marie, Mother will
be fine after she rests." Then he left our home.

I sat by Mother's bed worried about her, hoped
to see her well soon. I was glad the other children
were in school, so they did not have to see what
had happened. Mother had me stay home from school
to help her with this project of cleaning the pipe.

When she awoke she said, "You ignorant fool,
you embarrassed me by using Kotex to stop my
bleeding. Wait, until Edith gets home, she will
fix you, you ignorant fool." I went upstairs to my
room threw myself on my bed and wept, as I waited
for Edith to come home from work.

Kotex was of interest to me when I was very
young. I had seen Kotex in a bottom drawer and
thought it was netting. I asked my mother if I could
have some of this netting for my doll carriage to

keep the bugs out. She told me she did not have any netting and I insisted she did. I finally went to the drawer and showed her the netting. "That is not netting, its Kotex that only woman adults need in their lives," she snickered. I did not know this netting was only on the outside of this pad.

When Edith came home, Mother said, "Take Marie upstairs, lick the hell out of her, and put her to bed without any supper." This Edith did, but without the licking. I felt she must have known I suffered enough from the trauma of the event as it was, and maybe she loved me a little bit.

At about eleven years old, I found these net covered items useful. I was trying to get to sleep one evening rather early as I had a belly ache. Mother awoke me poking with her index finger at my stomach which already ached. "I am so sick of washing your brownish soiled underwear, if you don't start wiping yourself after doing your bowel movement, I'll wipe it for you," she said.

Each time I went to the bathroom I tried harder and harder to wipe myself clean so mother could not whack me anymore. Finally mother realized what this brownish-red stuff was in my underwear and simply gave me a Kotex and said, "Here stick this in your pants." I remembered these nettings - the stuff adult woman needed in their lives.

On the way to school the next day, I spoke of my belly aches. "Wow you started your period already?" one of my older friends said. She continued to discuss what what happened to her and how her mother was so excited for her. I never did tell her how my mother had acted, and what had occurred in my household.

In our kitchen before refrigerators became common appliances in every home, we had an ice box. Our nearby Nashawannuck Pond was utilized for the ice trader business. Mr. Graham our ice man in the summer chipped off small pieces of ice for me to have the pleasure of sucking on. He knew we were not allowed to play with our neighborhood friends. The kids in the neighborhood ran after the ice man, as they sang up a storm, and I watched out the window wanting very much to be amongst them.

Mother said, "Look at those snot-nosed kids begging for ice chips. What a disgusting sight!" I ignored her comment, still wanting to be amongst them. I still have the big black tongs that were used to hold this ice. One day my mother went to see a demonstration of the model "Frigidaire" at the Easthampton Gas Company.

She came home and said, "Refrigerators could never be dependable, the cake of ice was. I will never buy this new appliance."

After World war II we moved into a single house on upper Main Street. My mother said, "Our ice box has become an obsolete appliance in my new home." Shortly after a "Frigidaire", our first refrigerator, was delivered to our home, with a payment of $2.00 per week payable to the Easthampton Gas Company.

Speaking of the salesmen of yester-year, a rag man rode our street with his large work horse wearing a straw hat cut out for his ears. His wagon was filled to the brim with just enough room for the rag man to sit and guide the horse. "Rags for sale, rags for sale, come and get some wears," the rag man yelled. From my window he seemed to be a jolly man, extremely poor, and I longed to speak with him, to ask him how his day was going.

I was the special one. The only one to have my own bedroom. My bedroom was like a palace to me. I had a big brass bed that I had to polish monthly. It had a hand crocheted cream colored bedspread my mother made placed on top. I could close up my desk, which had inside pigeon hole places to organize my items, a little little drawer that pulled out, and this was where I placed that special news article with my name on it, I had cut out by myself. The desk had a special chair with the Queen Anne style legs and a wicker seat. The dressing table in my room had a three paneled mirror with three little drawers. I found two broken lamps in the attic and I glued them together. The lamps were lead crystal, urn-shaped, with a frosted leaf design and I convinced my mother to get me two pleated white fabric shades to match. Unfortunately, the glue was not like today's glue and I can not count the times I reglued and put rubber bands around the lamps to hold them. My favorite piece of furniture was a cheval glass mirror which is a full length mirror, the kind that is mounted on brass swivels so it can tilt. I danced up a storm in the mirror and even hugged myself as no one else did. As I got older I studied my face in the cheval mirror, so if I saw someone who looked like me I could know that was my birth family.

Mother's mood changes were so extreme that I felt cut off from her. I knew that even the heartiest singing, dancing and laughing could change her in a moment to a bitterness that seemed to last forever.

Mother played a silver harmonica with a blue stripe across it. She blew into the row of reeds which sounded tones when she breathed out or sucked

in across them. Tunes like Yankee Doodle she played
and very well at that. I listened with rapt attention
while mother played songs over and over again. I
do not know why it was, but the strains of that music
had a magical effect. I could not just sit quietly,
I jumped up and sang and shouted. I went into my
room, stood in front of my mirror and whistle all
the tunes that my mother played, making believe I
had a harmonica.

Mother scared me to death as she ran up the
stairs and said, "Stop that silliness. You are soo
stupid, I can not believe how stupid you are. Are
you mimicking me?" I was shocked she thought that
of me.

I said, "No, mother, no I am not mimicking you,
only playing make-believe." As a child, I never
realized how insecure and sick Mother really was.
I knelt in the corner for hours as my punishment,
thinking what I could say to make mother less angry.
Mother swatted me across the head several times when
she passed by because I became tired and could
not kneel upright. So I sat on my knees instead
and since that was not what she wanted of me, I was
whacked again.

Mother often read a thick bulky volume with
a stout binding of black leather. Some of the words
were faded, therefore I could scarcely decipher them.
It was the Bible. Mother said, "This book was better
than all the doctors and all the medicines in the
world." This book was her solace in every need.

Each Sunday, Edith brought us to church, mother
stayed at home as the flight of stairs was too much
for her arthritis. I, the special one, was always
in the front seat of the car with Edith. The others
were in the back seat. We sat in the same place
in church, Sunday after Sunday. It never occurred
to us to take another place, as that is the way it
was. As soon as we were seated in our pew we bowed
our heads, and then we looked about us. We saw the
beautiful feathers, fur, and velvet hats the woman
wore and the boring suits that all the men wore,
with their special Sunday chapeau (broad brimmed
hat) in their hands. I wanted someday to wear
beautiful hats like these woman.

I waited to hear the organ play, for then I
knew our junior choir was to start. I loved to sing
all the old familiar tunes, out of tune I am sure.
Our organist, Mrs. Strong, I loved dearly.

Our very good looking minister, Rev. Foster,
was the best. He was handsomer than ever when he
stood in the pulpit and preached. And the longer

he talked, the handsomer he grew in my eyes. I was
not restless at all, for he was my idol. No matter
what he said, it was fine with me. Edith was involved
in our church as a Sunday school teacher with at
least one of us children in her class. At church
Edith seemed to be happy among us children. In public
she was a very pleasant person and I felt she needed
to be away from this confusing household. At home
Edith sewed and stuffed different animals like
donkeys, elephants, and pigs dressing them in little
outfits. These were unusual, different than the
typical teddy bears and bunnies most craft people
made. Sometimes on different occasions Edith liked
to give an animal to church people she grew to like.
Today, my children still have the animals Edith made
for them in her later years sitting on top shelf
of their bookcases.

After church service, we were amongst coffee-hour
friends and crowded around our handsome preacher,
our hands filled with delicate cakes and
cookies. We were aware of everyone looking, so
we were only allowed two of these delicious treats.
"Don't forget," Edith told us, "you're still in
church, the house of our Lord." Affection was given
to us in public, but as we were driven home, reality
set back in with no affection at home.

I tried desperately to be a good girl, so I
would not be abused like the others. Living with
my adopted mother for five years before my adoption,
and being told I was so special, I assume was
supposed to ease the loss and pain of not being
amongst my birth family. But over and over again
I was told I must remain special, since I had been
given away once, I could be given away again. My
psychological journey as an abused child went like
this, Mother said, "Why are you always smiling?"
"Who, me?" I stammered, "It's natural, I guess.
I always have this expression." Mother said, "Well,
it's weird, you shouldn't smile. It makes you look
retarded." I loved to smile because people smiled
back at me, even my mother. She never stopped me
from smiling, since that was my nature and my shield.
I was afraid, to stand up for myself. I feared they
might abandon me, like she told me many had already
done in my young life. Looking back as an adult,
she must have truly hated herself, to view smiling
in such an ugly way.

When we sat at the long table in the dining
room, embroidering, sewing or crocheting, with mother
tatting away at a half-finished sunburst doily, the
phone rang, she dropped a stitch and somehow it

was our fault. All hell broke loose and everything we were doing was wrong. We were sent to our rooms or not given supper. This confused me, and again I wondered, how can I make mother happy. Mother seemed to concoct a reason; one of us said something or said it in a way that gave offense to her, someone criticized or did not praise her extravagantly, someone was not there when he should have been, or maybe someone was butting into her conversation. Though none of these excuses were true and the phone was the real culprit, she punished us.

We were excited when a new season began since that meant a new dress. The long dining room table was where Edith laid out the big bolts of cloth and I did the cutting after she pinned the pattern on the cloth. Cutting was not easy for me, as I was a south paw (left handed) and always held the scissors upside down. Edith told me over and over again how stupid I was. We were given the simplest things to do first, like I made big stitches on the seams and later Edith sewed these on the pedal sewing machine.

My middle finger was punctured over and over again, as the thimble never stayed on my tiny fingers while working on the seams. Sometimes I wished Edith pricked her fingers while she pinned the fabric together, just to see if she was human and she could bleed. It was hard for me to tell the right side of the cloth from the wrong side, and when I erred a swat across the head, first on the left side and then right was in order. Actually, I chose this sewing ritual rather than scrubbing the floors, sifting the coals outside, piling wood, or folding clothes, like the other children. Besides my mother had always said, "Marie, a needle had better fit your hand, as your head can't do anything." I worked hard at learning to sew, as I believed Mother, the person I needed and wanted to trust.

As I got older, my aunt, Edith Brouilette brought me hand-me-downs from my cousin Donna. I took the clothes completely apart, as they were much too large for me. I laid them on the dining room table and simply cut two inches around each piece and continued to sew the item back up again to fit me. They called me stupid again. When I picked up a piece of cloth with my thumb and index finger to protect my long fingernails, Edith called me an animal and told me I was monkeylike. I sure could not nurture, from those who were destroying me.

Home Hurts

My childhood home was like an earthquake. It quivered and shook without warning. My childhood home was not a safe place. My mother seemed to respond to all stress in a violent manner.

I was known as, "Pratt's adopted daughter." Being the chosen one was not an easy task. I was to be the good girl, an example for the others. Over and over again I lived and breathed to please my adopted mother.

Child abuse does not only occur in situations where poverty and ignorance are factors. These Pratt's were perceived by the community as wonderful people who served the public good by taking in state wards. This was something they could do, as they were uneducated and the pay was not so bad either. They dressed us, fed us, allowed us to have schooling, and took us to church. We sat at the 8th row up front, on the right hand side. My sister Edith taught Sunday School and we sang in the choir. We walked down Main Street every Sunday afternoon, all dressed up as if we were on display. We did all the right things at the right times - in public. When the social workers came, we were all lined up on the sofa, dressed in our Sunday best, with our broad smiles on. Or else! I was uncomfortable while mother spoke of me as perfect and not like the other children. In front of the social workers I was uneasy at being shown off and uncomfortable under the almost constant stares they gave me from across the room.

Eight state children were in and out of my adoptive home at different times. Anywhere from one to four of us lived in this foster home at any given time. When I arrived in what was then my foster home, there was already one teen-aged girl, Alice, who lived with them. Alice left to get married to someone she met in Easthampton. Then Mildred, about my age, came to live with us, and we were dressed to look like twins. Mildred was taken back by the state, hopefully home to live with her birth parents. Soon after, Barbara, a few years younger than me, came to live with us. Gloria, who was my age, came shortly thereafter. Years passed and Barbara was taken away. Gloria whom they did not want living with us, they got rid of using whatever excuse they wanted to use.

Shortly thereafter, came two birthsisters, Linda and Carol. While they were still with us, two more birthsisters Sheryl and Pamela (they were much younger than us) came. I left home to be married, and these last two sets of birthsisters were still living in the household.

Life in the Pratt home was anything but pleasant. Understanding the dark side of human conditions and my experience as a child, one trauma after another followed.

Alice was a tall lanky girl, not so pretty, whom mother said lied all the time. One day mother hung her upside down out the third story apartment window. She screamed, "Help me. Help me. Oh God, help me!" A man came running with his ladder to help, and when my mother finally pulled her back in, she whipped her with a handled wire mattress whip as punishment because she screamed and caused the man to come. I shook and with my hands on my head said to myself, "Oh God, oh God help her, help her."

Alice fainted and I thought she was dead. I learned later that fainting was nature's way to save people's sanity.

The neighbors reported this incident to the authorities. The agency called my mother and told her when they were arriving at our home to discuss this incident with her.

Meanwhile Mother said to us children, "If you tell the authorities anything, I will send you all back where you came from and things will be worse than living here; you will be institutionalized." Mother had described an institution as a jail for bad children. We never did open our mouths. Young at the time, I did not understand all that happened anyway.

One of Alice's jobs was to clean the large hallway and four flights of stairs weekly on her hands and knees. Mother handled this job for the landlord in order to pay less for her rent. This was an eight unit apartment house with very dark, putrid flights of stairs and scary areas. I watched as mother put Alice's hair up in a dirty old rag with a lock of hair loosened. Then she was put into one of mother's old housedresses and an apron. She yelled, calling, "Cinderella, where are you? Are you finished, yet Cinderella?" Kids who lived in the building with us mocked my mother and used this Cinderella name over and over again. Alice was in tears weekly. As tears rolled down my checks

I quickly ran to my room so Mother did not see me watching her.

Very close to this house was Gawle's man-made swimming hole, where the public swam. Gloria wanted so badly to swim. One day after we begged and begged, we were allowed to go. Gloria walked in over her head deeper and deeper. The farther I walked the farther away she seemed to be from me, and I did not know how to swim either. I was around ten years old. I panicked, ran and screamed. "Help - Help she's drowning." Someone ran in and helped her to the beach after she had gone under several times.

I was too scared to go home so early in the afternoon and yet scared that Gloria might go in over her head again. She was exhausted from the near drowning and promised me she would just lay on the beach. We vowed not to tell this incident to my mother.

A few days later, in the middle of the night I bolted up in bed screaming, I had a nightmare about the swimming incident. Gloria's voice rang in my ears, echoing, "Help me, help me." Needing the comforting and not wanting to lie about my nightmare, I was screamed at over and over by my mother, who said, "What's the matter - What's the matter, tell me or else." I confessed about the near drowning of Gloria.

Mother stared at me and asked irritably, "Why didn't you tell me?" She knew why I did not want to tell her of the incident, so I did not answer her and not answering made her really angry. Needless to say, all hell broke loose and we never did go swimming alone again.

Gloria was about to pass onto fifth grade and I was kept back. Mother got rid of Gloria, telling her she was going to be institutionalized because she showed off by being smart at school. I was held back because of poor grades, but I was also not emotionally ready to go on. Each year the school passed me through, as I knew just how to please the teachers enough to let me go on.

As I remember the day Gloria left, I was crushed and scared for her. Mother used to make us walk on different sides of the street when we came home from school so we could not discuss our problems at home. My life as a child was spent concentrating on saving myself from these crazy people. Concentrating on school work was impossible. I had a lot of trouble focusing and trying to remember things. Each time I brought my report card home, with stiff fingers between my shoulder blades, mother said, "Take down your pants and bend over."

As I got older I was mortified to be in this position. Her ruler fell with a sharp thwack. Many times the ruler cracked in half, sending the other half across the room. After these spankings, sometimes she dropped the broken ruler to the floor and hugged me tight. Strangely, those were the times I felt she did love me.

I never saw Gloria again. I remember seeing the look on Gloria's face and tears in her eyes, as she looked through the car window at me. I know she was looking at me, because we really cared for each other, even though we were told not to. I cried also, not knowing if she was going to be worse off elsewhere, not knowing what her future was to be.

Barbara was yelled at and criticized constantly. She often shrugged her shoulders, always a sign that she had caught herself at something she had considered unwise or useless to continue with. Most of the time it was nothing much. Barbara walked in a very slow motion. It took her a long time to go from one room to another. Sometimes she tilted her head one way and then another, as if looking both ways, with her head in a downward motion. Mother yanked at her hair, told her to walk with her head up, gave her a kick with her big black hard-soled shoes on her fanny, to move her on.

We felt tension and sunk our voices to a whisper and then looked shiftly around and quickly glanced over our shoulders to see what was up next. Mother had mirrors placed just right in some rooms so she could see us as we played or worked in another room.

Most every morning at breakfast there was a battle. Linda could not eat breakfast, especially eggs. When my mother figured that out, she talked about the egg-white being like snots and the shell came from the ass of the chicken with shit all over it, while we tried to eat them. Linda could not handle this kind of description and many times vomited the eggs into her plate. My sister Edith sat on the chair next to Linda, "Eat your eggs," she said. "I can't," Linda said.

My sister continued, "You're going to sit there until you eat your eggs."

Linda started to cry, "Please don't make me eat these eggs, it'll make me vomit."

My sister Edith warned her if she vomited the eggs again, she would make her eat the vomit. The next morning the same breakfast was served and again Linda vomited. My sister kept her word and spoon-fed Linda the vomited eggs, as she did this Linda vomited again. Sometimes this went on for hours, with Linda humiliated, with her head down. She cried and cried.

My sister told us that at the state hospital where she worked as an attendant, this was what they did to the patients when they vomited. The vomit that was spoon-fed that morning, was saved for lunch and done again, of course in a threatened way, until all of it was finished on that plate. Meanwhile I had a difficult time enjoying my first meal of the day. I quickly ate my breakfast so I could be excused and not watch any more. Sometimes even I felt squeamish and ran to my bedroom throwing myself across my bed.

When the toddlers were potty-trained, they were made to sit on the potty chair for hours. I was young and had very little knowledge of the next period of time, but even I could see that when the child was there from breakfast to lunch, it was an extremely long time. This was not a fun experience for these toddlers. Their little fannies were marked with a red circle by the seat of the little potty chair.

We were sexually mistreated. Linda was checked by mother after she showered to see if the hair on her head was clean, by pulling on it. If her hair squeaked, it was clean. But, it was never clean to mother's satisfaction. Coming out of the bathroom my mother laughed. "You should have seen her breasts as they moved up and down while I pulled her hair, she said to my sister, "Her breasts moved when she shook the water from her ears as she toweled her hair dry."

Bathing was very unpleasant at times, as they scrubbed us clean with a hard scrub brush. "You are bad, filthy, ugly, and this will cleanse you," she'd say. The water was hot and the heavy spraying made a stinging sensation as I held my breath, not saying a word, for fear of the incident lasting longer.

Tension was unbearable. Mother rose from her kitchen chair like a goddess breathing hard like she always did when she was mad, and hobbled over to where Linda stood. Linda had said something she did not like. Mother suffered from arthritis in her arms and legs, but when she was mad, you never knew she was in pain or half-dead. She proceeded to bend Linda back against the stove, with a knife in hand as though ready to cut her tongue off. Then grabbed her throat (the source of the words not liked by mother.)

Linda struggled, "You're going to break my back," she screamed. Mother was very tall, a big German

woman with much strength who could very well have
done that. She pulled Linda over to a chair, set
her down, and with a good farm-style hold, she held
the back of her neck.

Linda hollered: "No - No," as she tried to
twist loose. My mother had a grip that could crack
walnuts.

For what reason she was punished we never knew,
as none of us really did anything that was what I
called bad. Terror was a part of my life as I took
deep breaths then shallow breaths trying to become
calm.

Mother's negative thoughts escalated into other
malicious acts. I do not remember what Mother accused
Carol of doing. I only know and watched as Carol
was held up-side down and dunked in a pail of water
up and down, up and down. One time she did not catch
her breath and almost choked to death. Edith revived
her, gave her mouth to mouth resuscitation. During
this time I was praying to God and pacing the floor.
We were all told next time - no revival - she would
be dead.

On one occasion Carol's face was banged hard
on the sharp corner of the door jam repeatedly.
She let out a howl of pain that was like nothing
I had ever heard before as she fell to the floor.
Her hands were tied behind her back, while her hair
was yanked and her head banged over and over on the
sharp corner of the door. Carol cried and moaned
throughout the night. In the morning Edith finally
brought her to the doctor. She told me she had a
tremendous headache, and I could see her face was
so badly swollen. Her eyes were only tiny slits
and her mouth looked like a deformed bellybutton.
I tried, with all my strength, to pull my mother
off of her. When I interfered, Mother put up a
warning hand and pointed outside to the porch. I
obeyed, ran towards the porch. I did not want to
be next having this happen to me. This exposed
torture and trauma of child abuse made Carol look
like a monster, because her facial appearance was
out of proportion.

The doctor said, "Your lucky to be living with
them. This would not happen, if you could only be
a good girl." Wasn't he helpful?

One school night, no sooner had I shut my eyes,
than desolation came upon me. We were awakened and
made to sit and watch, while Mother and Edith forced
Carol to scrub the kitchen floor on her hands and
knees with a scrub brush. This kitchen floor was
big, not like today's kitchenettes. Needless to

say, Carol cried and cried all the way through this
ordeal. We were threatened this would happen to
us too, if we were bad.

Forced to watch her, though we were half asleep,
we nodded our heads time and again. When our heads
nodded, our hair was pulled up, jolting us awake
only to watch her again. I was exhausted while in
school the next day, after being kept awake during
the night.

I was expected to clean my room, which to
Mother's satisfaction meant in perfect order. As
I followed her up the stairs, I braced myself for
the fall I always expected she would have, because
she was so unstable on her feet as she climbed the
stairs. When I did not meet her standards, she went
into my room in a fit of rage, placed herself on
my bed, and stared at me for a period of time. She
then disrupted everything I had folded. When I
folded it again, she tore it apart again. This went
on over and over again, with tears in my eyes again
I folded my clothes, until I felt I was going insane.
When Mother finished with me, she disrupted every
one else's room as well, therefore I was forced to
listen to her over and over again.

Lack of privacy was the rule. Our rooms were
entered whenever they wanted to. They went through
our dresser drawers, desks, closets, they listened
to phone conversations, they discussed me with the
social workers even though I was adopted and not
still a ward of the state. All we ever heard was
screaming, ridicule, name calling and harshness,
day in and day out.

Once when I was a bit older, mother pushed me
through my bedroom door, locked it, and went down
stairs. I remember that awful clicking sound of
the key as it was turned in the lock. I stood in
the kind of anger I had not known before as a
child. I was a prisoner in my own home, filled with
fear. At such times, in my head, I went to the beach
or walked in the woods, things I was never allowed
to do.

If I did not like watching animals, I could
have gone crazy. From my bedroom on the second floor,
I sometimes watched my cat in the high grass spend
a great deal of time lying half-hidden from view,
making a few stalked runs as he rushed forward in
his flattened posture. He halted and waited again
before he pounced on a rodent. His tail started
wagging furiously, which exposed the movement to
the frightened intended prey. Later when I was
let out of my room, I found the prey, a mouse, at

our doorstep. The cat let us know he had done his job, wanted us to pet him, and acknowledge his work.

Carol had a destructive play pattern with her toys. She broke or destroyed them by kicking, as well as being cruel to our animals. This allowed her to express her dominance and rage without negative consequences from her actions, while abuse never allowed her expression. Carol played very rough with her dolls, struck her sister Linda, and kicked our cats around. I tried to help her by rocking a doll, held her sister Linda when she was sad and picked up our cat to pet him after Carol had been cruel to it. I felt she expressed her anger on the dolls, animals, and her sister knowing they would not fight back.

Sheryl was once made to act like a dog. Edith put a dog collar around her neck and made her urinate outside, eat dog food, lap water from the dog dish and walk on all fours. She had to sit up, beg, and bark. Mother and Edith laughed and laughed as they made Sheryl act like a dog over and over again. If we did not laugh too, we were told this would happen to us. Tears filled my eyes so freely. When put to bed, I prayed and prayed someone could help us. I wanted to touch Sheryl, hold her, comfort her, make her smile and kiss her abused face, but I was not allowed to go near her.

At dinner time, nobody but my mother sat in the arm chair. Nobody ever ate before the blessing was said over the food, or she got served last or maybe not at all. Nobody dared to get up before excusing herself from the table or she suffered the consequences. Setting the table correctly, with everything matching, was important to my mother. Sometimes we had to dress in our Sunday best in order to be allowed to eat, even when it was not Sunday. When we were elegantly dressed and perfect table settings with dishes, glasses, and silver, Mother released some rotten farts, while we ate at the dinner table. We had better laugh, when she did this or be reprimanded. Many times I could not laugh and was then punished for not laughing. Mother locked me in my room without finishing my dinner, again. I could not comprehend this behavior at all. But day after day I forgave and started again, I promised myself to be a good girl.

Our attic was suffocatingly hot. There were no windows, so there was a stuffy dry smell. As you opened the short door it creaked on rusty hinges. The spider webs hung from the ceiling and you felt them as you tried to find the light string. If I

made the mistake and touched the light bulb and not
the string I got a shock. Often we were punished
by being put in there for hours at a time.

One summer day Sheryl was not only put in the
attic, but was also stuffed in a trunk laden with
the smell of moth balls. When she was taken out,
mother screamed when Sheryl went limp in my sister's
arms. Meanwhile we were told to lay on the blanket
placed in the sun and to stay on that blanket until
she came to get us. After an un-Godly scream we
all ran into the house. Mother had smelling salts
under Sheryl's nose and Edith threw cold water on
Sheryl, and she awoke in a startled manner. The
terrors - nightmares we experienced and witnessed
were unbelievable.

One Halloween I wanted so much to go
trick-or-treating like my neighbors and friends.
During the afternoon I went up into the attic and
put together a costume. I had found an old black
dress, belted it, for it was too long for me, and
made a tall witches hat out of my black colored paper.
I took the old short broom which was used to sweep
up the coals in the cellar and put some coals on
my face. After dark I dressed up in my costume,
went outside, and knocked on my own door fooling
my mother. She laughed and laughed. She then let
me go to a few houses on my street. I was the
happiest witch around that evening. Several weeks
later I was punished for disobeying her on Halloween
night. She locked me in my room for two days and
only unlocked the door to pass in my food and
empty my slush bucket.

When Sheryl was very small, my mother stuffed
her naked into the oven to threaten her. Mother
said this time she just wanted to see if she could
fit. Next time she would cook her so we could eat
her. We children were terrified as we were forced
to eat blood sausage, pigs feet, and liver. We feared
my mother would cook her. Mother had already done
many frightening things, yet we forgave her time
after time.

Even our dog was affected by terror. She
sometimes moved her belly along the ground, and raised
her soft eyes to her master, my mother. With the
point of her nose she carefully rested on folded
paws, her eyes blinked and blinked, strange shivers
ran down her long spine, and she began to growl very
softly. Even she, our dog, did not know what to
do next. Mother then kicked the dog out of the room.

After supper, we were occasionally taken for
an ice cream at the Tastie Top in Westfield, a few

miles from home. One time Mother said, "Sheryl is
bad, therefore she will not have an ice cream."
We drove there in silence, elbowed each other in
the back seat and thought mother might give in.
You guessed it, mother did not give in and we felt
badly. I did not enjoy my ice cream.

"Sheryl is talking while I am trying to watch
television," mother said. "That's it." She exploded,
and slammed her empty glass down, stood up, and said,
"I'm leaving." When she left the room every one
of us remained silent, not wanting to provoke a
further outburst. I had seen and heard this before.

This evening happened to be Sheryl's birthday,
she was made to sit down with her sister and blow
out her candles on her birthday cake. Mother took
a picture of her doing this, and mailed it to the
social workers, so they could see what a wonderful
birthday party Sheryl had. What the social workers
did not know was Sheryl was not allowed to eat her
cake and received no presents because she was bad,
again.

I felt no matter what was wrong with a family,
the holidays could fix it. Edith read us her favorite
poem at Christmas called, "A Letter To Santa"

> Dear Santa Claus,
> Please bring to me
> A little tiny Christmas tree.
> I've never had one yet you see
> And I just thought if I
> Would write a note to you and say,
> Please don't forget me Christmas day
> You wouldn't pass me by.
>
> I wrote you last year
> Don't you know?
> But maybe you were busy though
> Or else your reindeers wouldn't go
> I don't know what it was,
> But anyhow - you never came
> And I'm sure I signed my name.
> I'm Jimmy, Santa Claus.
>
> I'm Jimmy Moore, have you forgot?
> I think you have, you've never brought
> One thing to me, but I just thought
> If once more I would write
> A note and ask you please to bring
> Not very much, just anything
> Well I just thought you might.
> I'd like some Toys, but I suppose
> I'd better ask instead for clothes.

And Santa Claus my little toes
Stick right out in the air
And gee-ma-nee! On days like these
I tell you what, I nearly freeze
But no one seems to care.

I guess that's all I'd better say
But won't you please,
Come past our way
And give me one real Christmas Day?
Forget that we are poor
Our house is where it always was,
Try hard to find it Santa Claus
That's all from Jimmy Moore.

This holiday was filled with disasters, one right after the other. All of us, except Sheryl, opened our two gifts each, while she was made to sit and watch us. Many a time I wished it was me, instead, for it was difficult for me to enjoy what I had received.

"Sheryl just sit there, wipe those tears from your eyes, be quiet, and don't cry or else," Mother said.

I particularly remember, large cardboard paper dolls, giant ones, they seemed to me. When Pamela opened hers, Sheryl thought she was going to have one too even though the night before, she was read Edith's favorite poem, and she was told, she was not going to have any presents. Mother kept her word and Sheryl received nothing. I could not believe what had happened.

Pamela and Sheryl were sisters, only eleven months apart. Mother often rocked Pamela before she put her to bed, held her very close, while Sheryl was sent to bed without being rocked or loved like her sister. We were allowed to push Pamela in the wicker carriage when we went for a walk, but Sheryl was not allowed in the carriage at all, even if we had gone for a long walk.

One day, I felt bad for Sheryl. A broad smile illuminated her face as I placed her in the wicker carriage and had Pamela walk for a short time. We stopped at Maryon and Attorney Donais candy house while on our walk. We ate our candy on the way home, as mother did not allow us to have candy. When my mother got wind of Sheryl being in the carriage, I was punished along with Sheryl. "Sheryl was never to go in that carriage again, and that it was none of my business," Mother said.

The consequences of not doing what I was told was worse than not doing what I thought was fair,

at least in my own mind. Therefore I never did this
again.
     We were threatened if we did not behave. Mother
hurt our pets or gave them away and we never saw
them again. This happened many times. Once I saw
my mother, in a fit of rage, throw my cat out the
second story window of my bedroom. "You're next,"
she said, "if you do not behave."
     I looked for my cat for hours, and he was not
dead. Now I know, a cat does a twisting reaction,
beginning both at the head and end of the body, the
front legs, they bring up, close to their face.
The upper part of the spine twists and then the hind
legs bend up, so the rear half of its body, catches
up with the front. The back arches, as a way to
reduce the force of the impact and that way, they
always land on their paws, and are not hurt. But
as a child I did not know this, so I was terrified.
     Edith gave our cat catnip stuffed into the shape
of a mouse. My cat washed and clawed at the mouse.
She sniffed, bit, chewed, and rubbed against the
catnip mouse repeatedly with her cheek and her chin.
The cat shook her head and rubbed the catnip with
her body. Sometimes she purred loudly, growled,
meowed, rolled over and even leaped in the air.
This was one more frightened experience for us,
for we were not told it was all right to give this
catnip to a cat.
     Edith said, "If you do not behave, I will give
you this chemical and you will react just like this
cat." We were scared to death and were extremely
careful what we said or did the rest of that day.
Later in life, I found out cat junkies were lucky,
unlike other drugs, catnip does no lasting damage.
After the ten-minute experience was over, the cat
was back to normal, with no ill effects. This same
drug, if given to a cat internally, can act as a
tranquilizer. The scientists say, how they can be
uppers and downers remains a mystery. It would have
been better if we had been told the experience with
the catnip was okay, but instead we were threatened
with this horrifying experience.
     If you have experienced owning a cat, you know
how they can be. When they are out they want to
come in, and when they are in they want to go out.
This can be frustrating and it did not take much
to frustrate my mother. We knew one of us probably
was going to be next, when my Mother kicked the
animals out the door with her heavy black shoes.
     Mother's voice, sharp, loud, and shrilling was
heard from the bottom of the stairs as she called

upstairs to Sheryl. I went upstairs to call her thinking perhaps she had not heard mother. I found her hiding under the bed. "My name is not Sheryl, Sheryl left," she said to me. "Sheryl you had better come out from under the bed, mother is calling you," I said.

"My name is not Sheryl, Sheryl left," she said again. This blew my mind, since I felt Sheryl was playing games, while Mother was angry. She continued to say Sheryl isn't here. I'm SAH." I never understood that name.

I said: "Sarah?"

She said, "No, SAH."

I said "Shawn?"

She said: "When I'm a man, they will hurt me no longer."

I smiled, "Sheryl, you will never be a man."

"SAH is a boy and he will be a man when I grow up."

I continued to tell her she would never be a man.

Sheryl said, "Never, not ever?

I said, "No, not ever."

"I want to, I want to, and I need to," Sheryl screamed and cried.

As an adult I now realize she spent numerous hours alone and began to move herself out of her body, being someone else made it easier for her to cope with the abuse. Constantly and mercilessly she was beaten without being allowed to cry. If she did cry she was told she was weak and then beaten longer and harder, often on the back of her head. The fight she had in her was literally beaten out of her. I now know head traumas received during childhood could have damaged those sectors of her brain that control primal emotions such as love, hate and fear. I do not know what happened later that evening, as I dated at that time and could not wait to be out in the world by myself. Forgiveness is a funny thing, it warms the heart and cools the sting. Forgiving mother, feeling she was a sick person, was the only means of survival for me.

Sometimes I felt sorry for Mother. It seemed mother wanted to do things the hard way. Some clothes she used the wash board, with its ridges for scrubbing the dirt out of our clothes. As she stood near the set tub, deep sink, she looked like a washerwoman, whose work was washing clothes, who was very washed-out and tired. Edith said, "Please use the washing machine upstairs, it is much easier and you will not be as tired."

We had a cold dark scary cellar with a dirt
floor. In the middle of the cellar, sat a pot belly
stove that heated our water. I saw black snakes
that lived in the wood piles and when the kids were
bad they were tied and made to stay on the wood pile.
As a religious torment Mother expressed the living,
breathing, presence of the serpents as God sent them
there because we were "bad" like Adam and Eve were
in the Garden of Eden. Therefore these serpents
threatened to drive us out of our home because we
were "bad" as well. Panic set in again, even if
it was not me being punished. Mother and Edith played
with our minds. They said, "The black snakes are
going to crawl on your bodies, bite and kill you."
The kids prayed to die, so everything could be all
over. Many of my nightmares were about these serpents,
but today as an adult when I dream of serpents on
my body, I find in my dreams I carefully and slowly
remove the snakes from my clothing placing them
on the ground carefully and peacefully.

I was only allowed to bathe once a week because
of the work involved in heating the water. I was
not allowed to heat pans of water and fill the tub
as we knew other people did. In the winter I froze
if it was not Saturday, as I tried to wash my
important parts. I could never wash my hair during
the week and in the winter our hair was not washed
too often either, as Mother believed I could become
quite sick. Today I know this was an old wives tale,
as the common cold to me is a virus transferred from
others who have it.

School for us all was disastrous. Once, when
first learning to color, Sheryl brought home a paper
from school, colored real dark. "You colored too
dark, you should color much lighter," mother said.

"My teacher told me to do it dark," Sheryl
insisted.

So my mother made her color for hours, really
dark, bearing down on her hands, to hurt her. Mother
banged her knuckles with a heavy wooden ruler, until
they bled, and the crayons broke in half. When I
tried to placate mother because her tone frightened
me, her jaw muscles tightened. "It's none of your
business."

When Edith arrived home from work mother said,
"Look at all the crayons Sheryl broke today. She
must learn to take better care of her crayons. "The
next day, I asked her teacher about Sheryl's work
and she said, "The darker colored pictures, when
hung on the wall, looked brighter. Sheryl colored
very well that day." I did not share with her teacher

what had occurred at home, as I felt ashamed and
I might have burst into tears. I was afraid when
Edith attended the next parent-teachers conference
this teacher might bring this up and happenings at
home might have been worse for us. Nor did I ever
mention this to my mother, as this was none of my
business and I was told not to intervene.

"My only complaint about Sheryl is she does
not interact with other children," Sheryl's teacher
said.

I know now that the beatings, neglect, and verbal
abuse left Sheryl with no sense of self-worth, and
therefore in school no basis for social interaction.
The experience of crayons was not enough. When at
school experimenting with paints Sheryl wiped her
hands filled with paint on the side of her dress.
My mother was furious, and in a fit of rage, slopped
household paint with a wooden stick to the front
of the dress where everyone could see. She made
Sheryl wear that dress to school for the rest of
the week without washing the paint off. Sheryl cried
herself sick everyday before going to school, begging
Mother to allow her to wear something else. I never
understood why the teachers could not see that this
child was abused. I suppose because Edith went to
every parent-teachers conference and convinced the
teachers of a patient, generous foster home they
had provided us with. Mother and Edith manipulated
doctors and ministers, as well.

Saturday morning was shopping day for Edith
and me. Later I learned of abuse being used while
we shopped. The rest of the girls dusted, vacuumed,
scrubbed, and cleaned the house spotless. This
Saturday mother needed me to help her by operating
the mangle machine. I did not mind helping Mother
with this chore. I liked placing the sheets,
tablecloths, napkins, and hankies between the rollers
of the mangler as it pressed these items perfectly.
It was this Saturday when I did not shop with Edith
I found myself, running around the house in a panic
because I refused to hold Carol down, while my mother
gagged her, tied her to a wooden chair, and whipped
her with an electric cord. If Edith was not available
to help mother abuse, mother's verbal abuse escalated.
Finally, my sister Edith came home from shopping
and she helped my mother by holding Carol down, while
Mother tied her. Carol was tied, stuffed under the
kitchen table and kicked with my mother's high laced
black shoes every time mother walked by her.

One morning I heard Barbara's screams. My mother
had her pinned on the bed, accused her of

masturbating. She said, "I can do that for you,"
and I saw her as she stuffed a banana up Barbara's
vagina. "Now you really will go blind," my mother
yelled. While mother abused, she said, "I'm only
doing this for your own good and because I love you
and want you to be good." We were so confused as
"good," and "bad" began meaning "hurt" to us and
totally confused about "love," and "right," and
"wrong."

Sexual behavior was sure a part of our
relationship with mother, but we did not understand
this at the time. My mother said, "You are to take
your nap in my bed with me."

The kids said, "No - no, I'll be good, I'll
be a good girl." They told me sometimes it hurt when
my mother's hands were on their body. Abuse required
coping throughout life, to separate the confusion
between sex and love. Many times the kids said over
and over again, "I love you, I love you, please don't
hurt me anymore."

My mother's reply was, "You had better say,
you love me."

Sheryl slept in a four poster twin bed. She
was very often tied naked to her bed, hands tied
high to the upper post and her legs spread and tied
to the bottom posts. Edith yanked at her breasts
and grabbed at her crotch as she walked by her.
Sheryl moaned, cried, and complained because she
said her arms ached.

"If you keep complaining we will make it
tighter," was their response.

Already in bed myself, I put the pillows over
my ears, but still I heard the hurting cries and
the angry voices. Again and again, I cried myself
to sleep. Later, Edith brought a straight jacket
home from the hospital where she worked, and placed
Sheryl in it. I often pray to God these abused
children have not turned to physical violence,
substance abuse, crime, suicide and even homicide.

A relative of ours gave us an old bed and
mattress that had been stored in a cottage. This
became Sheryl's bed and it was filled with bedbugs.
They bit her and naturally she complained.

The mind games went on. "These bugs are going
to eat you alive," Edith said.

Finally they gagged Sheryl so she could not
scream or complain, and tied her so she could not
even turn or hit the bugs. Her sniffles were so
bad, I sometimes thought she could not make it through
the night.

At the foot of the stairs was a sewing room

with a large sewing table, an oil tablecloth placed
on top, situated in the middle of the room. On this
table was a kerosene lamp which was lit each night
before we went to bed. I feared this lamp might tip
over and start the house on fire, so in my mind I
thought of what to do if this was to happen. Outside
my bedroom window was a small roof over the entrance
of the kitchen, and I visualized getting everyone
out that way. I had my double dutch rope under my
bed, so we could safely get out. Edith found the
rope under my bed one day and all hell broke loose.
"What's this for?" she said in a panic voice. "So
- your going to run away?"
     I said, "Oh no, I'm not going to run away."
"What else is this rope for? Huh - Huh?," she said.
I could not tell her why I had the rope under my
bed, as I was already told I was crazy. When I said
I was afraid of fire, punishment was a part of my
world. As my punishment the following weekend my
bedroom furniture was moved to another room, one
which had no porch roof to first get onto, so I could
not get out. Fear was worse than ever, not knowing
how we could now escape in case of fire.
     On a muggy, hot, summer day the water from the
garden hose felt so good on us as it came out in
a spray with the sun tingling amongst it. One day
when it was not summer, mother placed Sheryl naked,
with hands tied together and ankles as well, up
against the corner of the house where flowers were
not grown because of its shadiness and forcefully
sprayed ice cold water on her. I returned home from
shopping with Edith, headed   for the back steps
to give my dog a quick hug around the neck. I heard
Sheryl's screams. As I turned the corner, Sheryl's
eyes were big with fright. She was pleading with
my mother to let her go and at that time, mother
aimed the water from the hose full-force at Sheryl's
mouth, gagging her. An awful sinking feeling gnawed
in my stomach as I knew the force of water stung
and hurt. I felt helpless and a lack of control
over my life and the others around me. Mother stopped
and glared at me to leave them alone. I ran past
Edith who was putting the groceries away and went
straight to my room. I knew if I butted into Mother's
business, as she called it, the abuse would continue
longer. Soon after they came back into the house
and Sheryl was sent to bed.
     When I was around twelve years old, after school,
Edith and I went to visit Sheryl in the hospital.
"I brought her to the hospital as she became
dehydrated," Edith said. I felt scared of what I

was going to see in the hospital because Sheryl had
been gagged and tied to her bed. Edith said to her
as she lay in the hospital bed, "See I told you,
you will become so weak you will have to be taught
to walk and eat again." Sheryl feebly shook her
head and closed her eyes, as I gave her a hug. I
told Edith I needed to go to the bathroom and instead
I spoke to a nurse at the desk about the abuse at
home, as I was shaking. The nurse with her arm around
me followed me to the bathroom and said, "We are
looking into abuse, thank you for telling us." I
was able to walk back into the hospital room smiling
so Edith would not know what I had done. Slowly
Sheryl got better and returned home.

After this hospital stay, Edith and Sheryl were
instructed by the social system to attend therapy
sessions. Edith told mother, "This therapy session
is just routine, no big deal." I was scared and
wondered if at therapy, Edith would find out what
I had told the nurse. Meanwhile Edith threatened
Sheryl, pulled at her ears and said, "When you are
alone in therapy, if you tell you were not allowed
to eat, next time I will succeed in starving you
to death." Out of fear Sheryl was scared to tell
of the abuse and denied what I had discussed with
the nurse. I was never asked to go into therapy,
they just believed Edith, the adult, in this case.
Therefore Sheryl was never taken out of our home.

I had one way out, that I took, to shut up about
the abuse, and hope this was not going to happen
again.

Many times I became the peacemaker for all,
as I greeted Edith at the door when she came home
from working at the hospital. I felt if I gave her
lots of love and let her know she was missed, she
would not abuse us as much. I am sure she thought
her job at the hospital was sometimes a thankless
job. I sincerely felt most of the employees who worked
there cared deeply about their patients and the
hospital. A few years ago this hospital closed its
doors and an article was in our local newspaper,
stated inevitably, some employees were abusive,
I know Edith had to be amongst them.

Sheryl's hand was all bandaged up and as she
left to attend school one day. "If you ever tell
I burned your hand with an iron, I'll kill you,"
mother said.

When I was able to talk to Sheryl, she said,
"Grandma did it, but it is okay, because I am a bad
girl." Sheryl was told over and over this was for
her own good, and that it could never change, for

she was born evil and would die evil.

Pliers were on the kitchen table one morning. I watched as mother roughly bandaged Sheryl's bloody hand. Her fingernails on two fingers had been ripped from their beds and stood perpendicular at the cuticles. Her fingertips were bloody. Mother talked about infection and gangrene setting in as she wrapped Sheryl's hand back up. I prayed to God that evening that Sheryl would not lose her fingers.

It was difficult having friends, since when children came to our door wanting to play with us, Mother sent them away. "My children do not want to play with you," she said. If I was near the door after the children left, Mother grabbed my arm and spun me around and spoke in the tones of quiet reasonability, which were to me the marks of her greatest anger. She hated people knocking on our door. After all, Mother and Edith could not have anyone around when they controlled a household of abuse.

We abused kids had the weight of the world on our shoulders, but we still protected our abusers. When I spoke of our problems to another adult, the kids did not back me up, because they were afraid they would be killed or taken away. Not knowing the unknown of being taken away, might be best - as they were told a bad grandmother was better than no grandmother. Bound with chains of fear, I was trapped. Minorities and women had technically been set free - but we children were still enslaved. Our minds and hearts were poisoned by acts of uncontrolled brutality and sustained torture.

Today I still feel like I could weep, just lay my head in my hands, and let go with some great flood, that would drown the world.

          scared to death   adopted white
        4th home in 4 years   flared dress

        I lived & breathed   Dressed alike
     to please my adopted   wicker carriage given away
       Mother and Sister   because I was a bad girl

Me

At one corner near the back of the house, where the sun shown often, giant hollyhocks blossomed over my head. I thought to myself, when I can touch the tips of my fingers to the highest hollyhock, I will not be a child anymore. I never realized how I wished my life away.

Playing make-believe was a big part of my childhood. There was no rock and roll, television, cafeterias, supermarkets, shopping malls, frozen yogurt, personal computers, nuclear submarines, contact lenses, birth control pills, digital watches, hand calculators, fax machines, electronic copiers, plastic garbage bags, disposable diapers, polyester sweaters, cat scans, laser surgery, heart transplants, space rockets, or satellites.

Nothing was ever permanently mine. Punishment often meant taking away toys I connected with. I played house with my dolls, my favorite one was a 12" cloth body Shirley Temple. Instead of looking like a baby, my Shirley Temple doll, made of vinyl, looked like a little girl with flirty, sleep eyes, dimples, and a big smile which showed her upper and lower teeth. She brought joy and sunshine to me. I had a matching trunk, her special clothes - a sailor outfit being my favorite, and dishes. My mother had ordered these items through General Mills after we had saved enough Wheaties box tops. It was like yesterday when the mailman knocked on our door. He carried a large box which mother took from him. I was happy, excited. I jumped around, and waited for mother to open it. "There is no reason to be so excited - because sooner or later your luck will change," mother said.

At this time I did not ask her what she meant when she made that statement. She finally opened the package, and for a moment she was happy.

Later mother collected a Shirley Temple pitcher and blue glasses to match, with a picture of Shirley on each one. On what I thought was a very good day, Mother asked me, "Which doll is your favorite?" I responded (never saying Shirley Temple) and that doll would be the one given to someone else, thrown away, or burned in front of me in the old barrel in the back yard. While tears rolled down my cheeks.

She never threw away my Shirley Temple doll. I think she enjoyed Shirley as much as I. After I became an adult I am not sure what happened to my Shirley.

Sister Edith made two baby dolls the size of real babies. I pushed a small sized baby carriage with this handmade baby doll in it and covered the doll like a real baby. People who stopped to converse with me (Old man Mitchell, people called him, gave me fifty cents whenever he saw me) peaked in and said, "Wow, I thought your baby was real." I felt like a real little mother. These two dolls were never given away or burned, as a matter of fact, my daughter Donna has them on her bookshelf.

One day I missed my little wicker doll carriage, and when I asked where it was, Mother said, "You were bad so I gave it away."

I was confused and cried hysterically. "What did I do to have my wicker carriage given away?"

Mother screamed, "You know, you know what you did."

I still cried, as I tried to think of what I might have done wrong. To this day I never did find out what I did to deserve that kind of treatment. I tried to be perfect and win my mother's affection and approval, but her unreasonable standards could not be met.

Later that very same day mother seemed sad. "Mother is something the matter? Can I get you something," I said.

She looked at me disgustedly, "Go to your room," she said. I wanted to hug her, to make things better for her, but instead I went to my room, threw myself on my bed and cried.

Gloom settled on Mother for no apparent reason. A sunny day could depress her because tomorrow it might rain.

All possessions seemed to be mine on a temporary basis. If I cried, I was punished for being ungrateful and reprimanded for being unwilling to share. I realized at this early age that I was helpless and powerless. But again Mother and Edith said, "We are doing this because we love you and want to teach you a lesson. I, as a child, assumed what my mother did was "right."

In 1951 I was twelve and mother turned sixty-five. Edith had made her a birthday cake and we ate ice cream on the side. Later we played cards and among the cards (glued to the back of one of the cards was a poem) called 'Whoopee, Grandma!' It went like this;

> Cheer up, Grandma, don't you cry
> You'll wear diamonds by and by,
> Uncle Sam has money mills
> Made to grind out brand new bills.
> He will help you in your cause
> With his old age pension laws.
> No more worry over bills,
> Butchers' duns or doctors' pills.
> No more panic over rent,
> Leave that all to Government.
> Dine on squash and caviar,
> Sport a streamline motor car.
> When the blizzards bliz a bit,
> Off to Palm Beach gaily flit.
> Lead a life of pleasure bent,
> But you must spend every cent!
> Whoopee, Grandma! Stay alive!
> Life begins at sixty-five!

Mother laughed and laughed. We had a good time playing cards that evening for a short while.

My Shirley Temple playing cards were being used, and I enjoyed the moment. Mother sat as she thumbed the cards a long while, but as soon as she laid a card on the table, she regretted it and wanted to take it back. I became very very impatient during this game, as I allowed her to take back her card. On most of my turns I had good luck, at first, but later I got a poor hand and lost. When I was close to winning, I felt so nervous that I had to hide the hand that held the cards under the table so no one could see my hand trembled. Again Mother wanted to take back a card she regretted playing.

I stood up, threw all my cards on the table.

"I won't play with you any longer, for you don't play fair," I shouted. This was unheard of in our house, for me to throw my cards on the table and to accuse mother of cheating. So naturally, Mother rose at once and came toward me. I burst into tears, ran up to my room, with Edith after me. All the while I shrieked hysterically. "It's not fair, it's not fair." After Edith spanked and yelled she said, "In the morning you will tell Mother your sorry."

Of course by then, I said, "Yes."

"Say your prayers, asking God to forgive you," she said. Obediently I complied.

Then she said, "I'll sit here until you fall asleep," I felt then that she knew I was right, and it made me feel a little better.

In the morning, I dreaded getting up. I knew the first thing I had to do was tell Mother I was

sorry for something that happened over and over.
I wanted her to say she was sorry to me for the way
she cheated at cards, especially if she was not
winning the game. But, when my cat hopped up on
his hind legs, placing his front paws onto me, and
wanted me to have face to face contact with him for
a second, I felt better. I proceeded to walk down
the stairs. I told my mother I was sorry. All hell
broke loose. She did not think there was any feeling
in my voice. She was right.

"No breakfast for you or lunch either, if you
can not say you are sorry with meaning, then you
do not deserve to eat," Mother said. This went on
forever, it seemed. By supper time, I finally managed
to say, "Sorry", to her satisfaction. Then my stomach
was satisfied.

God was brought to our attention, over and over.
Mother read her Bible, many times referring
to it when she punished us.

"In the book of Job, God told us to act in such
a way or be punished and I am the one to punish you,"
she said. I feared God and did my best to be a good
girl. When one of the girls cried out, "Please
God help me," while being abused, my sister laughed
and told my mother. She too laughed. As a child,
I believed my mother to be knowledgeable and
strong, especially with a Bible in her hand. I
depended on her for everything.

Something frightening happened to me one night,
when my mother noticed my light was still on in my
room. It was late and I was seen reading Mother's
Bible. My bedroom door opened. I was caught cold.
It was too late to try and hide such a large book.
The truth was out in the open. I tried to find
the passages Mother had been talking about. Mother,
her face flushed, reeled before me, glowered
menacingly. My body started to tremble. I knew
I would be beaten, because this was her Bible. I
tried to apologize, but the Bible was slapped from
my hands before I could finish my pleading. Mother
left my room with my light bulb and her Bible in
her hand. I became so confused, I had no sense of
right or wrong. Being hit by my mother was demeaning
to me and left me with the message that I was
worthless.

I read in bed at night every chance I could.
I finally used a small flashlight under the sheets
before going to sleep so Mother did not see my light
on in my room. I wanted to see how the other world
lived. Reading for me was like a lifelong journey
of learning. Whenever I was caught, I was punished.

This was difficult for me to understand, because
when I was younger she read to me before going to
bed. I lay down and watched her chin move as she
was reading (I saw a funny face on the chin) and
this made me laugh and laugh. Not allowing me
to read before bed never stopped me though. I was
drawn to books by curiosity. I needed to pretend
I was elsewhere. I was scared, vulnerable, trusting
and innocent. I often prayed to grow up strong,
so Mother and Edith could not hurt me anymore.

My homework one evening, was to write an
advertisement I saw on television. As television
was not always available for us to watch, that evening
I peaked down the grate in the floor to do my
homework. Mother thought she had heard something
and I was able to run back to bed before Edith had
climbed the stairs.

One time Mother burned my diary in front of
me in the large barrel in our back yard.

"All my dreams and lies were thrown out and
burned to death," she said. That was just what
it felt like to me as I watched from the window with
tears in my eyes. Mother said, "You were hiding
your diary, and I do not like you when you hide
things." Mother batted me across the head as she
said, "You know what you said, don't you, don't you,
you know."

I had trouble trying to figure out what it was
she was talking about that she had read in my diary.
I wrote a very pleasant diary, mostly the weather,
my happy moments, and never happenings in the
household that were unpleasant because I knew someday
Mother might find my diary, and besides I wanted
to forget most instances, anyway. I did not sleep
much that night, I was wakeful and felt I had lost
a part of me.

It was difficult when I realized I was not like
most other children. I had no mom or dad. I
received much teasing from the kids at school.
Questions upon questions that I could not answer.
Children can be cruel and not even realize it. I
felt, as I became an adult, the Massachusetts social
system was, in those years, dysfunctional. I knew
the importance as I kept up the facade of being
normal, so people at school never find out about
my nightmarish life at home.

My one joy at home was my cat, Tiger. When
I came home from school, my cat who might have
been sleeping, responded to my friendly words as
she rolled over on her back, stretched out her
legs as far as they went, yawned, exercised her

claws and gently twitched the tip of her tail.
Sometimes Tiger pressed against me with the top
of her head or the side of her face, then rubbed
all along me, her body slightly twined its tail around
me, while she looked up into my eyes.

I am left-handed, and this was the cause of
more punishment. I got my hair pulled or smacked
across the face for things that I could not help
doing, or did not remember to do it her right-handed
way. When we boarded the bus to shop, I dropped
my coin in with my right hand and hung on with
my left. If I did it her way, I could have been
all twisted up. I had more confidence as I held
on with my left hand, for I was petite and did not
have much strength, in my right hand. She called
me stubborn in front of everyone and complained
that I had trouble following directions.

I wound my watch the wrong way, therefore I
ruined my watch. Mother called me a Social Misfit.
Staircase railings are always on the right side,
but I went up on the left because I did not trust
my right hand to hold me if I fell. This often meant
that I walked into the people who were coming down
the stairs. "You are doing this to get attention
from strangers," Mother said.

When I washed my hands, the hot water faucet
was on the left, so that was the first one I turned
on, and since we threw the coals on to make the hot
water, this was a problem. I was accused of wasting
the hot water and mother reprimanded me time and
again without taking the time to find out why I
did this.

My hair turns counterclockwise at the back of
my head, and I knew how I needed to comb it so it
would not stand on end. She thought I was crazy
or stupid and combed it her way. My hair stood
on end, as she pointed at my colic she said, "Look
at Marie, kids. Her hair stands up." She sometimes
said, "Can't you do anything, right?" This pun made
me laugh, and a swat across the face, was in order.

Whenever I put her new phonograph on, I reached
over the record with my left hand to place the needle
on the record. "Your ruining all your records that
way," mother often said. Finally she gave me the
old Victrola that had been stored in the attic.
"How Much Is That Doggy In the Window," I ruined,
not because I reached over the record with my left
hand to place the needle on the record, but because
it was my very favorite record and I played it over
and over.

I made my circles counterclockwise and got my

knuckles smacked. I also drew check marks going in
the opposite directions. When I wrote as a lefty,
I could not see what I had written. My hands were
in the way, so I had to stop, look, and then go on.
     These criticisms never did keep me from being
left-handed, even though my mother gave me the
impression that I was almost a different species.
Today, I still use my left hand, confident that I
won that childhood battle, to say, Right On!
     Mealtime was not a pleasant experience for us
children. Our rules of etiquette, I swear, were
from the Colonial Days. We never sat down at the
table until asked to do so. We were expected to
listen carefully to the blessing said by Mother,
as it forever contained God helping us to be good
girls, and I might be questioned about the prayer
content later on. We waited to take the food from
the serving dishes, in front of us, since Mother
and Edith served themselves first. I was, at all
times, served next, before all the rest of the
children. We at no time asked for anything, we waited
until it was offered to us. Salt was at no time
used, as that was considered an insult to my mother,
and by the way, she cooked very blandly. We were
not allowed to bite our bread, but were expected
to break the bread. "That's what the Bible said to
do," Mother said. After we buttered our bread we
were expected to lay the knife upright, but sloping,
on the right hand side, with the blade on the plate.
We were not allowed to smell our food before eating
it, or to make any noises with our tongues, mouths,
or lips while we ate. Some of these were reasonable
requests, but most were not. We could not sing, hum
or wriggle while mother or Edith talked, even though
the conversation was often boring to a child. They
spoke about politics and what our town meeting had
discussed. We were never allowed to interrupt their
stories to make a correction or question a fact.
We never, never said we heard that before, or we
were sorry girls. To speak unless asked was unheard
of, and when spoken to, we were expected to stand
up to respond. We had to finish everything on our
plates and then wait until we were excused.
     School was very difficult for me with tyranny
and chaos surrounding my life. My mother said, "Your
problem is that you don't listen and you just don't
care." She could not know how much and how painfully
I did care. I struggled to survive my relationships
with my teachers. I liked my junior high teachers.
They treated me like an adult. Any teacher who
disagreed with my mother was dismissed from my life,

and teachers close to me became someone my mother
decided to hate. I struggled, barely able to keep
up as my teachers passed me from grade to grade.
By fifth grade I grudgingly gave in to the thought
that maybe I was not all that bright.

Then one day my teacher changed my thoughts.
After class, she called me aside, showed me the test
paper I had turned in. I hung my head, embarrassed.
Most every answer was marked wrong. "I know you
understand this material," she told me, "so why don't
we go over it one more time?" She sat me down and
asked the same questions that made up the written
test. One by one with a teary voice I gave her
many correct answers, orally. She decided to mark
most of my answers correct, changed my failing grade
to a passing one.

I have lost touch with many of my teachers who
helped me along the way, but I forever will remember
their kindness while I struggled. They were very
patient and encouraged me as the school year went
on. Obviously they detected a learning disability
and helped me compensate for it.

School and society considered it a problem
for a person to be different. How embarrassed I
was when I was asked to make a family tree. This
was rather difficult for me because I was adopted
and many foster children lived with me in our home.
I had no dad to put in that place as I was adopted
by a widow. I did not know how to list the children
I lived with, not wanting to leave them out. I said
to the teacher in a whisper, "I have no father."
Everyone laughed, including my teacher. Family trees
were difficult for me as an adoptee since I didn't
know the names of my parents. As an adoptee I knew
I had two sets of parents, both real and both crucial
to me. I never asked Mother or Edith to help me with
this homework. I did not feel like being hassled
or getting into an argument. I felt this family tree
was impossible for me to accomplish.

Amazingly enough, in spite of my home life,
I had many friends and often took a leadership role.
Like being secretary of our Junior Class and Young
Peoples' Group at our Congregational Church. Even
though I was not allowed to have my neighbors or
friends come to my house, we still had good times
together at school and church. I look back now and
read what was written on the back of my friends'
school pictures and in my yearbooks. One neighbor
friend wrote, "Remember running home from school
to meet the mailman?" In those days the teachers
mailed a note home with our report card, which told

of our progress or failure in school. The mailman
handed us the mail and we took out the note and
left just the report card in the envelope. This
sure made my evening much more pleasant, for mother
punished me for any sign of imperfection. The
biggest complaint was that I daydreamed a lot and
did not always complete my work. I had to concentrate
on living, not learning.

In my teen years, I was not allowed to date.
I dreamed and made believe I had a boyfriend. It
seemed everyone else had. I wrote a love note to
myself scribbled like I felt a boy wrote, and said
what a good time we had on our last date and asked
myself for another date. Of course, signing, "love,
Ray." I told my friends at school Ray was from
Connecticut. That was easy for me to remember my
fictitious boyfriend's name because I had a brother
named Raymond and he lived in Connecticut. These
letters I brought to school, so all my friends could
read them. They grabbed my letter from me, gathered
around me and read the letters as they whispered,
out loud.

Since I was not allowed to have a boy come to
my home, the animals in my life provided an escape
for me. I walked my dog down Main Street, to meet
my boy friend on the corner of his street. We
talked, giggled, flirted, as we held hands and stole
a few kisses, even in the pouring rain and the bitter
biting wind of a blizzard.

David attended a prep school called Williston
Academy, located in our town, so I was not able to
see him at school. He did belong to our Youth Group
at our Congregational Church and there I was allowed
to be with him. One Sunday after church his mom
said to Edith, "Don't they look cute together."

Edith came home told my mother what Mrs. Fasser
had said, in a disgusted way. This statement hurt
me, as I liked Mrs. Fasser and I did not feel this
statement was fair.

It is fun to read my high school yearbook years
later. One school friend wrote: "Remember the
Christmas dance. Who stole the mistletoe, huh?"
In my loneliness, I took the mistletoe that night,
a symbol of the romantic love of which I felt I was
cheated.

I was not allowed to try out for the basketball
team, because sports were not a, "Girl thing," my
mother told me.
I loved to play basketball. So during my free time
at school and especially during lunch time, I could
be found in the gym playing basketball. I was short,

but making a basket was something I could do. I
dribbled down the floor and with a high jump the
basketball went into the hoop. One of my friends
wrote in my yearbook, "What a swell basketball player,
we sure could have used you on our team."

Another friend wrote: "Good luck in everything
you want, keep that smile. Next year is your senior
year; have fun, because it is the very best." I
never did see that senior year for Mother decided
it was time for me to work for a living. A few years
later, I graduated from Holyoke Evening High School
fulfilling my dream.

To find a job was no easy task for me. I applied
for several office jobs in different mills in our
town and was never hired. I finally took a bus
to Northampton, about five miles from home, and
applied for work at McCallum's Department Store,
where I was hired as a clerk for the stationery and
gift department.

McCallum's was considered "the" store to work
at in Northampton. This building was four stories
tall, of Gothic design, with mahogany railings on
each side of the wide staircases. Merchandise sold
in this store was of fine quality and I was proud
to be associated with this business. When I returned
home all excited because I had been hired right away,
I was put down. "You were told to get a factory job.
You deceived us and did what you wanted to do. You'll
see, that this job is going to cost you money, taking
the bus to work everyday. You'll never make the kind
of money you would working in a mill," Mother said.

When I started working at McCallum's, I met
fellow employees from Easthampton, and they offered
me rides each morning and evening. Being stubborn,
as mother was, she did not offer to help pay for
their gas. I was sure glad they never asked me
to pay my share. I was grateful for the free
transportation, as it made my life a little simpler.
My money was not mine. "You owe your paycheck to
me for adopting you," Mother said.

Not having money to buy clothing for myself,
I continued to sew my own clothes and adjust anything
I could to fit me, as everyone dressed quite nicely
in this lovely store.

Later, there was an opening in the advertising
department: I applied, and was transferred
immediately. My responsibility was to change the
store windows, advertising different merchandise
provided for me by the buyers of the different
departments, as their sales progressed. I also
gathered a list of clothing, furniture, jewelry

and gifts to find pictures in the files of
advertising, at the gazette office to use in our
cut and paste full page ad.

This was like working in heaven to me, until
one week when my boss left for vacation. I was
dying to clean up our filthy office and ran around
quickly accomplishing my routine duties, leaving
me time to scrub and clean the messy office. I was
proud to take control as I cleaned, fixed, and
changed everything I could. When my boss returned,
he called me into his office. "What have you done
while I was gone?" he said. I proceeded to tell him,
as I was proud to have accomplished what I did.
In an upsetting voice he said, "I am sorry,
unfortunately I must dismiss you." By this time I
was too upset to ask him why I was being fired?
I know someone had complained about me because I
left a mannequin in the store window naked for they
said, a long period of time. Perhaps he was not
happy with my upsetting his mess and I am sure he
felt I could have used my time more wisely.

I was fired and cried in the car all the way
home, wondering what I was going to do.

My mother never encouraged me or helped me to
just go on, but said, "If you had a factory job,
this would never have happened. See I told you,
you couldn't do it." Tears flowed freely again,
since I felt I had failed. Then my former boss
Marion heard of this. She called me on the telephone
and asked me to come back and work with her, again.
This was difficult for me to do, as I felt stupid
and ashamed, but I put on my best smile and returned
to work as a clerk in the stationery-greeting
department.

"You are so stupid and you should be ashamed
to go back and work there," Mother said. After all
the bitter battle at home to acquire this job
and now I felt everything had been ripped from under
me. Mother said, "Call her back and tell her you
cannot work for her." I dialed and then held my finger
on the button as I spoke in a teary voice. That
took care of that for that moment, and the next day
I returned to work as a clerk.

After a very short time, I found a man friend,
who soon became my husband. He worked in the shoe
department, which was adjacent to the
stationery-greeting department. My adopted mother
often said, when I did not do what she wanted,
"We chose you and you're special, so you should set
an example for the state wards."

When I started to notice boys, she said, "You

think you're going to be like your mother? You're
not." This comment was usually accompanied by a
swat across the face. So the past, as she wanted
me to forget, she never did forget, and always brought
it up. Therefore, I was led to believe that my birth
mother was a bad person.

Kids at school said, "That's not your real
mother, she's too old and how come your mother didn't
want you when you were born?" I never did know the
answers to those questions. My response was usually
a shrug of my shoulders and a smile, instead of
crying. All the information given to me about my
birth mom came from my adopted mother and was
negative. She was big like a circus lady, mean,
stupid, un-lovable and uncaring. Later these
descriptions all turned out to be untrue. I was unlike
my adopted family - I invented myself. What I really
felt was a genealogical bewilderment.

My adopted family feared that I might take after
my mother, they did not want me to marry. They were
very suspicious of me and became extremely strict.
I was determined to break this cycle in my life.
I wanted not to be a victim, as I got on with my
life. Thus I chose the most perfect man I could
find, a handsome older looking man not sexually active
right away, but caring and a good listener. Everyone
loved my Johnny and I knew I had it made.

Jackie, my pal and buddy wrote, on the back
of her college graduation picture, "Good luck in
all your future endeavors. I'll never forget our
wonderful friendship, hold onto John, he's a swell
guy." My friend Jackie's father taught ballroom
dancing in our town and Jackie and her father picked
me up, so I could learn to ballroom dance and Jackie
and I talked about my Johnny and her boyfriend, Harry.

Harry was stationed at Westover Air Force Base
in Chicopee. Her parents were not happy about that,
as servicemen were not to be dated by us good girls.

When Johnny came to pick me up for a date, my
mother and sister questioned him. "Why do you want
someone like her." They said he had already been
around, was five years older than me, had been in
the service and dated many girls. What did he want
with me?" Johnny went along with mother and tried
to win her over. "Well she is sweet, I enjoy her
company," he said, as he hugged me by the shoulder.
Before Johnny picked me up on a Saturday night -
my face was covered with blotches and my eyes were
red and swollen from weeping over some incident.
I looked so hideous even I wondered why anyone wanted
to look at me.

One morning after our Saturday date, Mother and Edith threw me on the bed, held me down, and Mother stuck her fingers into my vagina. Moving with an in and out motion, she caused me pain. "Is this the way he puts his finger into you, and when you go to bed, do you do this to yourself, as well?" she said.

No - no, he doesn't do that, that's not the way it is," was my answer.

At that time we had not had any sexual experiences and I was essentially naive, almost child-like. "I had inherited Bad Blood," Mother said as though it was a disease. This was extremely humiliating to me, but I wanted to be a good person and not leave this house before marriage, as only "bad girls" left home before marriage in my time. I had no money to live on anyway because I owed my paycheck to Mother.

Sex was always spoken about in a very cruel manner. I never told Johnny of my childhood, nor about the cruelty at home at this time, for I felt isolated and ashamed. This was not a secret I wanted to share with my boyfriend. I wondered what he would think of me. I did not want him to marry me just because he felt sorry for me. So, I struggled to survive my relationship with my mother, believed that to find peace as a Christian, I needed to forgive her. She stared us down, with rage and hate, as if she could kill. Sometimes I wished they drank or were on drugs. It would have been easier to understand if I blamed their behavior on those dependencies.

One day I needed a ride home from work. When Edith picked me up she said, "What's the matter with you? You haven't said a word for our ride home." Talking led to a scene as well as silence.

"Nothing is the matter," I said not wishing to hear her lecture about what was.

I never cared to take up life's problems with her, but suddenly something inevitably infuriated her and set her off. "You know what I'm talking about. Stop pretending," Edith said.

"I don't know what your talking about, Edith," I said.

"You know damn well, your not going to marry John or anybody else for that matter," she said. Edith never married. She shifted around, was uneasy, and that was always one step in front of irrationality. I should have been ready. After a few minutes of nagging, by the repetition of "Spit it out, Spit it out," I told her she didn't have

to worry, we decided to break up for awhile, date
others, just to be sure. I was hurting, and had
not spoken to her very much that week because I sensed
that she was on the verge of a temper. The mishmash
she talked was too hard to follow, but mostly I had
already learned that I could not, did not wish to
explain. I felt she did not want to understand.
(I was to realize in the years to come that sadness
often looked like temper, or turned into it for her.)
Johnny and my separation lasted about three weeks
and we were back together again, Edith never did
understand.

A few days before Christmas in 1958, Johnny
came to pick me up at my house to attend a party
sponsored by McCallum's, our employer. He handed
me an early Christmas present wrapped in a large
box with my favorite color blue bow. I gasped as
I uncovered the most beautiful dress I had ever
seen. I had admired it for weeks at the store where
we worked. Immediately I tried it on and it fit to
a tee. I was thrilled.

"My you look beautiful," Johnny said as he kissed
me lightly on the check, and pinned a corsage of
red roses on my dress. This dress was white and
black in color, had puffy sleeves, and was ballerina
length with many crinolines underneath. I was in
heaven as I enjoyed this romantic stage of my
courtship. Johnny was emcee at the party, and in
front of everyone he asked me to marry him. He put
my diamond on my finger at that very moment. I was
extremely happy and could not believe my eyes or
my ears. This was happening to me!

All hell broke loose when morning arrived.
Clothing was not a gift, in Mother's eyes, that any
man should give his girlfriend. He was considered
a man, but I was not considered a woman, even though
I was nineteen. My diamond sparkled on my finger,
but again I was told, "You are not what we expected
you to be. You are NOT getting married, return that
ring immediately. You are a big disappointment to
us," my mother said," I adopted you to take care
of my Edith, and that is what you will do." So,
off went the diamond, hidden to wear at work and
with Johnny, but never again at home. I never told
Johnny what occurred at home, I figured I could
eventually convince them to accept the engagement
and then the marriage.

The highs of being out in the world and the
lows of surviving home life continued. I was being
surprised by engagement parties, along with kitchen
and personal showers given by John's family, our

friends and associates from work. I still have many
of these gifts and have treasured them. My happiness
began to work on Mother and Edith and gradually they
seemed to accept the engagement as a reality. So
at this time I had our engagement announced in our
local newspaper, the Daily Hampshire Gazette.

Shortly before we were to be married, my sister
found an apartment which needed a lot of work, for
us on Main Street in Easthampton. Our landlord gave
us our first month's rent free as our wedding gift.
That gave us a month to paint and furnish our very
first apartment together. This was an absolutely
wonderful time and I lingered over the swooning and
craziness of it all.

The first room of furniture Johnny bought for
us was our bedroom set. It was of light blond veneer
set with cedar chest to match.

"No one buys a bedroom set first," Mother said,
as she tried to make me assume this was wrong. We
painted our bedroom walls navy blue, hung white
Pricella curtains, and placed a white bedspread
on the bed. To me this was the most beautiful bedroom
I had ever imagined. There was a method to my
sister's madness in having our first apartment nearby.
She came to our third floor apartment, sat on the
stairs just outside our door, eavesdropping. Sometimes
we opened the door and invited her in to help us
clean and paint, but her answer was always, "No,
no just checking up on you."

Johnny was a strong Catholic and wanted to bring
our children up Catholic. I could not be married
in the Catholic Church if I did not promise to bring
our children up Catholic. This I did, participating
in their Caticism classes and was baptized a Catholic
myself. My mother had brought me up as a Protestant.
Mother was not happy about this religious matter
to say the least. Having to be baptized twice was
ridiculous to her.

I was only allowed to date once a week. So
while I was taking classes on Wednesdays to become
a Catholic, in preparation for our marriage, Mother
considered that Wednesday our date. I worked near
Johnny daily so I was able to survive this for a
short length of time.

One Saturday evening Johnny decided to pick
me up for a date. My mother would not let me out.
She stood and blocked the door. Johnny became very
upset and said, "We are going out tonight, even if
I have to call the cops to do so." Mother got very
angry so Johnny walked across the street to a
neighbor's home and knocked on Pontbrant's door

to call the police.

Mother opened our door and shouted, "Get over here and take her out of this house, and I never want to see either of you again."

I gathered what little I could of my clothing, and out the door I went, Mother hitting me with the broom on my head and back. She grabbed me by my arm and moved me to the kitchen steps, there she pushed me down the stairs towards my Johnny.

Obviously there was no date that evening, because we never expected this to happen. We drove around, tears in my eyes, trying to think of where to go. We ended up going to John's sister Dodo's home, asking her to take me in.

I was embarrassed and disappointed, while I had put up with all this abuse, had no money, and began to believe my mother and Edith had accepted my marriage to my Johnny. I would not live and could not live in our apartment, because our furniture was not delivered yet and I was not a strong enough person to live on my own. For me, that was doing exactly what I did not want, earning a reputation as a "bad girl." Being good and a follower of the rules was extremely important to me. I did not want them to say I was a bad person, like Mother believed my birth-mother was. Sometimes I felt, I stayed in this situation to be able to protect the others living there, even though I did not seem to have a big impact on what happened.

Holy matrimony took place at St. Catherine's Church in Leeds, Massachusetts, according to the ordinance of God and the laws of the church on the eighth day of August in the year of Our Lord 1959. This wedding day started out with an overcast sky, and I hoped it would not rain. Jackie, my maid of honor arrived wearing a white dress with pink sash, and a pink flowered hat to match. Her boyfriend Harry drove her to John's sister's home where I stayed, to be with me getting ready for my big day.

Jackie helped me get into my wedding gown, which I had ordered from the Sears catalog. My ballerina length gown had Chantilly lace bodice with iridescent sequins, front and back V-neckline, and my skirt of misty double nylon net formed a billowy swirl, accordion pleated under-skirt with matching acetate taffeta lined lace panels. Jackie gave me a blue garter to wear underneath all of this. My friend Mary let me borrow her fingertip net veil with a crown of white flowered pearls, as a head piece. John had given me a beautiful drop cultured pearl and white gloves trimmed with pearls.

Before ten o'clock, the skies opened up and God
gave us a spectacular summer day. Jackie, my friend
and maid of honor, started down the aisle of the
church carrying a blue, pink and yellow floral fan
while a friend of John's played the traditional
wedding march accompanied by our soloist. There were
no men in my life so John's brother Richard walked
me down the aisle as the tears flowed onto my cheeks.
I carried a prayer book with a white orchid marker.

The church was beautifully decorated with
gladioli flowers. I skipped once to catch my step
with Richard's and limped slightly from the misplaced
lucky penny in my shoe. John's mother looked
beautiful in her pale blue lace dress, set off with
a pink rose corsage. All of John's family was there,
but no one was there for me. I did not feel free
to ask my relatives, still not wanting to hurt
my mother's feelings, as she did not get along with
anyone of them. John's family planned and paid for
everything, therefore I felt I should not invite
my friends. John's mother and sister Dodo visited
with my mother and Edith and told us what wonderful
people they were. I did not want them to know
anything about my household and Johnny did not want
to speak of the night I was told to leave. Dodo
invited Mother and Edith, while they visited them,
to attend our wedding. Their response was, "No,
no way."

I could not cope with rejection again, and I
did not invite them personally, feeling they would
not come anyway.

A warm and wonderful reception was held for
our guests from Massachusetts and New York at the
home of John's parents in Leeds. His parents, sisters
and brothers gave us an abundant and tasty buffet
and a friend of Johnny's, Ray Gosselin made us a
lovely wedding cake. Our cake had three tiers, with
pedestals holding it up and a bird bath with pink
roses in the center and bells all around the cake.
This was the most beautiful cake I had ever seen.

After I changed into my new brown paisley print
suit with a white collar and white accessories which
John had bought for me, we headed off for Hampton
Beach in New Hampshire, for our honeymoon, stayed
at the Beachcroft, a minute's walk from the Casino
and beach. The manager had a vase of flowers brought
to our room. They knew right away we were
honeymooners. The card read, "Best wishes for a long
and happy married life." Hard to believe, but this
was the first time I had ever seen the ocean with
its waves building up at sea and rolling slowly

towards shore, reaching a peak and crashing on the
shore. Then the waves withdrew and built again at
sea. I savored the smell and taste of salt on my
lips. We oiled our bodies with suntan lotion and
enjoyed the warmth the sun gave us as we indulged
ourselves in relaxation. We ended our day in the
still air and the sunset seemed spectacular.

After a few days at the beach we drove our
overheated car, stopping several times for it to
cool down, on to New York City. I toured the city
just like a child I am sure, as I looked up at those
grand buildings. I was totally enraptured with New
York. I could not imagine anything half so beautiful
as Broadway. Stopping at Radio City Music Hall,
I saw my very first show called, "The Unsinkable
Molly Brown." It is one of my favorite musicals
and I still like to view it on video cassette today.
My new husband said, he took as much pleasure in
showing me New York as I did in seeing this exciting
city. We lingered and enjoyed our candle-light dinner
in an expensive French restaurant, where I wore an
elegant pink silk pant gown. In the evening, we
walked along the shore of the river where all the
trees were hung with lamps, as they twinkled through
the branches. The summer air was delightful on this
moonlit night and the music coming from the boats
on the water front made everything so romantic.
I was so happy, I cried.

Upon our return we resided at 14 Main Street,
Easthampton, one of the oldest homes in town, our
newly decorated apartment. The following week we
both went back to work at McCallum's Department Store
in Northampton. John was excited and scared, for
he had received a promotion, going from the shoe
department to become a children's wear buyer.

At the same time I needed to leave because two
married people were not to work at the same place.
It did not matter since I was in the family way.

My Babies

Before pregnancy, I lived with my own life.
Once egg and sperm met, and the dance of creation
began, a new life was in me. It seemed unbelievable
that I produced a baby, out of me, from my loving
husband. Me, myself as a man's wife and a child's
mother. Biologically someone to look like me.

In the 1960's I conceived three lovely daughters
within four years. All my babies heads were shiny
and bald, blue eyed and beautiful. I felt very
fortunate to have girls, because in my childhood
I never had male role models. Uncles, grandfathers,
fathers, and brothers were never in my midst.

My Johnny told everyone how radiant I looked
while I was carrying his children. I felt very proud
and admired myself in the mirror seeing my changing
shape and new curves. I felt fully alive knowing
there was a life inside me. This was incredible
to me that my baby was growing weightlessly and
floating in the fluid of my sac.

Johnny went to New York quite often, as a buyer
of children's clothing. On one of his trips he bought
me a lovely royal blue maternity suit. The skirt
was straight with a comfort panel and the top had
long pushup sleeves, with a vintage-look collar that
had mink attached to it. Each time I wore my suit,
I felt like a millionaire. He wined and dined me
as often as our modest means allowed.

Once in a while I tried to talk to my mother
by telephone expressing my self discovery and
awareness of my pregnancy. At the time I was
expecting my first born, John and I cared for his
youngest sister Tassy and his mom during the day,
because his mother had had a nervous breakdown.
When his dad finished work for the day he joined
us for dinner and the three of them went home for
the evening, then came back the next day. I cared
for and felt comfortable with Johnny's family.

Tassy is a retarded child whom I love, and my
mother said, "Oh my God, don't care for her, your
child will be born retarded."

I knew in my heart this was not possible. Mother
was playing with my mind even in my adulthood. I
continued to care for Tassy as I sewed her a new
dress, which she modeled for her brother when he

came home in the evening. She loved Johnny's old records of musicals, playing them over and over again, as she sang along. She knew most of the words. We watched television together and she knew the actors and actresses names who stared in the different films, and shared this with Johnny after work when he joined us for the evening dinner.

I wanted very much to take John's mom and Tassy for a long walk, but was told not to by his dad, because she had already tried to walk out into traffic. His mother paced the floor most of the day which worked out well, as our apartment went from kitchen, living room, and hall in a circular walk, but was on the third floor. I kept the key to our front porch in my pocket, I feared she might want to jump from there.

"Unlock this door, I need to go out there," Mom said. It was winter, snow was on some parts of the porch near the railings and I was afraid she might slip and fall, or jump. As she persisted, I felt perhaps she needed air. I opened one of the small windows that lead to the porch just a crack.

Mom said, "How do you expect me to crawl out that window?"

"There is no need to crawl out the window, it's too cold to be outside," I said. Wanting to defer her thoughts, I suggested we start dinner, even though it was early morning. I pushed my last load of washed clothes through the wringer that squeezed the water from my wet clothes, of my old tub washing machine, as it had just finished its swishing and bubbling. I felt like an old washer-woman when using this unique machine. This tub was paid for and was mine and that was all that mattered for me. When I finished washing I hid this washing machine in a kitchen closet, because it was an ugly sight.

Mom started cooking dinner. She loved to take charge in the kitchen, indisputably her domain. I felt it was the only place in the entire world where she felt she mattered. After many hours in the kitchen, interrupted by Tassy's excitement of her television shows, Mom was happy. "Wait until Johnny gets home, he will just love this. It's his favorite," Mom said. Everything mom cooked, Johnny made his favorites. She could not wait for Johnny to arrive, so he could taste her cooking. He winked at me. "Boy, does it smell good in here," he said. After tasting dinner he said, "My this is scrumptious, is there more?"

My first child Deborah Anne was born at 8:55 P.M. on February 18, 1960, weighing in at 6lbs.4oz.

18 inches long. Diane Mary my middle child, was born at 1:35 P.M. on June 29, 1961 weighing 6lbs.15oz. and 20 inches long. Donna Jean born at 8:36 AM on January 24, 1963 weighing 6lbs.7oz. and 19½ inches long was my last child. I have silver spoons inscribed with this information, along with the silver cup they all drank from, displayed in my living room.

I carried, not complaining, each baby in my womb for nine months. Uncomfortably at times, but this was a happy time in my life. I carefully ate the right foods to assure my babies a healthy start.

"When you have morning sickness," John's mom said, "nibble a few crackers and sip a cup of tea before getting out of bed." Each morning before Johnny left for work he brought me crackers and tea.

I feared the unknown of childbirth as months later I felt turning and twisting inside me. This no longer was just a lump, but a live baby.

As time got closer and closer Johnny shared our event with his mom. She walked us through labor by phone, telling Johnny to help me bathe in the tub, on my knees, through my contractions. After I sat on the toilet and my water broke. When my husband shared that bit of information along with my face was flushed and I was feeling shaky, his mom said, "Quick, quick go to the hospital, your about to be a mom and dad."

We had no formal birthing classes. At about nine centimeters, my doctor said, "you must take control," which meant breathing at prescribed rate and depth, while staring at a focal point. I needed to cope silently appearing not to be in pain during my contractions. I knew this was pain with a purpose and one step forward to having baby in my arms.

"Women were made to have babies," he said and seemed very ruthless. My nurses were cheerful and friendly spending time with me, making up for my doctor's demands.

When being wheeled into the delivery room ready to have Donna, I saw no mirror. I screamed. "I need a mirror to see my baby being born!" A mirror was found, I was quickly placed in a lithotomy position. No time for the miniprep, delivering extremely quick as I focused in the mirror.

"Why is my baby crying for so long after being born?" I asked the nurse.

With a good sense of humor she softly said, "They know they're going to be on their own and never again have the protection and safety of your womb. If you listen closely, you can hear them saying, 'Hey. Wait a minute. What are you doing...put me back!"

At the end of my last pregnancy, my husband was about ready to leave for a week-long business trip when I started to have slight abdominal pains. I asked him not to go. He kiddingly said, "Give me a break, you know I must go, you are not expected to deliver for weeks, you're just anxious!"

I cried and pleaded with Johnny not to go, until he finally said, "Okay, I'll wait and take the next train to New York. If you are not in labor by then." I cried whenever he left for his business trips and he knew I hated to see him go.

Four hours later I delivered a beautiful baby girl with blue eyes and almost bald. Daddy was not there. He had to drop off our other two daughters at our friend's home, and by the time he returned I had already delivered, (Husbands in the 60's were not allowed in the delivery room.) I delivered quickly. Johnny laughed and said, "You made it happen now so I could not go on my business trip." He was home with me for the next week, caring for me, our newborn, and our other two toddlers.

The maternity ward was a twentieth-century invention, with the nursery glass wall separating my baby from everyone. All parents and grandparents (not mine) viewed the newest family member through the dividing glass.

I stayed in the hospital a week with my baby in nursery, except for daytime feedings. I didn't mind staying, though I did miss my toddlers who needed to stay at home. Thanks to many, I had a remarkably short hospital labors of natural childbirth.

I do not remember who I was before these totally dependent-on-me creatures arrived. My left and right sides were totally lopsided. There were no Kiddie Packs to be worn on your back or Snugli Soft Infant Carriers to wear in the front. The one and only way to carry our babies was on the hip. Tired as I was, I held my baby with my "new body" and felt a tenderness as I looked into her eyes and soon I felt un-tired again.

I wondered many times why through the night, "Muuummmyyyy" was heard over and over again and not, "Daaadddyyyy." Morning came and half asleep I heard, "Uppy, Mama, uppy uppy." So I rolled out of my bed, not sure when my day began. It seemed like one never ended. Standing at the foot of their crib unquestionably awake, arms raised high, they said, "Uppy, Mommy uppy!"

"It's not time," I said and I tried to give them a bottle. It never worked for very long.

There were times when I changed one of my babies and discovered an awesome amount of poop which covered her from navel to knees. I stood there for a second stunned, then ran with her to the bathroom, held her at arms length. A dip in the tub was the easiest way to handle this situation. We ran back to the changing table and said, "All done, all clean," very cheerfully as if it was no big deal. I even loved them at these times.

As each of my children was baptized I watched nervously as a white-clad stranger, a priest, poured cold water over my infant daughter. I knew this water was a sign that we shared Jesus' new life. The old Gothic style Catholic church was extremely cold and empty. Unexpected tears filled my eyes as I watched our young ones dedicated to our church. The Godparents raised their right hands signifying their willingness to help support this young family member. We accepted responsibility to aid in nurturing this little baby girl, to help lead her to Jesus and as her extended family the church, to love her.

I tried blocking out the memories of my own childhood, putting aside my life, as I brought up my own children. My childhood had not prepared me to function well in the world. The "Ideal" family was symbolized by television's "Father Knows Best," with a father who worked outside the home, a mother who did not, and their three less-than-perfect children. Responsibilities were rigidly divided, Mommy made supper, Daddy made money, Mommy did dishes, disciplined the children, and Daddy loved us all.

Feelings of being thrust into a new job of motherhood about which I knew very little - yet one at which I wanted to excel in - often drove me close to breakdown. Sometimes I thought I was losing my marbles. My goal was never to be abusive to my children and my love allowed me never to have this happen in my own home.

As a new mother each time I recovered from the stress of childbirth or experienced dramatic physical changes, I was often brought to tears, now known as post-partum depression. I read every book I could get my hands on. Advice about feeding, sleeping, dressing, bathing, outings, baby sitters, and parent child interaction.

My babies cried, which was their way to communicate and a sure way to get me as their mom to come to them. I did not believe I could spoil my babies as they were too young to be taught any lessons about the cold, cruel world out there. When my babies cried, I fed them, and believed that when

tummies were full they slept better. I swaddled
my babies, covered them to become warmer, and music
helped. I felt perhaps my human heartbeat was music
before their birth. As I made faces and sang to
my heart's content they smiled, they did not realize
how badly I sang. Daddy made up a song while we rocked
our babies and changed the names of each one as
we went along:
    Deborah, Deborah Jean, Deborah John, Deborah Anne
    Deborah, Deborah, eat as fast as you can
    Deborah is her Daddy's girl
    Deborah is her Mommy's pearl
    Deborah, Deborah Jean, Deborah John, Deborah Anne
Often we improvised words as we sang.
    I held my babies close to my heart, the constant
motion as I walked, and talked to my babies kept
them from crying. I yearned to love, touch, hug and
kiss my babies. I felt mothering as a positive
experience. When I spoke to my babies, their whole
little faces smiled, eyes twinkled, and their tiny
noses scrunched up. Eye contact, and as they smiled
it sent tingles of pleasure through me. Their reaction
rewarded me, as if they knew I was someone special.
    Johnny, a clothing buyer, left for a few days
trip to New York City, and I feared for myself and
my baby. I had never been alone in a house before,
and I was afraid of what my mother and sister were
capable of doing to harm us, as they had threatened
me often by phone.
    Johnny had already, to some degree, been shaped
by his upbringing, his culture, his fears and
anxieties. His relationship with our babies developed
and blossomed very quickly. A simple smile from our
little ones and Johnny exclaimed, "Hey, I think she
likes me!"
    I wanted to make time for my Johnny and to be
alone with him, hold, and hug him. We tried to
understand each other's struggle to help and be
supportive. It brought us closer than we had ever
been before our babies were born.
    When I strolled on an afternoon walk with my
babies, my favorite Aunt Edith paused to stare at
my babies in the carriage and then bent down and
sniffed them. "You have the sweetest-smelling babies
in town," she said.
    I came home and told their daddy and he said,
"Of course it's true, they smelled fresh as flowers."
All I ever seemed to smell was pee - no diaper service
was affordable to me and throw away diapers did not
exist.
    I wanted so much for Mother and Edith to share

my joy. One day I walked the mile to upper Main Street.
I gripped the carriage handles and I felt the tires
as they passed crease after crease in the sidewalk
as I got closer and closer to my mother's home. I
anxiously wanted to be accepted by her and to see
the other children who were still living there.
I missed them and hoped they were fine.

I knew Mother was home. She never left that
house. I knocked on the door again and again but
there was no answer. Finally, I looked into the
nearby window and I saw my mother as she watched
me knock. Rejected again. Still pleading I held
up my baby's bottle pointed to it and told her I needed
it heated. Even this did not open the door to her
heart. Tears flowed again, as I gripped the carriage
handles and passed cracks and crevices on the sidewalk
back home. I did not believe she would not melt
in the presence of a beautiful granddaughter.

I never wanted to give up on my adopted family.
I tried to stay in touch, talked on the telephone,
tried not to judge. I wanted to connect as one adult
to another. Many times this gave me discomfort.
Tears filled my eyes, but I have no regrets. I
realized that what happened in that household happened,
and I had to let it go, to proceed with my own life.

My Babies
bald and beautiful

Our family outfitted alike:
patent leather shoes and
white gloves.

Diane, Donna and Deborah
LaBarge passed out oranges
from tiny baskets throughout
the clothing store.

My Toddlers

My toddlers let go of my hand, spread their
arms ever so slightly to get their balance and took
off, 8-9-10 steps to daddy and the wide world beyond.
Then they looked at me, turned their palms up, like
they did when they wanted me to carry them, and
started back to me. Oh, how we clapped and rejoiced.

While playing peek-a-boo, my girls hid under
the sheets. We tunneled after them as we kissed
them, from head to toe, when they let us catch them.
With their arms tight around our necks, our daughters
told us they loved us, "A whole bunch." Hearing
the belly-laughs of our toddlers, when they touched
the soft fur of our cat for the first, time was
wondrous.

Each day there was a slap-happy bath with a
flotilla of plastic boats and ducks in the tub.
One evening, I ran to check on the dinner, which
smelled like it was burning on the stove, and the
bathroom door locked behind me. Frantic, I ran to
my neighbor's home asked the man of the house to
please help me get the bathroom door open. All three
girls were locked in as they splashed and played
in the tub. When I ran back I said to the girls
very calmly, "Are you having fun?" When we got the
door open, they never knew circumstances of my being
locked out.

After this fun time in the tub, my girls ran
naked into our bedroom and used our bed as a
trampoline. When Daddy entered the home, everyone
was spanking clean and sat at the dining room table
while they waited for their dinner. I called this
hour of waiting for Daddy to come home for dinner,
the witching hour, for during this time before their
baths, the children were dirty, tired, and hungry.

When my four year old girl desired to go to
the men's room at a restaurant, with Daddy, rather
than the women's room with me, it was a major scene.
It was not easy to explain to the girls they could
not go with daddy. Our girls clung to daddy whenever
he was around, and they did not realize the difference
between the ladies and men's room. With a frown
on their faces, I dragged them to the correct room.

Remember bubbles? Home made bubble recipes

like; six cups of water, three quarters of a cup
of glycerine and two cups of liquid Joy. The aroma
of dish-wash filled the air while being thoroughly
stirred. My girls and I took the little wand, made
from a pipe cleaner, and had a great time as we
ran with the bubbles. They ran, with those tiny
feet, into the middle of the dish, as it burst like
a small dam across the driveway.

They were mischievous too. One day when I ran
upstairs (for only a second) the spice rack and all
the spices in them were poured all over my kitchen
floor. After my screaming was finished, I was struck
with their curiosity, "Yes they do smell good, don't
they?" I said without hollering again.

The girls said, "I can do it Mama, I'm big."

Then I said, "Yes, I know you helped with all
the other messes and that is good enough."

As soon as Daddy awoke, the first place he went
was the shower. He turned that water on and he stood
there luxuriating, slowly he woke up. He seriously
cleansed himself, turned the water off, wiped to
get the excess, shook the water from his hair and
daddy smelt clean and ready to start his day.

Every-so-often I needed to shower. But this
was how it happened for me. I shouted, "I'm going
in the shower," and I ran fast to the bathroom to
find that the water that gave Daddy all that pleasure
was now as cold as ice. In the background I heard
a chorus of, " Mom, we need you."

"I'm in the shower," I shouted. I washed my
essential parts, sprayed a sweet smelling cologne,
and rushed out. No relaxation for Mom in the shower.

When coaxed by my daughters to the window on
a sunny summer day to see the belly of a caterpillar
outside the glass was a great experience. That morning
and several thereafter, the girls squashed their
noses against the pane and studied in hushed wonder,
the caterpillar's flowing crawl, saying, "Wow!"
As I broke the silenced awe, "The caterpillar will
turn into a butterfly and fly away," I said. After
a few days I opened the window, only to find the
caterpillar was dead. I thanked God that the girls
were out playing, I told them, when they asked,
that the butterfly must have flown away.

Teaching the girls to dress themselves, I laid
out their clothes on the floor, in a design as
I dressed them. They laughed and laughed as I placed
hat, dress, socks, and last of all, shoes.

Then I said, "Please get dressed."

Sometimes I heard, "I hate that shirt."

To which I said, "Get another."

Then they said disgusted, "Never mind, I'll wear it."

My phone rang and it was my mother, who seemed to be in good humor, and I preceded to tell her how I laid out the children's clothes. Her good humor turned immediately to anger. "God damn it, that is the silliest stuff I ever heard anybody talk about, grow up." She hung up, and I could not believe what she had said, but I ignored her anger and continued to have a good day.

That night before retiring for bed, I told John about my conversation with mother, and I cried wishing things were different. John understood my needs, but sometime he wondered why I bothered to keep in contact. I have to confess, for a moment as usual, I thought maybe she was right and it was silly of me to lay out their clothes.

My neighbor always dug up the weeds in his yard, he was one of those lawn freaks. While I enjoyed the dandelions as they covered my yard each spring with fine yellow flowers. The young leaves make a spicy salad and the flowers were magic. We did not spread weed killer. When they turned to seed, if I blew just right, all those little seeds flew away and I got my wish. If dandelions were rare and fragile, people would raise them in greenhouses, but they were just about everywhere, so we called them weeds. Dandelions were the makings of the first bouquets I received from my children. I was weeding my garden one day with my little toddler when I heard her exclaim with delight: "I pinely dot it up!" She ran to show me. "See Mama, I pinely dot it up!" She had proudly dug up my tomato plant, root and all.

When we went food shopping, my girls wanted to help push the basket, instead of sitting in it, they tried to control its direction. I strived to get only what I needed, but I had forgotten my list. I found the needed toilet paper, toothpaste, juice, pasta, and they found some sugar coated cereal.

"That's not good for you," I said, but ended up throwing both the sugar free and the kind they had chosen in the cart.

As each of my girls turned two, I introduced them to CRAYONS, the short fat thick ones. I'd put one in my toddlers' hand and she just held it and stared at me. Then I held her hand and made a big red mark with the crayon on a sheet of paper. A light bulb went off in each one's head. Now, there was no stopping this. They experimented with their first box, using every color, and tried to get them

in the box in order again. They left them in the
hot sun as they saw them melt. They even tried to
eat them. Crayons were amazing things to them, just
petroleum-based wax, not much to them, until I
added the imagination.

"Mommy! Mommy! We found some real fish
(tadpoles) in the pond down there." We had picnicked
at Look Park, a beautifully landscaped park a river
flowed through, ponds of lilies and paddle boats,
olympic size swimming pool, as well as kiddies pool,
tennis courts, baseball fields, picnic areas located
in Florence. All afternoon the pond lay flat and
still in the early evening with its shiny pads dotted
with pink and white lilies. I had hoped there were
no tadpoles so we could leave. There was still bath
time and a bedtime snack yet to be had that evening.
Daddy enjoyed his latest novel as the sun began
to disappear on the horizon. I found some paper
cups that the girls could put their tadpoles in,
and settled down on the bank to watch and said to
myself, "Well I do not have to get involved and it
will keep the girls busy for a while." The girls
unlaced their sneakers and waded into the water.
They chased everything that was in there. Time and
again they grabbed and missed. The tadpoles' radar
seemed tuned to avoid little girl's clutches. They
wanted me to join them but I said, "You can do it.
Don't make so much noise. Walk slowly, your stirring
up the water too much."

They were young and full of wonder and how could
I not help them now. "Okay, okay," I called out.
"Let me get my shoes off." In I waded as the muddy
bottom squished softly through my toes. I wiggled
them, as the feeling was gross. The four of us stood
quietly in the tepid water as we waited for our prey
to return. In a moment inch-long brown shapes darted
around our ankles. Slowly I lowered my cup, ready
to scoop the first tadpole that passed my way. One
was not enough, we needed three, one for each
daughter.

"Yeah, now we can watch them turn into frogs,"
they said.

I could not wait to leave. All I wanted to
do was collapse, prop my feet up, drink something
long and cold, sit in silence and ponder all the
chores I had to do. It was nice to know that the
magical vision of a child had not died in me. It
only needed to be re-discovered.

My Children

John and I decided to look in Easthampton, to purchase our first home. Easthampton was settled in 1785.

Payson W. Lyman, in 1866 said, "This thriving town is beautifully situated. It is such a spot as a lover of nature might select for a residence. Its streams, flowing down from the mountains which encircle it, bearing fertility on their bosoms, the mountains themselves standing like watchtowers guarding it, its variation of hill and dale and plain, its beautiful trees and streets, all combine to render it a delightful retreat from the cares and turmoil's of city life. Its steeples, educational institutions, factories, and well cultivated farms, tell that it is inhabited by an intelligent, enterprising, and industrious people, and that here education and religion have not been forgotten."

We decided this was a great town to bring up our children. In 1965 we purchased an eight-room home on East Green Street, in Easthampton. Here our children played in our yard. We had a vegetable and flower garden, an above the ground pool in the backyard. Our home was the next to the last house on a dead end street. It had a kitchen, dining room, living room, family room, library, bath and a half and a screened porch on the back of the garage.

I had just turned twenty-six and John was thirty-one. John was the sole breadwinner. We had the responsibility of our three children, and some acquaintances made remarks like, "I hope you know what you are doing?" We were extremely excited, but also scared to take on this big responsibility. I still tried to keep in contact with my adopted family. I called my mother and Edith and told them of this great accomplishment. Confusion set in, probably because everything about their life, present and past, was a jumble to me. By this time Mother was seventy-nine, in a wheel-chair, and did not care to see my new home. Our home was all on one floor, not like the apartments we had lived in, and I was sure she would be happy to see it. Edith said, "You are crazy to attempt this responsibility," and she, for many years, never came to visit us. Even though I was upset most of the time after calling

them, I kept calling. I thought the calls would
no longer cause a negative reaction. Tears flowed
and I was wrong again.

Several years passed and I wanted the inside
of our home remodeled. I felt the only way to be
able to remodel was to find a job, for a few hours
at night. The Log Cabin, a very fine restaurant,
build on the edge of our mountain, which overlooked
the valley of Easthampton, advertised for a waitress,
evenings. I applied and was immediately hired. John
came home from work around 5:00. I left at that
time to earn the extra income needed to remodel our
home. Out of a porch, situated in the middle of our
house, we made a family room and library. In the
kitchen I painted the cupboards in the fashionable
color of the time, olive green, with a white
background.

I learned very quickly, when I took on my part
time job, how to cut corners in housework. I made
our bed before I even got out of it. I sat in the
middle as I pulled up the sheets, blankets, and spread
smoothed out all folds, then slid out of the side,
and finished it off the way I liked it. When I dusted
I used two soft gloves with furniture polish sprayed
on them and dusted with both hands. Having all girls,
hair clogged the drains, so I used baking soda and
a cup of vinegar, then flushed with very hot water.
Scrubbing food dishes was a chore I hated, so I used
throw-away aluminum foil as a lining. To quickly
clean the bathroom, I used Windex and paper towels,
and worked from the top down. If I was out of toilet
cleaner, I threw in a denture tablet, (I had false
teeth.) I let it foam and bubble while I laughed
away with my brightness. I prepared my meals all
in one dish, like chop suey or macaroni and cheese.
In that way success was guaranteed. I did not need
eight hands to tend all the pots and pans, or worry
as I kept everything hot.

There were memories that came in a steady stream
that sweetened my days. When I became a mother, my
occupation and hobby was motherhood. I was determined
that my girls have everything physically and
emotionally. I wanted them to live what I would have
liked to live. When John had time away from work,
we planned day trips. We introduced our family
to the glories of the ocean at Hammonaset Beach
in Connecticut, only two hours away from our home.
The day splashed with sunshine as we stood on the
beach, smelted the salt air, as the Atlantic roared
at our feet. Daddy, with the smell of coconut lotion,
sunned himself, while we girls held hands and showed

no fear, we took the plunge into the ocean and
loved it.

Our vacation at Lake Winnepisocki will never
be forgotten. Carol, Carl, and their children Beth
and Carl Allen, close in age to our children and
friends of ours, Daddy our girls and I were there.
Early one morning Johnny decided to take the girls
out to breakfast while I slept a little later.
Our youngest infant had slept in the bottom dresser
drawer, and the two toddlers in their playpen in
our motel. At the restaurant, my oldest daughter
Deborah, told the waitress, when she asked where
Mommy was, "Mommy is dead back at the motel." (She
had heard Daddy say Mommy is dead tired, so let's
allow her some sleep.) The following morning, with
the aroma of bacon in the air, I had breakfast with
my family, the same waitress was there and remarked,
"This must be the dead mom."

Daddy, girls and I whisked off to the Catskill
Game Farm in upper New York State, where the zebras
were in striped pajamas and the lions were not afraid
of anyone. We saw camels who were humpy and monkeys
using their feet as hands and hands as feet. Then
the big tiger cat with stripes, and the leopards
with spots. Not at all like our cats at home. Some
of the tortoises were as old as the mountains and
the parrots must have been born on a day with a
rainbow, they were so colorful. As we looked at
God's creation through the eyes of our children,
this experience opened us to a sense of wonder.
We were real lucky, though this day ended in rain,
the windshield wipers frantically waved to each
passer-by.

On a crisp September morning, I sent my children
off to school for the first time, each in turn as
the years went by. Hand and hand we went as I turned
them over to their kindergarten teacher (only private
nursery school was available at this time) with tears
in my eyes, each started as they smiled away.
Freshly bathed, they wore their new dresses (pants
worn only on gym days) bought from daddy's store,
with shiny shoes, hair curled, they made their first
steps up the sidewalk to Maple Street School. Off
they went to the big world of pencils, blackboards
and knowledge. When the teacher asked me what I
expected from school for my child, my outgoing
daughter answered, "friends and fun." Then they
asked me if she could hop on one foot and she did.
School days meant the beginning of new friendships.
A knock on our door was often a schoolmate asking
if the girls could come out to play. We hugged at

the end of the school day when I picked them up, as if in celebration of a giant leap forward.

They became actresses in plays at school. For 'the theater' we rehearsed lines night after night. John was president of the Maple Street Parents Teachers Association, and he directed several plays, which helped raise funds for our children to go on field trips. On the day of the plays I was seated in the first row of the auditorium and saw only one girl, mine. One was a bunny dancer in one drama, and in another one was the scarecrow. They were the leads in the play as far as I was concerned. My camera was extremely busy as I captured my girls.

My daughter Deborah wrote a poem about her sister Donna and named it, "A Little Girl!"

> I know a little girl,
> Who has a lot of curls.
> She fights with her sister,
> And she calls her Dad Mr.
> She is very funny,
> Like a little bunny.
> She is in a play,
> All stuffed with hay.

This poem was published in her school newspaper.

John and I felt we wanted our children to have their feet on the ground, so we put responsibility on their shoulders and used Girl Scouting to introduce them to various activities, with Mom often serving as leader. To earn their badges, our scouts explored different subjects, initiated a project, then worked one-on-one with experienced adults. Once we hit on something that made our kids' eyes sparkle, we encouraged them to pursue that project.

One summer, Connie, a friend of mine, and I became girl scout camp leaders as they attended our girl scout camp. Not having a summer job, we were able to help them as they cooked, camped, and hiked to earn special badges.

In my first experience at the amusement park, many tortured screams were heard across the land. My girls wanted to ride the roller coaster in Agawam, our area's amusement park. It was an old-fashioned wooden coaster, the kind you remain right side up and seated, unlike some new rides of today. We waited in line for a half an hour, listening to the tortured screams, and seeing the white faces on many who came off the ride. Scared as I was, I took my seat along with the girls. This was not something Daddy's stomach could handle. The long clanking trip to the top of the lift drew out the deepened sensation that something awful was about to happen. The train

went over the top. I had never been so scared.
This felt like we drove a car with our heads out
the window 50 miles an hour. We started hurtling
down and then went into a loop. I opened my eyes
to see how I was to spend the next three minutes.
I saw a boomerang ahead of me, I gasped and the
inner feelings began to pop in my rib cage, then
my teeth clenched, and my knuckles clung around the
lap bar. Then we slowed down. I thought it was
over, and someone yelled, "Here's where it gets good."
Ahead it looked like a corkscrew and I felt I had
left my heart somewhere back on the tracks. This
was the most spectacular coaster we ever imagined,
which made our wait in line worthwhile. It had just
enough breathing room in between the loops,
boomerangs, and corkscrews for us as we realized
the titillation we already had been through. The
girls were overjoyed with every moment of the ride.

After we wondered who invented such a device,
a little research told me the Russians. Americans
take about 300 million scream trips per year. A
leading designer of Roller Coasters, Mr. Cobb, now
in his 80's, described the coaster we rode on, the
Riverside Park Cyclone in Agawam as, "the most vicious
cyclone ever."

At the end of this day we walked the midway
with a candy apple in one hand and a balloon in
the other. I had suggested to Daddy that each one
purchase a different color balloon to keep from
arguing whose balloon was whose. Deborah chose a
blue one, Diane a pink one, and Donna a red one.
Before arriving at our car the pink one had floated
into the sky, while in the car the red balloon had
popped, and the blue one hugged the living-room
ceiling for a few days.

The minds and mouths of my kids kept my life
fresh and excited. I forever washed clothes as I
outfitted them in smocked dresses, all alike, with
little patent-leather shoes. How very proud I was
when people remarked how cutely they were dressed.
Daddy was a buyer in the children's department of
fine stores, like Forbes and Wallace, Steiger's and
Blakes. Therefore the girls modeled all the latest
fashions, obtaining their clothes at a good price.
In the middle of winter our girls were seen as they
walked around the store in bathing suits, passed
out oranges and grapefruits from 'Florida Fashions.'

My friend Jackie, who owned a dance studio said,
"Children should dance for it's the finest exercise
to build up healthy bodies." Attired in little
leotards and dance slippers they lined up before

a large mirrored wall. They learned fast turns, and
swirled around with eyes fixed on a single point.
Simple tap, the time step, and some soft-shoe as
they tried not to look down at their feet. This
was repeated practice until every motion of dance
became like a walk. Seated with other mothers on
folding chairs against the wall, we waited, did crewel
work, gossiped, and occasionally speculated about
our children. Then came the recital and there I
sat at the dining-room table, my fingers flying
over yards of shiny satin, stitched tiny, shiny,
silver sequins into place (Not like today's bought
costumes.) The dance recital was here, again.
I was the typical backstage Mom who quickly changed
costumes, combed hair, and swayed them to smile.

The girls were fascinated with animals, and
just like me, they had our cat Missy to share their
childhood. This also provided an education, as giving
birth was a lengthy process for our mother cat, Missy,
and she never seemed to mind if the girls and I,
along with our French Poodle, Dutchess, watched.

Missy broke away the birth sac, as she cleaned
the nose and mouth, which enabled the kittens to
take their first breath. She then cleaned up as
she bit through the umbilical cord and ate it up
to about an inch from each kitten's belly. Then
she ate the afterbirth, which provided her with
valuable nourishment to see her through the long
hours of total kitten-care that was ahead of her.
Missy licked her kittens all over, which helped to
dry their fur, and rested about twenty minutes
between each kitten in the litter.

The girls were anxious to see how many kittens
she delivered. Afterwards the kittens started to
move around and searched for their mom's nipple.
Our poodle dog, Dutchess acted as midwife, when she
helped to chew through the umbilical cord and cleaned
up the newborn offspring. The girls watched in
fascination, overwhelmed by the mystery of new life
before their eyes. Later our dog Dutchess, cleaned
the kittens, put up with their play like a babysitter,
while our mother cat Missy, walked outside.

When she needed the fresh air she went to the
door and was immediately confronted by an unfamiliar
dog. Missy pulled herself up on fully stretched
legs and at the same time arched her back in the
shape of an inverted U. While her fur stood up,
she hissed and growled. The cat knew this was
the best way, because if she ran, the dog would run
after her and might actually break her back if she
was caught. By this time I was able to call Missy

into the house.

Daddy was often away in New York on a business trip, or studying a play, so he could direct it for The Circle Players, a theatre group in our area.

Knowing Daddy was extremely busy, the girls and I took the opportunity to learn softball in the middle of our street. They learned to whack that ball with the bat. We practiced to hit and catch many evenings in the spring. At every softball game, I was there cheering them on. Watching my children during their game hit the softball, I was exhilarated, and I cheered in the bleachers as I jumped up and down when they scored a run. They were the stars, in my eyes, of every team they were ever on. Nonotuck Park in Easthampton, was a great place to spend our evenings. Many of my friends and neighbors were there and we all cheered the kids on. When the girls made the "All-Star" team I was filled with great joy and pride, even though it meant more running around as taxi driver.

I wanted to push the pause button and freeze those days. I often felt Daddy lost out on many of these events and the girls sometimes wished he was there. The girls were in my arms as they giggled, kissed, and played Barbie dolls. I needed to share this with my mother, but after a brief intense exchange, I hung up and this time I wondered why I even bothered to call.

Living on a dead-end street, we were able to fly our kites in the early spring. The girls wanted so much to fly their newest animal kites. Working at home as an Amway Distributor, I left my paperwork on the desk to be with them. It was a perfect kite day, filled with sun, wind, and a turquoise sky. I watched as the girls tried to coax the kite into the slippery fingers of the wind. I decided to try to help. All at once the kite caught a current and soared higher and higher. My laughter traveled with it, just like I was a kid again.

I taught them to play hopscotch as I threw a flat stone into each of the eight boxes and hoped down and back to home. The one of us who completed the most boxes won. No skidding or handsies were allowed and we could not step on a line or a crack or we were out of the game.

The girls had two goldfish they named Salt & Pepper. They watched them swim in the early morning before school. They told me they blew kisses at them with their little puckered mouths. I wondered if these goldfish knew more than me about my girls, as the girls seemed to tell them secrets. One day

after school the girls asked, "Do goldfish sleep?"
Their fish was lying on its side on the top of the
bowl.   They mopped their faces with their sleeves.
"Next time we go to the store, we can pick up a new
goldfish," I said. We preceded to dig a small hole
in the middle of our flower garden, placed our little
Salt, goldfish there, added a small flag and marked
where we had buried him so Daddy could see when he
arrived home, where Salt had been buried.

     When each girl was ready to ride a bicycle,
a real one as they called it, I held the seat,
and when they did not realize it, I let go and down
the driveway they went.   Later when the inevitable
fall came, after the bump, bump over the roots of
a tree, there was a wailing cry of "Ma-a-a-ma!"
They lifted their skinned knees for me to kiss.

     Climbing trees was a fun part of their life
and I said, "If you fall out of the tree breaking
a leg - don't come running to me!" My girls still
laugh at that one.

     When I wanted time alone, where did I go but
to the bathroom, for definite private space, so
I thought. Time out was mine. Directly from the
toilet an overdue letter was written. Outside the
door I heard names called, like, "You boogerhead,
you are soo stupid." One daughter, now in tears
by her smaller but intimidating sister, gave up and
said, "Fine, take it, who cares."

     There were days when it was not fun as I raised
our children. Like the times they sulked their way
through a day on the beach or zoo because some small
detail was not right. The girls made life miserable
for me when I refused to let them snack before
dinner, made them sleep in their own bed, or insisted
that they clean their room before they played outside.

     Each Sunday afternoon we visited John's parents
in Leeds, a small village about five miles away.
My girls still remember their PePe LaBarge, who wore
coveralls, with candy in his pockets as he smiled
and played with them. Grandma LaBarge always had
a wonderful Sunday dinner waiting for us to enjoy.
The aroma when we entered their grandparents' home
was sensational. (I longed for my mothers home to
be the same.) We had never been invited to a Sunday
dinner, or even invited to stop in for a visit.
I knew the toughness of my mother's criticism, the
coldness of her praise gave her a certain pleasure.
I did not want to hear it anymore, so I just kept
in touch by phone, as best I could, once in a while.

     Very often John's family came together to share
as we celebrated a family members' anniversary.

This one stands out, My sister-in-law, Virgie and her husband Jimmy had a cookout at their home, a beautifully decorated ranch home with an attached garage. You walked into the kitchen area from there, then the living room and down the hall were the bedrooms and baths. It was a rainy day, and they had the grill in the garage. It was a circular iron grill which tortures with heat, the good old grills that used charcoal, not like the grills of today with gas and lava rock. This was picnic ware for the great outdoors. They lit this with a match. The lighter fluid was then sprayed on, which started the charcoals burning. This created a flame with a very pretty glow.

My family and I had a previous commitment and arrived late. When we entered, my husband said, "WOW what a party - they did not wait for us, they just indulged as they drank glass after glass of the good stuff." One relative had fallen and broken a tooth, another passed out on the bed, several almost out on the floor and chairs in the living room. Our brother-in-law, Bill, who walked in behind us, pushed us aside, ran into the house, threw the garage door (which was closed) open and told us to immediately go outdoors. He threw open all the windows and carried this pretty glowing grill out to the back yard. Bill was a fireman and had realized what had happened. He said, "The carbon monoxide caused a loss of consciousness as a result of too little oxygen and too much carbonmonoxide in the blood. If this stopped their pulse, they might have all been dead." Thank God, for our fireman hero.

My girls loved to go to the doctor from toddlers to teens. They laughed, for our family doctor called them, "Joe - Joe Pete & Repeat." Even when I brought them in separately, our doctor always knew who was Joe, Joe Pete, or Repeat.

I rushed one of my girls to the hospital because she was in pain. After I sat in the waiting room for what seemed like hours, our doctor came out to me and said, "Deborah (Joe) is a sick girl, she has appendicitis, and needs to be operated on immediately." That evening I sat in the dimly lit emergency room, with hospital smells around me, by myself as usual, for Johnny was away on another business trip. Nervously, I waited for the nurse to come and tell me I could see my Deborah. As I raised my children there were worrisome times, but it seemed nothing drastic ever happened while Johnny was home.

I tried desperately to plant the seed of

character in my children, I let them know that, just
as there were actions for which they could win praise,
there were others like lying, cheating, stealing
that were unacceptable, and for which they received
punishment. As parents, we tried to mold character.
We as a family attended church, school and girl scouts
with them.

One time one of my girls stole a toy from
Grants Department Store, while we had shopped. I
had said, "No" to the toy she wanted, but when we
returned home, there was the toy. My daughter and
I got into the car and returned to the store to
apologize to the manager for what she had done.
I felt she needed this to teach her a lesson. When
Daddy was informed, by his daughter, how I had
handled this, he was furious with me. Daddy never
felt his children ever did anything wrong. As it
happened, I knew the manager and he understood what
I was trying to accomplish and helped me with my
lesson. He went along with what I wanted to
accomplish. I felt my daughter was embarrassed by
the confrontation, and yet relieved by the opportunity
to confess and be forgiven. She grew in understanding
that day without even knowing it.

I still feel the hurt when my girls lashed
out at me and said, "I hate you." What awful words.
Even though I knew in my heart, my child's
feelings of anger was short-lived, it was hard
to hear those words. I told them, "It's okay to hate
what I have done, for I knew they loved me."

The girls' father was a wonderful provider at
this time, but did nothing around the house to help,
and very little with our three children. Cooking
was one thing he enjoyed, but "Jack Daniel's," (the
whiskey bottle) was most always by his side. Our
girls were expected by me, not their father, to
complete their chores and had to be told day after
day to please do them before going out to play.

One day sadness came upon our family. John's
nephew, Skip, died in a car accident and John felt
very close to his family and wrote his feelings:

SKIP

God was lonely.
He decided that the only thing Heaven
Needed was a smile, so He sent for Skip.
He wanted a real American kid,
A Hunter. A Fisher.
Someone who played the game well -
Not only to win,
Someone who always was kind -
With a built-in grin.

God knew the mother and father of this boy
Would be lonely without him -
But He said:
I've only loaned them this boy with the friendly
grin,
With the joking voice and the body thin.
Someday they'll thank me through memories tears
That I've loaned him to them for eighteen years.
Eighteen years filled with love and so much
more.
With a "Howdy" as he came through the door.
With a twinkle in his eye as he looked at a
girl.

As he polished his car - as he combed each curl.
As he played his guitar - as he went his way.
Skip managed to brighten everyone's day.
Skip had a way that was all his own.
Whether in a crowd - or at his home.
His way was to be one heck of a fellow.
As he joked you along, or gave you the elbow.
Skip loved: The Guys, The Gals, Grinders, Uncle
Rich,
Jill, His Folks, Pepe, Grandma & Grandpa
Burrows.
His cousins, His car, Father Dan Crowley, His
brothers
Life, Fun, Being systematic and neat, Being
good looking
But thoughtful, Being popular, Being clean,
Being Skip.

Skip loved people and people loved Skip.
Some people live eighty unhappy years.
Skip lived eighteen happy, funfilled years.
When Skip died he didn't have an enemy.
Not many people can say that.
Yesterday he was a boy - but he died a man.
                              John LaBarge
                              His Uncle
I felt this poem had great feeling. As I read
it tears flowed onto my checks. Skip was a great
kid. We loved him very much. John wrote this poem
when we arrived home from the funeral and after
finding it on his desk, I persuaded him to have this
poem printed and framed for his sister and us to
be hung in our homes, as a remembrance of Skip.
     One evening it was cool enough for a fire, so
I lit one. I loved the smell of wood as it burned.
It took the chill off the air and was company for
me as Johnny left for another New York trip. I had

begun to miss him the day before he left, I hated
to see him go. We stayed in the Brulett's Log Cabin,
owned by a cousin of mine, which was lost in the
forest of Huntington, Massachusetts. There were
four bedrooms, a bath, kitchen, large living and
dining room, and two screened porches. Norwich Lake
was a part of these forests where the kids swam,
fished, went boating and roamed the woods to their
hearts content. In the summer of 1968, we stayed
in the cabin in exchange for watching their kids
and mine, while they took a trip to Europe. At this
time their Caroline was twelve and Bradford was
eleven. Our children: Deborah was eight, Diane was
seven, and Donna was five. The evening was cool
so after the kids were nestled in their beds, I
watched the firelight as it flickered on the old
beams of the ceiling and fell asleep. What a
wonderful time the kids and I had, and yet with my
Johnny off to New York, how lonely it was.

Halloween found me the witch
stirring my brew

Holiday Memories

My childhood memories of mealtimes and holidays was not good. I wanted to be sure my children had a different experience. When the girls were real young, we picked up the toys, took a bath, shut the television off and waited for Daddy's hugs and kisses. I knew that what we do not resolve we repeat, and that the extra effort to make this time special would be worthwhile.

Some of these meals and traditions are still carried on by my children for my grandchildren today. I lived to make each holiday special. I put my personal touches of decorations on the walls, television, bookcase, coffee table, buffet, dining room table, and on the outside of my front door.

Advent, the four Sundays before Christmas, we waited, expected, prepared, not only for Christmas, but for the birth of Christ. This was the time when each Sunday, at church, a candle of the Advent wreath was lit by families as we waited for Jesus. Our family sat in the front of the church and hoped to be chosen by our minister for this event, as our children loved to light the Advent candle.

During the weeks we waited, our family, along with friends of ours, took a ride to the big city of Hartford, Connecticut, to see the Festival of Lights and the chorus from the Hartford University as they sang our favorite Christmas carols. When I heard Christmas carols, something happened inside me: I thought of mistletoe, holly, and snow. All my friendships seemed to make me glow as we celebrated the holidays.

Year after year our church friends and my family loaded onto a bus in the evening, to go caroling to all our confined members and associates in the hospital, and nursing homes. In and out of the bus we trampled along in the snow. We sang at the top of our lungs, most of us out of tune, but had a great time as we hugged and kissed our less fortunate church families.

The girls, Daddy, and I dragged through lots of trees, heavy boots and winter coats part of our attire, as we froze but tried to find a Christmas tree that was beautifully shaped. The kids ran ahead to find the best tree, until we all agreed that tree

was the best tree for us, and the keeper at the tree
farm sawed the tree, as the air filled with the aroma
of pine.

With sincere enthusiasm for Christmas and the
kids' excitement, anticipation, and hope, we decorated
our tree, strung lights, ropes of popcorn and
cranberry, and we linked stripes of colored paper
glued together to form strings, like garland. All
the ornaments were added to the tree, as we included
the specially inscribed ones that said, "Baby's First
Christmas", which told them that one was especially
bought for them, when they were first born. We hung
the red inscribed stockings, which included one for
our cat and dog, on a artificial fireplace. A genuine
fireplace was not part of our decor.

Christmas Eve arrived and we ate delicious snacks
like chips and dips, English muffin pizzas, cheese
and crackers, as we waited to attend midnight mass.
This reminded us that Christmas morning, was the
birthday of Jesus, as we exchanged gifts because
God gave us our first gift (his son). After we
arrived home from midnight mass our girls opened
one gift, new pajamas to be worn that night to bed,
how excited they were. As they became older, they
laughed and said, "I bet I can't guess what is in
this package?"

On December 25th, after the gifts were opened
in their new pajamas, photos taken, and wrappings
cleared, we indulged at the dining room table.
Christmas was special with the aroma of roast turkey,
dressing, mashed potatoes, carrots, and squash not
so well loved by my children, but eaten occasionally.
We started our meal with fruit salad and ended with
pumpkin, apple, and mincemeat pies and fruit cakes.

In 1970, for Thanksgiving Day, our day to thank
God, held on the fourth Thursday of November, we
brought our kids to Plimouth Plantation" in Plymouth,
Massachusetts to see how the pilgrims lived and played
in those days of 1620. This plantation on acres
of land was able to help our children understand
why we celebrated Thanksgiving. Deborah said, "Where
is your television?" The pilgrims spoke in their
English dialect of thee's and thou's said, "What
are you talking about, television, what's that?"
Daddy explained when we arrived at the storehouse,
"This was all that was available to be purchased,
no television, or toys." Everyone was historically
dressed and shared the life and work of the
sixteen-hundreds.

Diane asked, one little girl who lived there:
"Why is your dress so long?"

The girl's mother replied, "This is not long, she has grown a lot this summer and her dress is getting to small for her, it is almost time to sew her a new dress."

Donna looked for the playground at the schoolhouse and the girl's mom asked, "What is a playground? This is where we do book-learning."

We were able to go aboard the Mayflower II and heard the story of the famous 1620 voyage. The colonists and crewmen portrayed the sailors and passenger who made the sixty-six day voyage. They had the challenge of building a colony, as they experienced a terrible first winter there in the New World. Our girls jumped when they heard the ship's bell rung to mark the hours of the "watch" or shift, each of four hours while the men were at sea.

"How did all those pilgrims fit on the Plymouth Rock?" Deborah asked. She was told by our guide they stepped on this symbolic rock, the stepping stone from the old world to the new. Everyone on this tour, had a little chuckle over that remark.

We ended this day with a Thanksgiving dinner served family style at a restaurant in the area of Plymouth. The owners gave our girls tiny Plymouth children dolls dressed in long dresses and bonnets, with little boots on their feet. The dolls kept our girls busy while we waited for our Thanksgiving dinner. With full bellies our girls snored in the back seat of our station wagon, giving us a peacefully quiet ride back home.

As a child myself, I envied those kids in my class who came to school in April with ashes on their foreheads, for I as a Protestant, did not do this ritual in our church. As an adult, we brought up our children Catholic. They came home from church with ashes on their foreheads in the shape of the cross which reminded them to follow Jesus. This was the first of forty days of fasting before Easter. It seemed candy was the item to give up for my Catholic children, as that was a big sacrifice for them, at that time, in their lives.

On Saint Patrick's Day we became Irish, dressed in green we ate a boiled dinner that consisted of rolled ham, cabbage, potatoes and carrots. Beets were served on the side and (green) pistachio pudding was a treat for desert, Daddy's favorite.

For Valentine's dinner, we had red candles on the table and after licking the batter from the bowl and scraper, the children and I baked a red cake, called Red Velvet. We served shake-and-bake chicken,

mashed potatoes, carrots and corn. The kids came
home with school Valentine cards that were priceless
and Dad gave me the largest card he could find.

We celebrated Palm Sunday, a day of rejoicing,
as each of us received a palm branch, a sign of
peace, as we left the church that day. Palm branches
were laid on the ground as the people followed Jesus
into Jerusalem. Easter lilies, which Daddy brought
home for us, were a sign of beauty and goodness.
We heard the church bells ring as we entered our
car, headed for Grandma's and Pepe's home for a
delicious Palm Sunday dinner.

On Maundy-Thursday we remembered Jesus' last
meal with his disciples, his betrayal and his arrest
as men of our church acted out the last supper as
they sat at the long table, placed near the pulpit
in the front of our church. As we celebrated a
service of Tenebrae - which meant darkness, the
children liked to extinguish their candles to
symbolize the temporary victory of evil; I felt the
darkness represented the betrayal of Jesus.

Then came Good Friday, the most solemn of all
holy days. It reminded us of the crucifixion of
Jesus. My young girls came home and told me it was
God's Friday and that they had to be quiet in school
for a very long time. I shared with them, that Jesus
spent three hours on the cross, therefore we had
a three hour worship service of silent prayer and
meditation in our church on Good Friday.

Easter, the first Sunday that followed the full
moon that appears on or after the vernal equinox,
I found in research, referred to the season of the
rising sun and rebirth. The Angels of the Lord rolled
back the stone and the tomb was found empty for Jesus
was alive again. He had risen!

The EGG symbolized "new life" - Jesus shared
his life with us - as we colored our Easter eggs.
The CANDLES told us Jesus was the light and helped
us do good things for others. The BUTTERFLY was a
symbol of Jesus, for he was free to be everywhere,
as the banners hung in our church. The CROSS, hung
in the front of our place of worship brought Jesus
death, but brought us life. And the sign of PEACE
was what Jesus said to his disciples. "Peace be with
you," as we hugged, or shook hands with our neighbors
sitting close by and said, "Peace be with you."

Easter dinner in our home consisted of baked
ham, carrots, rice, yams, rolls and lemon meringue
pie along with (before and after Easter candies.)
Off to church we went with the girls outfitted in
new Easter dresses, patent leather shoes, gloves

and hats. The pink ham, white rice, orange yams
and yellow pie seemed like pastel colors, as were
the dresses for the occasion.

Later in the day an Easter Egg Roll contest
was held at Look Park in Northampton, and the earth
seemed to come to life. Everything was fresh and
new as our little ones hunted for eggs to put in
their baskets. Our children received tiny wrapped
presents for finding so many eggs. I found egg shells
all over the floor of our car, as the eggs were peeled
and eaten on our drive home.

One Easter weekend, when the girls were older,
we joined their Dad in New York City. Fear lay ahead
of me, for I had to catch a train to the big city,
by myself with my three children. I do not know
how I did it, as I was far from a traveler and quite
the country girl. The girls clung to me (as I did
not have three hands) tired, crabby, and cried while
we walked as fast as possible from the train to a
taxi cab. John, as a children's clothing buyer,
had been on a buying trip for the week. After we
taxied our way to his hotel, I napped for hours after
all my stress. Daddy had received tickets to see
the Radio City Easter Show that weekend and we
attended St. Patrick's Cathedral Easter Mass extremely
early Sunday morning, because we needed to board
the train back home that day.

Each year Mother's Day breakfast was special.
Bacon aroma with eggs and fried bread-dough with
our coffee, cocoa, or juice. Dad loved to cook so
that day was wonderful, as fried breaddough was his
specialty.

Saturday was Beanie and Weenie night as I placed
baked beans in the oven with frankfurters, then shook
ketchup on top, to look pretty just before I placed
the meal on the table. The aroma of brown bread warmed
in the oven made everyone hungry, for this was sliced
and served with the meal. Chocolate pudding, the
girls' favorite, ended their meal. Saturday was
Mom and Dad's night out on the town, so probably
our baby-sitter's thought beans and hot dogs was
all we ever fed our children.

Speaking of BEANS, one day a friend of mine
wanted to shop with her sister and asked me if I
would baby-sit for their children. Many a favor
had been done for me, therefore my answer was, sure.
Over came six children, plus my three. As I tried
to think of something easy to feed all these kids
for lunch, I came up with beans and hot dogs. Very
easy, I thought just throw the beans and hot dogs
in one dish, and bake them in the oven. I fed the

children on the picnic table outside which saved
me lots of work. This I did, and decided to wait
and eat with my adult friends when they came back,
as the children played outside after their lunch.
As my friends entered my home they said, "Oh,
something smells good." After we admired all the
wonderful items they had purchased, we sat down
enjoyed our beans and hot dogs. All of a sudden,
my friend screamed, "Oh, my God, there's worms in
here." I could not believe my ears and eyes. I
very quickly got on the phone to our doctor explained
that I had just finished feeding these beans to nine
children. He laughed and laughed and said, "You
just fed them a little more meat than expected."
They had been baked very well. He told me not to
let the children know and they would be fine. It
was we adults who felt sick, as we thought about
our children eating worms. I am not sure I believed
the doctor therefore I was extremely scared and
embarrassed. I thought the kids might be deathly
sick. I wrote a letter to the bean company and
explained what I had found and they compensated me
by leaving five cases of beans at my doorstep. You
can imagine what I wanted to tell this company to
do with their beans, because our family and I could
not eat beans for a long time.

Some Saturday nights if money was not available
to go out for the evening, we had friends with
children over for a meal. After the children were
asleep we played several adult games like cards and
Monolopy. Johnny was the cook and I cleaned the
house and cared for our children. Many times
spaghetti was our menu with a rich thick sauce made
from scratch, simmering for hours. Johnny served
salad and garlic bread (prepared with sliced French
bread and brushed butter and garlic on it) with this
meal. The aroma of the sauce and garlic enticed
our company's taste buds.

All my girls and I, as leader, were involved
in Girl Scouts as we marched in our Easthampton
Memorial Day Parade. We marched from cemetery to
cemetery, honored our dead soldiers and sailors and
decorated their graves. During this week we put
an urn of flowers on my adopted mother's grave, even
though the girls around age seven, did not really
know their Grandma Pratt. Later in the day, our
family went to Leeds, just a few towns away, where
John's mother was buried and left flowers there as
well. Our girls were around five when Grandma LaBarge
passed away, so they vaguely remember her.

Our Chinese Night was fun. Just before dinner

we got the globe out to see where they ate this kind of food. We felt we broadened their cultural culinary horizons. Daddy brought home the Chinese food. I made rice, cookies, and cut pineapple into a stemmed glass dish to add to our dinner.

My girls loved to be busy in the kitchen with me. Once one of my girls told someone how we made ice cream. "All you need is ice and cream - but you also need the recipe," she said. My girls told our company how they ate an Oreo Cookie broke it open and ate the inside first, you know what they meant? While the girls helped me fill the crackers with peanut butter they learned very quickly, as they held down the peanut butter jar with one hand and unscrewed the lid with the other.

Bells rang all day and American flags flew from homes and public buildings in Philadelphia, Pennsylvania, on July 4th. This was the city where the Declaration of Independence was first read aloud and where the first 4th of July was celebrated.

We heard firecrackers as they popped and snapped in the streets of Philadelphia. Black powdered fireworks large and small, went off with a bang. The fireworks were beautiful as they exploded in colorful patterns against the night sky. What a special time to vacation in this big city, while Daddy was interviewed for a buying job in a large department store. The salary John was to receive sounded wonderful, as we contemplated it on our ride home. We seriously studied the differences in pay, weighed everything and saw that this salary could not compensate for the high cost to live in the city of Philadelphia. I am glad he never took the job, for our family ties were very important to us and our children.

In our little (cupcake valley) of Easthampton, even today we have some of the best fireworks displayed for us, sponsored by many of our local clubs. On television, we can hear the Boston Pops give an outdoor concert along the Charles River in Boston. The displays are staged to music and color-coordinated and electronically timed. Each year it seems they soar higher into the sky and last longer.

Halloween the holy evening is the evening before All Saints' Day. The bedtime story Daddy read to our girls said, "A man named Jack, who lived long ago, was so stingy he walked around the earth carrying a lantern. Today we call our Halloween pumpkins Jack-O-Lanterns."

Weeks before Halloween, we went to nearby farms

and found three of the best size and shaped pumpkins and brought them home for Daddy to scoop out the insides. He carved their pumpkins into odd faces, then lit the pumpkins with candles in the hollowed-out centers.

Just before our children prepared to go out for Halloween fun, we ate a Soup Supper, which consisted of tomato soup, grilled cheese and brownies for desert. Also hamburg and tomato soup over mashed potatoes with corn as a vegetable became a favorite meal at that time of year.

The anticipation of Halloween brought thrilled smiles to my youngsters. The TRICK was for mom, who frantically improvised costumes, and the TREAT was for the kids, who gathered and devoured the candy.

I spent the week prior to Halloween as I sewed, fixed, and made different costumes for them to wear to their school party and trick-or-treating. I used crepe paper or felt in brilliant colors as this was inexpensive, strong, stretchable and flameproof. Pipe cleaners for antennas or headbands, flexible wire for halos or spectacles, lamp shades for hats, fur for mustaches and busy eyebrows and beards, pom-poms, tassels, ribbons, lace, buttons, yarn, and glitter I used. Sometimes, my sweet little girls became ghosts, devils, goblins, and witches.

As our make-up, I used 6 T cornstarch and 3 T solid shortening which was enough to cover 3 little faces white or I added food coloring if they wanted a green face.

When our costumed trick-or-treaters knocked on the door, after it was opened, they happily shouted (nothing.) In the background I said: "Say trick or treat, nice and loud." I believe they did not know the door was open, as their eyes never seemed to be lined up with the eye-holes in their masks.

Mrs. Strong, a lovely lady in our town opened her home for children, adult children included, who could go through her Victorian spooky house. This home was three stories high with winding staircases, scary halls, frightening music, figures of goblins, ghosts, and witches.

Later, in our church, our youth group and some of we adults, made our church hall into a haunted house. A cemetery was situated on the grounds as you entered our church hall with eerie saying written on the stones. Inside the hall was hung weird decorations of goblins, ghosts, and witches. People popped out of coffins, a dislodged head from a body was placed on the table as blood dripped, and a jail with stripped prisoners behind the gates. In a separate room a white-faced person, white piano keys, with white candles in a pitch black room were amongst this haunted house. I was there as the witch, stirring the brew. Only on Halloween can we pretend we are ghosts, witches, as we played make believe. They left our church Halloween hall with wet heads as they bobbed for apples afloat in a large tub of water, not being able to use their hands the apples needed to be caught with their teeth.

Soup always seemed to smell so good as we entered someone's home. On a cold winter day just after my first baby was born, I decided to make home-made turkey soup with rice. I ended with four pots of soup on the stove, because rice swells as I found out. "It sure smells good in here," Johnny said as he entered the door, and then laughed and laughed at the four pots on the stove. This was sure a center of discussion for laughs, as was a time when I wanted to make fish and chips for supper. I served fish like the adds in the newspapers said with potato chips instead of french fries. Daddy laughed and laughed, and I cried and cried for I was embarrassed. In my childhood days we never had fish and I never ate a meal in a restaurant either, beside why should french fries be called chips anyway.

Graham cracker cheese cake was a favorite desert we made for New Year's day. The girls crushed $1\frac{1}{2}$ packages of graham crackers with the rolling pin as some were eaten and many crumbs landed on the floor. To the graham crackers they added 1 T sugar and melted $\frac{1}{4}$ lb. of butter. Then we took 1 lb, cream cheese, $\frac{1}{2}$ cup sugar, 3 eggs, and 1 tsp. vanilla together and added to the graham cracker mix which was already in a 12 X 9 Pyrex dish. We baked our cheese cake at 350 degrees for 20 minutes. Then we mixed 1 pt. of sour cream, $\frac{1}{4}$ c sugar and 1 tsp. of vanilla placed on top of the cream cheese already in the Pyrex dish and put our dish back in the oven for 10 minutes. We topped all of this with cherries making it look colorful.

Steak fondue which consisted of top round cubed steak, rice, and green beans mixed with mushroom soup was a favorite for New Year's day. Each of us had a different colored fondue fork which made the evening even more enjoyable as we never did remember whose color was whose.

John sat here, read his book
smoked his pipe, bench now
dedicated to him

Master of Ceremonies
Director
John C. LaBarge

Alcoholism

The first day of a new year meant to me, a chance to start over, to avoid repeated mistakes of the past. Johnny looked extremely pale and sick. I felt sick for him and wanted to be part of his healing. Lying there in the darkness, I remembered how much Johnny meant to me. He was the center of my life. I held onto my belief that we still loved each other, somehow we could make it. As the sun began to rise, pressing through the closed draperies of our bedroom, I told myself that we could be happy. The holidays worked their magic again.

I could not tell you when Johnny became an alcoholic, the number one question people ask me. He served in the U.S. Army in the early 50's just before we met. He did not hang out at the bars while we dated, or the first ten years of our marriage either. It seemed alcohol was always there, wherever we went. At family occasions, in the neighborhood, and as part of his job.

As a children's clothing buyer for Forbes and Wallace, Steigers and Blakes, at different times in his career, he was expected to entertain on buying trips to Boston and New York. Amongst our relatives, neighbors and friends drinking was only talked about in a joking way: "Hell you think you've got a drinking problem, kid. I've spilled more than you will ever drink." He believed that alcoholics were just skid-row bums. He, in contrast, was a well-employed respectable family man.

My Johnny obtained a great level of success in his profession. A short resume of his life appeared in a theatrical program in 1974 and listed a host of community contributions:

Serving as director for tonight's pageant is John C. LaBarge. Mr. LaBarge appeared in or directed over 45 plays, most recently he appeared in the Easthampton Community Theatre production, "The Crucible." He is a graduate of the American Academy of Dramatic Arts in New York, and has served as commentator and Master of Ceremonies for many area fashion shows and theatrical productions. He was a part of all three productions of the Cooley Dickinson Hospital "Follies." He performed in plays with the Northampton Circle Players, former Valley Players, Smith College and for

Circle Players, appeared in "The Rainmaker" and
directed "Night Must Fall." Mr. LaBarge appeared
in plays while in Special Services in the Army
and made several tours with the All-Army Chorus.
He is a member of this Pageant's Board of Directors
and served as Master of Ceremonies for the 1971
Pageant and as Director for the 1973 Pageant.
He is a past president of the Circle Players and
of Maple Street P.T.A., a member of the Easthampton
Lions Club and a board member of the E.C.T.A.
He and his wife and three daughters reside at
40 E. Green Street here in Easthampton.

How could this talented man be an alcoholic?
Rehearsals, publicity, auditions blurred the line
between reality and fantasy in Johnny's life. Praise
sometimes was out of bounds with the photographs,
interviews, "appearances," and party invitations
were so dazzled that you could not wait to go into
the next play with confidence. The air of the theatre
was unmistakable. Things went well or they did not.
He, as a good actor, knew by the first twenty minutes
if he had lost the audience, maybe friendly as it
came in, was soon restless and uncomfortable. I
could tell on the ride home, Johnny lost his
confidence. Failure in the theatre was more public,
more brilliant, more unreal than in any other field
of work. He lost his confidence in his theatre work
first, then occupation, and home followed quickly.

When he came home from work, Johnny ran into
the kitchen and fixed himself a drink, took a sip
so when he kissed me, I thought this was indeed
his first drink. When I brought up the subject of
his drinking, he said, "I can stop on my own."

He lost one good paying job after another, always
finding another job as quickly as he lost the last.
When questions arose about losing his latest jobs,
he said, " Why does everyone blame me for everything?"
He said it so indignantly that I dropped the
discussion. Our marriage suffered from arguments
that were too short. We never argued long enough
to find out what the argument was about. When we
were counseled, the therapist said, "You two don't
know how to fight."

One Friday morning, when I attended the weekly
meeting, as I entered I said hello to John and gave
him a kiss. I tried having conversation with him,
again he did not response. I became extremely angry,
stood up and said, "I'm out of here and you can remain
here this weekend."

Normally after the Friday morning meeting we
drove home together. Everyone clapped and the

therapist said, "about time you got angry." I
continued to storm out of the conference room. The
next day John's sister drove him to our home with
a   few   angry   words   directed   to   me.
     I was sick of the angry silence in our evenings
and tired of being hurt by disappointments. John's
energies were too often directed towards satisfying
his own compulsion to drink, instead of meeting the
needs of our home and those of us who lived there.
As   a   non-addicted   partner,   I   frequently   became
correspondingly caught up in the chaos created by
the addiction. As a result I was often unavailable
to my children.
     John's touch never failed to make me feel desire
as I loved him dearly, yet his breath made me want
to vomit. I did not say anything to anyone, I felt
everything was closing in on me. He finished another
glass of booze and then poured the rest of the bottle
down the sink. He began to cry and I held him.
I felt his anguish enter into me and felt that my
heart was going to burst for him. He must have felt
that and he pulled away from me, carrying his knife,
he went to bed. His knife as he put under his pillow
he said, was to scare the demons away in his
nightmares. He was more of an alcoholic than I could
have imagined.
     When I entered the kitchen early mornings John
stood at the sink pouring vodka into a glass filled
with ice cubes. "John, no!" I yelled, as I grabbed
for the glass. "You know what the doctor said, This
could kill you!" The doctor had given us a drug
called Antabuse. This was a pill to be taken once
a day. Our doctor said, "Marie, give this pill to
John each morning," then turned to John and said,
"Don't drink while taking these pills or you will
become nausea, vomit, or become violently ill."
     "Leave me alone and stop telling me what to
do," John said. I knew that look and tone of his
voice meant nomore words could be said. He pushed
me aside as he stumbled into the living room. "I
don't want to hear any of that," he shouted. "I
need this." He sat in his favorite chair, book in
hand as he nodded off to sleep. I knew better than
to interfere with him in this mood, so I went about
as I cleaned, cooked, and took care of our girls,
worried all day that he was going to become violently
sick. Later I found out after I gave him the Antabuse
pill, he went into the bathroom and spit it into
the   toilet,   he   flushed   before   leaving.
     Things grew progressively worse as John wrecked
the car, passed out, almost drowned in our pool,

and became verbally abusive. He often said, "If you leave me, you'll end up exactly where you came from - The Welfare System."

His personality changed when he drank, he abandoned all pretenses of being civilized. I sincerely loved him and wanted to understand and ease his problem. Yet, not infrequently I wanted to wring his neck.

Finally, he agreed to enter Brattleboro Retreat, a residential treatment program in Vermont, after a yes-no-yes-no-yes secession. When we pulled up to the retreat he said, "I hope you're proud of yourself for putting me in this crazy house." I felt humiliated and put down. He checked himself in at the office and signed some papers. They told him he would be regarded as a medical patient for the first few days, wearing pajamas and a robe. We had just gone over that before we arrived, and I had assured him that this was a retreat, not a hospital, to make him feel better. If his eyes could have killed, I would have been dead. He turned around grabbed me and said, "Sorry, this is not for me." He never knew all the phone calls and begging it took me to arrange for him to come to this retreat. My company insurance agreed to pay most of the bill, plus the time taken away from my desk job to make the phone calls needed to be made.

Money was rather tight. I was the sole breadwinner at this time. At my job as a bookkeeper, I made peanuts, compared to John's salary when times were good.

So back home we drove, where again I convinced him to enter a place to help him help himself. The next try was The Veterans Hospital, since John had been in the service before we were married. They helped us financially to help ourselves. Again, after yes-no-yes-no-yes, we drove to the Veteran's hospital. Again I was told by John: "Aren't you proud of yourself for doing this to me."

This time my response was, "I thought you wanted this for yourself, I am only dropping you off." By this time my feelings were not quite the same. I only cried on the way home, not in front of him. When I stopped the car he said, "Aren't you coming in?" So of course, I did go in again, watched him sign the papers and heard them tell him again that he would be regarded as a medical patient the first few days, wearing pajamas and a robe. He could only use the phone when permission was granted and no pills or aspirin were to be used unless prescribed by his doctor and given to him by a nurse. Again

if those eyes could have killed, I would have been
dead. This humiliated him, to wear bed clothes to
meetings, in front of strangers, in the middle of
the day, for he was very proud of his personal being.
"This is ridiculous," he told the nurses. "I can
stop whenever I want. I'm only here to satisfy my
wife." I wonder how often they had heard that story?
     "It is only a six week stay," the nurse said.
"You will have lectures on what alcohol does to you
and you will be examined as to why you drink. Toward
the end, your family will come to see you, but mostly
you will have to do it on your own. I am not going
to kid you," she said, "It will be tough! People
will tell you things about yourself that you will
not like. You will be angry, lonely, sometimes you
will want to quit. But we will save your life."
I am sure he thought of what his so-called friends
had told him, "You can handle it, you just have to
drink in moderation, you do not need a treatment
center."
     Everywhere we placed our eyes in the hospital
there were posters, "The Twelve Steps of Alcoholics
Anonymous," or signs that said, "Don't Ever Quit
- Don't Look Back!"
     John called me several times the next few days
and told me about the daily group sessions. He said
he had to tell everyone else how he felt and he
did not want to tell them. When I asked why, he
broke all composure, sobbing like a baby. I felt
maybe this time was for real, but the real never
happened for us. He told me he had attended lectures
on the effects of alcohol. He was scared to hear
that alcoholism was a progressive disease. The
lecturer said, "A person can lay off for ten or more
years and then if he starts to drink again, things
can be worse than ever." They told him he had to
talk about his garbage and get rid of the garbage
as our higher power did not make garbage.
     Starting the twelve steps of Alcoholics Anonymous
was easy for him as he was a great speaker, but he
did not realize how emotional this could be. He
told me he cried and cried, and afterward the nurses
gave him a big hug. Part of his homework was to
make up a Drunk-a-logue, a list of things he had
done while he was powerless. I looked forward to
seeing my Johnny again, holding him close to me.
     While driving on the beautifully well kept
grounds, I looked around and thought, he is not
like any of these people, all sick and lost. Perhaps
I thought this because my friends kept telling me
John does not need to go to the hospital, he just

needs to cut down on his drinking. But after we
talked to some of the other patients, I realized
they were human beings, with problems that could
be solved, just like ours. I said to him, "I don't
care if you ever make big money again, I only care
that you never drink again!" Making big money was
important to him, as being in the spotlight and
a leader.

While we took a stroll on the retreat grounds
with John, some of his anger, fears and sadness came
out slowly: Anger at being used by people around
him, fear of never getting out of these retreats,
sadness at being an alcoholic when he wanted to be
the best at everything he did, and guilt for he gave
his family so much pain.

Johnny was always funny, using humor as a way
to be accepted and wanted. As he laughed and joked,
this got him through the hurts, made life palatable,
as he said. Throughout our married life, we went
over and over as to why was this happening to us.
We wondered and wondered, why us? Why us? Until
I could not take it any longer and divorced him.
He had chosen the bottle, and I wanted to choose
life!

As relatives and friends said, "He had everything
going for him, great jobs, good community life, family
and friends who were proud of him and a wife who
just worshipped him." All this was being threatened
by an addiction, a disease, he tried desperately
to deny deep inside him.

My Teens

As I raised three teen-aged daughters I was both frustrated and rewarded. There were times when I felt defeated and alienated. There were other times when I felt a deep bond and fulfillment. With teen girls, the entire house was filled with adornment. Rings and bows and barrettes and perfumes. Also stress!

I finally learned the teen language. Teen-speak is a different language. I nodded and smiled as a parent and I believed that I knew what had been said. Words like cool, awesome, and bogus had a variety of meanings which depended on the tone in which they were used.

When they said, "All right," they really meant don't bother me or that they resented the authority I had over them, in response to an ordinary request I as a parent asked. "Great!" meant, not that again. "Yeah or Sure" meant that was just what I expected from a parent. All of these expressions meant, "You've ruined my life." Life refers only to the next thirty minutes!

"There's nothing to eat," meant we were out of junk food, and, "Is this all we're having?" meant green things did not count.

"I don't want to talk about it," indicated that I had touched a nerve. "Thanks a lot!" meant why did I do that? "I'm coming," meant when they were ready. "Nice," meant, I as a parent, had really screwed up.

During a discussion when we said, "Do you understand?" They said, "Whatever," it meant why are you still talking to me when you know I've stopped listening.

Sometimes I used some classic "momolies" such as, "Your not, the only pebble on the beach." "Go ahead, cross your eyes and they will stay that way," was another one I used. "Wait, until Daddy comes home," was not a line I could use in my household, as he was not a disciplinarian. "I know, I'm just the worst mother in the world," I used over and over again. My teen-age girls counted the days until they got their drivers' licenses. They washed my car, then turned to me and said, "Spin Dry?" And off I went in the passenger's seat again.

From earaches and heartaches I tried to be there.
From first bra to last blemish, I stood by. Through
eating jags, crying jags, nasty insolence and
desperate adolescence, I waited and welcomed them
back. Being a single parent was not easy. There
were times of anxiety, fatigue, uncertainty. I felt
like an amateur confronted with these teens, whose
needs and wants I could not always identify.

Bathroom talks were the greatest - if only the
walls could have told me more, as we put our make-up
on and styled our hair. You know the telephone?
Sometimes I thought the phone was a part of my
teen-ager's ear.

If I were to make up a calendar based on some
teen-age feelings, I should say - there were six
Saturdays and one Sunday - nothing in between.

Once when the girls were older they tried
skipping school and I received a phone call, at work,
from my sister-in-law Marianne who said, "How come
your girls are home?"

I responded, "They're in school where I dropped
them off."

"I don't believe they stayed, because they
answered the phone when I called your house," she
said.

Not being able to leave, I called my sister
Edith and she went to pick up the girls. When she
arrived at our home, the girls were back in bed in
their pajamas. My sister had them get dressed,
brought them to the principal's office, and back
into class. The girls were not happy with me. I
had dropped them off at the front door and they had
walked through the school and out the back door.
They told me their daddy, who was intoxicated, said
they could stay at home. Daddy was intimidated by
my sister Edith and never said a word when Edith
picked up the girls to bring them back to school.

Dancing lessons, competition, and recitals were
a big part of our life. During the girls' lessons
they faced the large mirrored walls which stretched
to gracefully reach the ceiling and they bent forward
until their nose's touched their knees. They walked
beautifully for four counts, circled around the
room with their arms out and head held high.
Sometimes they stood on one leg with their other
leg extended out behind them and then a run, run,
grand jete. Diane with her pretty pink satin toe
shoes with satin ribbons carefully wrapped around
her calves clear up to her knees danced very
gracefully. Her pink chiffon skirt spun out in
a perfect circle around her. Sometimes I caught

her as she smiled at her reflection in the mirror
and she was embarrassed when she saw me watching.
At the recitals the music changed and the dancers
wove their arms and bodies in and out of each other
in complicated patterns. "That was wonderful!"
I said as I clapped loudly while the dancers made
their exits.

When our girls were young I put them to sleep
at night with a bedtime story. As teens, they came
in at bedtime and told me stories that kept me awake
all night! When the girls started a sentence with,
"OH," it meant they lost or needed help with
something, or perhaps needed a ride. Many times,
"I've cleaned my room," meant that the mess that
was in the middle of the room, was now on the side
or under the bed. Teens never seemed to put anything
away, so they never did know where away was. When
they said, "I have nothing to wear," they meant that
the laundry was hidden so well, they couldn't even
find it. "Everybody is wearing it," meant they saw
the advertisement on TV.

If I asked, "How was school today?" Their "Okay"
meant don't ask. Most of the time "I don't have
any homework," meant I've misplaced my book. "Can
you help me with this?" meant it was due today.

Life was good for our children. They were raised
in a comfortable home as middle class Catholic family.
I did not have to work to live comfortably, therefore
I was very active in their lives. I attended all
sport events, was a Girl Scout leader, and attended
all dance competitions. Their father was a buyer
of children's clothing for only the finest children's
clothing stores. Therefore our children were dressed
in the newest fashions. He was involved in their
school plays as the director and very active in the
town's entertainment events. Like I said, "Life
was good in their early adolescence."

At the breakfast table, one Saturday morning,
I informed our three girls that their father had
a disease. This disease was called Alcoholism.
I told them their father was what they called a
"closet drinker." He went to the store purchased
his alcohol and hid it, drinking straight from the
bottle throughout the day at work, as well as home.

Our girls were naive to the problems of the
world. The look of confusion was on their faces.
I continued my conversation by telling them we were
going to attend meetings as a family to educate
ourselves on the disease, and life around our home
would change. I now needed to work and our three
girls would have to help around the house more, as

well as our spending habits needed adjustment.

Life sure changed. Our girls took on more
responsibility as I was thrown into the big job
market. At the Al-Ateen meetings, the girls heard
other teen-agers talk about the verbal, physical
or sexual abuse they were living with in their homes.
Our girls, nor I, did not have to contend with
physical or sexual abuse in our home, so the fact
that their father was an alcoholic was not a reality
to them yet.

On a warm August morning, while I was at work,
my girls watched their unemployed father in the pool
through the dining room window. He tried to climb
out of the pool on the ladder. He climbed a few
steps up and then fell back into the pool. At this
point they giggled and had no idea how serious this
event was. After several attempts of this climb,
their father fell from the ladder. He had passed
out and was now under the water. They ran to the
pool and Diane jumped in to try and help him. Their
father was a large man but in the water it was easy
to help him. The problem was how were they to get
him up and out of the pool?

Diane held her father's head above the water
and Donna ran and asked our neighbor, Mr. LaPinski
for help. Finally, with the three of them, they
managed to lift him out of the pool. Diane ran
in the house, called an ambulance, because her father
was in and out of consciousness, and then called
me at work.

When Diane returned her father was conscious
again and pleaded with her not to let anyone take
him to the hospital. Later on she realized the reason
for his request was he could not drink there. The
ambulance came and Diane rode the long ride next
to her father to the hospital. Donna waited for
me to arrive home from work so we could join them.
Their father stayed for a few days for tests as to
why he blacked out in the pool. Diane had terrible
guilt inside her for not being able to help her father
stay out of the hospital. It was years later that
my girls actually understood what had happened to
their lives. Life changed drastically for them in
their early teens.

Our oldest daughter Deborah, had to cope with
the adverse effects of her father's addiction to
alcohol and her difficulty with the upset in the
family. As she was our oldest child I felt all of
a sudden the bottom dropped out and her security
was gone. John and I persuaded her to succeed in
life and work hard for her wants and needs. At

this time John was without a job, therefore many
of her wants could not be met. We as her parents
were on the verge of separation when disaster
happened. I tried to cope to keep my family together
financially and emotionally. It was tough and it
was now to be even tougher. Deborah responded with
a drive to succeed, cared for no one but herself.
For her, this was a way to be safe, to not have to
deal with the problems of others around her, to
survive at a difficult time.

One evening after watching Deborah play in a
softball game, she asked me if she could go out
to eat with her girl friend and family. I agreed,
but I panicked when she did not come home at what
I thought was a reasonable hour. The evening became
later and later, and Deborah had ridden her bicycle
to the game and I knew there had been plenty of time
for her to eat out and return home on her bicycle
by then. I got into my car and drove around town
as I tried to find her, but with no luck. I tried
to tell myself everything would be fine.

Finally she rode her bike into the garage.
I yelled at her. "Where have you been?"

She responded with, "Just riding around,
thinking." Even though her Dad was not physically
abusive or a raving loud drunk, there were unexpected
and uncontrollable circumstances that happened.

I said, "My god, you had me worried to death,
being on your bike this late at night. You will
be grounded for this behavior. I will not sit here
worried to death, you know better." She went without
comment to her room and I went to mine.

The next thing I knew my slumber was shattered
by the shrill ring of the phone at about two o'clock
in the morning. It was the voice of the mother of
her friend who she had gone out to eat with that
evening. "Don't get alarmed:" she said. "Deborah
is here in my home with me. She was about to run
away from home and stopped at my house to say good-by
to my daughters. I convinced her to stay here in
my home. She does not know I am calling you, but
she told me she left a note for you under her pillow."

I said, "No way, Deborah is in her bed, I saw
her going to her room just before I retired for
the evening." Dropping the phone I ran into her
bedroom to retrieve the note. While reading the
note over the phone to the woman who called me, I
could not believe what I had read.

Deborah's note was addressed to: "The Person
Who Is Married To My Dad." Her note said, "I can
not stand the sight of you. Why did you not realize

that, when I moved my bedroom down to the cellar."
When Deborah asked to have her bedroom moved down
to the basement, I figured she was a maturing
teen-ager, who needed her own space. I even painted
the whole cellar for her, the floor gray and the
walls white. Her father failed to meet his financial
obligation, so we had no money to refinish it for
her. I hung some old drapes across the beams to
block off her section to make it more private.

The note went on to say, "There was no food
in the house, only hot dogs, hamburgers and peanut
butter." She was right. The steaks, lobsters and
other specialties had to go, for I was now the sole
breadwinner.

At one time I smelled vitamins when entering
her room. In her letter she said, "You were right,
I was taking vitamins because we had no food."
Meanwhile, her two sisters ate what I could afford
to buy for groceries and seemed to be fine. Deborah
took over responsibilities, wanted to give me advice
as to what her sisters should or should not be allowed
to do. Each child was different with different
feelings and wants. Divorce was not mentioned at
the time Deborah was still at home. I am sure it
was a thought in her head. She had said many times,
"Why do you put up with him?" I knew this was a
crucial childhood event, knowing her father was a
patient in the Veterans Hospital. She decided to
run away while he attended the alcholic program
that was available to him.

I felt that Deborah, being my oldest child and
I had a good relationship, as we discussed changes
that had to be made for our family to function at
this time. Maybe she resented all the responsibility
of this business called survival.

Letters written to me, were strewn about the
porch one day. I picked them up returned them to
the box they had been in, and wondered why they
were thrown about. These were very nasty letters
written by my mother addressed to me, which
contained many lies. She was not very nice as she
described me as a teen-ager dating young men. I
was called every bad name you could possibly call
any teen-ager, and I am sure Deborah believed all˙
I wondered why they were thrown about, but I had
enough to think about and too tired working two jobs
to get into any discussion over this. Now I do know
for sure she must have believed what was written
in these letters and probably at that time needed
some reinforcement that I was a bad person.

Deborah said in the note: "There isn't a doubt

in my mind that I'm doing what is best for me. I
can not and could not stand you anywhere around me
and you wanted kisses when I left for school, NO
WAY, Lady. They were too special for you."

Deborah left on a Thursday evening on her new
10 speed bike which she had bought with her own
money. As I looked around I discovered she packed
her tennis racket and balls, clothes, vitamins,
and had taken her money out of the bank. It looked
like she departed with a backpack full and heavy
on her ten speed bike.

That Friday morning I went to the Veterans
Hospital for an alcoholic rehabilitation meeting.
John was scheduled to come home after the meeting
to spend the weekend with us as a family. I was
then to bring him back on Sunday evening. I cried
and cried, as I tried to understand what had happened
to make Deborah want to run away. I knew it was
not easy for her or any of us, but I did feel
we had discussed Dad's sickness and how we had to
tighten the reins until things got better. When
I arrived at the Veteran's Hospital, I felt drained
and tired. I waited until someone at the meeting
asked me how I was doing, and then I blurted out
between tears what had happened early that morning.
The doctor screamed at me and said, "Why didn't you
call John immediately and tell him Deborah had left
home."

My response was: "I did what I thought was best,
thinking what could he do at 2:00 am being here
in the rehab center." I felt I had done all that
could be done. I was told Deborah would be spoken
to in the morning and we could then try to get
together and discuss the best way to proceed. The
doctor had expected me to run into the meeting,
hysterical, screaming about what was going on in
my life. I felt the doctor was unfair when he said
why didn't I call John as together we had established
our parenting rolls; John was the breadwinner and
I was the disciplinarian. I told him I coped with
my problem, cried and cried by myself, knowing that
John did not need one more guilt trip and had enough
to contend with at this time. I was not used to
discussing events with John as he was a very quiet
alcoholic who did not want to face life as it was.
He said, "The children were my responsibility and
that it was my job to cope with them." This made
sense to me since John was either working, directing,
or acting in the theatre.

John came home with me that weekend and I talked
to the mother of Deborah's friends. "It is best you

just let her alone for now," she said. She feared that if I came near, she might really run away. Meanwhile, I kept in touch with the doctors at the Veterans Hospital, who told me to leave her there for now. I followed their advice for two weeks and kept in contact with the family with which she stayed.

Finally I could not eat, sleep, work or function and decided I must just go to their house and talk with Deborah, demanding she come home. They had a beautiful large home with five bedrooms and many bathrooms. Fuel and plumbing was their business, therefore they did not need to worry about surviving. When I arrived, Deborah was still sleeping. Her friend's mom offered me some coffee as we talked and tried to sort things out. I saw Deborah coming down the stairs, so I got up from the table and headed for the stairs to speak to her. She pushed me aside, ran out the door, and said, "Get out of my life."

Hours went by and she did not come back to this house. Meanwhile I had gone home to my other girls. By dinner time I panicked and went to the police station. They insisted she would return before dark that evening, and that there was not much they could do at this time. Several hours later the phone rang! Her girlfriend had found her in the woods behind their house. She stayed with them after that incident, and that scared me as I felt it best she live with them, rather than roaming the streets of California, New York or Florida. Questions like: Where is she tonight? Is she warm? Is she hungry? Is she lonely? I could at least put these questions aside for now. My hands that held this tiny first-born child had to open up completely and let go. It was not easy. I thanked God, for at least I knew she was taken care of and I knew where she was.

After a few weeks had gone by, I received a call from the family she stayed with. They said they had some papers for me to sign. I was intimidated because they were a prominent family in town and I was confused as whether to love them for helping me or hate them for taking my child. Deborah had gone to a lawyer and had papers drawn up that said I could not bother her, and made her friend's parents her legal guardians. Deborah threatened us. "If we did not sign, she would leave and we would never know where she was."

I sincerely believed her and did not wish to put Deborah nor myself through that kind of torment.

My therapist at the Veterans Hospital said, "Think of it this way, if you were a rich parent you might have placed your child in a boarding school and that would have been accepted by society and not even thought about twice. But now society puts shame and disappointment upon you, which makes life rather difficult." Society, relatives, and friends seemed to shy away from discussing my predicament and sometimes this was awkward for all of us as my tears flowed easily.

Deborah had worked for this family while still at home with us, banking her money for college. Knowing the amount of money she had already saved for college, I did know she could have easily started her way across the country. The following weekend, John and I went to their house and signed the papers allowing them to be her temporary guardians. I tried to talk to Deborah, but she would not talk. John just sat in the chair and cried as if he was depressed, and never even tried to say anything to Deborah. She looked quite stern as she stood in the room only long enough for us to sign the legal papers. Then she poured herself a glass of milk and proceeded to go upstairs to the bedrooms.

Meanwhile Deborah and my other two children attended the same high school, dance studio, scouts, and softball games. When someone said to Deborah, "Here comes your sister," she said, "That's not my sister." Deborah many times called her friend's mother, "Mom" in front of my other children. That hurt them very much. Diane and Donna loved their big sister. I always thought Deborah took a supportive, nurturing role in relation to her younger sisters. I guess I was wrong. It was not easy for me to watch while someone else brought my daughter Deborah to attend the bus trip, while I brought my Diane and Donna to the same bus.

Occasionally we saw each other downtown, but Deborah crossed the street when she saw me. I never had the joy of being able to express my pride in her when she received different awards at school and graduated from high school or college. Deborah and Diane went to the same Junior-Senior prom looked at each other with amazement for they had each bought the exact same gown only in different colors. Not living in the same household this was amazing to me. I told her friend's mom, "Deborah will be good for you," as she seemed to mind me and do what she was told most of the time.

John and I were active in our town's Junior Miss Pageant Program. This particular year I was

a chaperon for Sharon Ostrander helping her to become
our next Junior Miss. I cried, so happy I was able
to help Sharon succeed, but I cried sadly too, because
I was not able to help my own daughter in life.
In her senior year Deborah was announced as the
daughter of her friend's parents. That really hurt.
I was there to see her do her best as a Junior Miss,
with tears rolling down my cheeks, as I was not
seated where my friends and all the other parents
were, not recognized as her parent (by her.) She
never placed in our town's Junior Miss Pageant.

Deborah went on to graduate from Philadelphia
College of Pharmacy, again not naming us as parents
at graduation. Over and over the denial and identity
as her parents hurt us tremendously.

My middle child, Diane often tried to have a
relationship with her sister Deborah, but whenever
I was mentioned Deborah said, "I don't want to be
with you, if you keep mentioning her," meaning me.
In those intervening years, Diane and Donna had
no relationship with their older sister. It hurts
me to think that she has involved her sisters in
this family relationship. If she hated me that is
one thing, but why her sisters? Hating me was alright
because she could not hate her father, a sick man.
I tried not to bad mouth their father but help them
understand he had a disease. Most conversations
on the phone between Diane and Deborah never seemed
to have much feeling. One of the last conversations
Deborah and Diane had, Deborah said, "If you knew
what I know, you would hate her too."

Diane responded, "What could you know that
I don't? We were only one and a half years apart."
After that, Deborah refused to talk anymore, and
remained quiet. It would be helpful to know - what
she has held over my head, so that we could deal
with it. Perhaps, I will never know. I am sure
relatives, friends and acquaintances after reading
this book might wonder, since I was an abused child,
was I also an abuser? The answer to that is no -
I blocked out my childhood while I brought up my
family. I read every book I could get my hands
on - with information on how children should be
brought up. The family Deborah was living with mailed
me a poem called, "Children Learn What They See"
and I did not know whether to consider that an insult
or not. That was exactly what I tried to do when
I attended Alon, to help us as a family help
ourselves. I am sure I made mistakes along the way
- it's a fact of life. There are mistakes along
the way which I wish I could erase - but I realize

it is all a part of parenting. I am not infallible.

Someone else announced the engagement of my daughter, as theirs and her father, sister, nor myself was welcome to attend her wedding. Our minister asked her, "Do you think you could make amends with your Mother, Father and Sisters before you go on with a new life with your fiance?" Our minister wanted her to write the bad debt off emotionally, so that she could go on with her life.

She simply said, "Forget it," and got married in Stevens Chapel, a prep school called Williston Academy in our town of Easthampton. All of my friends and their children attended her showers and her wedding, while we were disappointed and left out.

My friends gave me photos of her shower and wedding. She looked beautiful in her wedding gown of white taffeta featuring a high neckline, leg of mutton sleeves and a fitted bodice. It was trimmed with Alencon and silk Venise lace and pearls. Her bridal hat was trimmed with matching lace and an illusion pouf. As she walked down the aisle on someone else's arm, she carried a bouquet of white roses and baby's breath. Her father never got the chance to walk his first born down the aisle.

Her reception was held at the Wyckoff Country Club with "Thursday's Child," an exceptional band playing their favorite music. Following the reception they left on a cruise to the Caribbean.

Deborah received a bachelor of science degree in pharmacy from the Philadelphia College of Pharmacy and Science in Philadelphia, Pennsylvania. She was employed by DuPont Pharmaceuticals as a sales representative. Her husband Matthew attends C. W. Post College of Long Island University in New York. After their honeymoon they resided in Port Jefferson Station, N.Y.

I thought when she had a family, maybe she would come around and realize how very hard things were for us at that time. She wanted as I did: a healthy family life with Mom, Dad and siblings, as she saw her friend's family as a perfect family. Deborah had a strong need for control, placed a high value on being successful. Having her own family and the bonds of her own children did not seem to matter, as I have two grandchildren I have never seen, and a son-in-law I will never get to know. She does not find it necessary or even possible to make peace with her family and her past. I hope to be able to make peace with her, as forgiveness helps me regain my emotional freedom and peace of mind.

Some fifteen years after Deborah left us, my

job took me to a community in Pennsylvania, the
state Deborah lived in. I was to be there for ten
days, having a Saturday off in between. My husband
Michel, not her father, and I had decided to
go to her house, knock on her door, and demand to
see our grandchildren. Having Friday morning off,
I ventured forth to find her house, so that on
Saturday morning when Michel was with me, we would
know where to go. I found her house though no one
was there, for I figured they both worked during
the day. I took pictures of the front, back and
sides of this lovely home, I thought at least her
sisters could see what her house looked like on the
outside. It was a very large new home situated in
a beautiful neighborhood.

When Michel and I drove to their home at about
ten o'clock on Saturday morning, we knocked on the
door, only to be informed they did not live there.
The people who bought the house from them had no
idea where they had moved. We knocked on the
neighbor's door and the woman said, they thought
they had moved closer to where their work was, but
where that was she was not sure. Extremely
disappointed we decided to go to the post office
and see if they had left a forwarding address, but
they had not. We drove to adjoining towns and looked
in the phone books. I found two names spelled the
way Deborah spelled her name, in two different towns.
By the time we had traveled to these different towns
it was dark, and we never did find their home. We
had spent the day being detectives.

God moves in mysterious ways and perhaps that
was not the time to re-unite. I was angry and had
intentions to demand to see my grandchildren.

My grieving goes on and on with all kinds of
feelings. Sometimes I am not sure what my feelings
are. I do know that she was conceived and raised
out of love.

During the girls teen years John and I separated
and spoke of divorce. Many unanticipated events
were capable of changing our days. John was an
alcoholic and in spite of recovery programs, the
situation only seemed to worsen. I knew that we
could not continue as we were. Confusion and
uncertainty caught up with me and I could not handle
life any more, as it was. I felt divorce was best,
for all of us, including the alcoholic.

One evening when I returned home from work there
on the dining room table was a note. It was from
my daughter Donna whom I had grounded. My heart
went in my mouth.

She said, "Dear Mom, don't bother looking for me
in this house, for I am not here. I will be home
tonight around 10:00pm. I'm sick of everything that's
going on and I have to get away. We can talk tonight
when I get home. I promise I will be home tonight.
Love, Donna."

I waited and waited and around 10:15pm she did
come home and we had a real good talk. Life was
not easy at this time for any one of us. Donna had
stressed in her note, she would be home that evening
and she kept her word. By the way she was grounded
again, with more of an understanding this time.

Donna seemed relieved when we divorced, as
embarrassment about today and the uncertainty of
tomorrow was difficult. One day after school she
came across her father passed out on the sidewalk
in front of our movie theatre about a half a mile
from our street. Donna and her new friend just walked
over him. She pretended he was not her dad. This
type of recurring experience caused Donna much pain.
Donna did have a very good friend named Patty that
she could talk to. She was always there for her,
one of her best friends, even today.

Donna, my youngest, played guitar and a memory
popped into her mind. It was a memory she tried not
to think about, soon enough she wrote and heard her
own voice break the silence.

Oh Daddy:
Oh Daddy, take me onto your lap
tell me it's Okay
Read me a poem from the big green book
sing me that song our old way.

Oh Daddy my eyes are filled w/tears,
I hurt so much inside.
The man who filled my heart w/love,
left me with all his lies.

Oh Daddy he told me of his love,
I believed his every word.
Then Daddy he turned and walked away,
left me an empty world.

Oh, Daddy why can't I turn my back
dry my many tears?
Oh, Daddy why can't I find someone new
forget these last two years?

Oh, Daddy I cannot stop thinking and
feeling,
that I never really did know him.

Oh, Daddy my heart has so much more love,
I just need time to show him.

Oh, Daddy please take me back in time,
When we had our own secret world.
But, now he can't help me anymore,
Cuz my Daddy forgot these words.

Donna never spoke to us about this, opening
up to moms is something teens do with great
difficulty. Expressing herself with her guitar was
okay with me as I knew she was sensitive,
introspective, and troubled. Looking into and
examining her own thoughts and feelings made me feel
in a round about way she had succeeded in helping
herself.

Even my mongrel dog was running away. Again
and again Muffin broke away from her leash. "Catch
her! Catch her!" I screamed to my girls. Muffin
paid no attention to us. Her feet on asphalt, she
went fast, putting as much distance as she could
between herself and us. Panting, exhausted and
hungry, Muffin was showing up at Laurie's doorstep
over and over again. Laurie was a good friend of
Deborah's and Muffin was Deborah's dog and followed
her everywhere she went. Muffin missed Deborah,
almost telling me she did not want to live at my
house if Deborah was not there. Having to work two
jobs to make ends meet, I did not feel it was fair
to my dog being alone. My other girls were never
lovers of dogs, and a friend of Deborah's paid much
attention to her. Finally I knew Laurie loved my
dog Muffin and so I decided the dog would be happier
living with Laurie, and that Muffin did until she
eventually passed away. This was not good for my
ego at this time, as it seemed everything was falling
apart.

Diane reached for a tissue, dabbed at the corners
of her eyes. When she was able to go on she said,
"I miss Daddy, he was like one of us kids. He told
us stories, shared his fantasies." Diane had a great
capacity for compassion and understanding. Separated
from her father, Diane, my middle child, reached
out for love that she hoped would satisfy her need
for a secure and affirmed relationship. Missing
her dad she needed to feel love and closeness to
someone other than her mom.

As each one of my girls were born, we named
them with all the same initials D L and as each
married, they chose a spouse with the last initial
C so they all still have the same initials.

When my middle bundle of joy Diane, decided
to leave the roost, it was an August morning in 1978
as we faced each other, across the kitchen table,
across the years. It was our last breakfast together
as mom and daughter; she was almost someone's wife.

Diane's sister Donna helped her into her gown
of organza featuring a scoop neckline, empire
waistline and sheer ruffled cap sleeves, as her
bridesmaids Beth and Brenda looked on. Her chapel
length skirt with deep ruffle was trimmed with lace.
Later that morning, I adjusted her bridal hat of
Chantilly lace trimmed with seed pearls, arranged
with a back bow of matching organza and long split
veil, and for a long moment we cried in each others'
arms.

The blurring of endings and beginnings was scary.
But, I smiled my bravest, she smiled her most radiant
sunburst smile. We walked down the aisle of the chapel
together, with her dad on the other side, propped
up on a cane. John had fallen in the tub one day
when he was sober, and preferred not to go to the
doctor, therefore the healing process became longer
than usual. I arranged for both of us parents to
walk her down the aisle, just in case her dad was
not capable of doing this.

Hands full of white daisies and baby's breath,
heart filled with hopes and promises. She took the
hand of a young man, to whom I entrusted the most
precious treasure I had yet received, one of my little
girls. They exchanged their rings which marked the
beginning of a life journey together filled with
wonder, surprises, laughter, tears, celebration,
grief, and joy.

We invited Deborah, her sister to join us at
our home before the wedding ceremony took place.
I was extremely happy she accepted to join us in
our home, even though she walked past me as if I
was not present. I needed to enjoy the precious
moments of this day and not dwell on past feelings.

We had the pleasure of being amongst our
relatives and friends at Diane's reception immediately
following the ceremony at the Pulaski Club in our
hometown. Afterwards my home filled with conversation
and laughter, as adults and teen-agers interacted.

I watched as my daughter married and knew in
a few months she and her husband would be separated
for a period of time as her husband Timothy was
to be at sea aboard the USS Philadelphia, our Navy's
newest nuclear attack submarine. Frequent phone
calls during those few months let me know how hard
it was for her to be away from her family. Then

I watched her go through the fear and joy of the birth of her first child.

We had been joyful together, foolish together and exuberant together. I survived Hippies, Yippees, Wars, assassinations, and their childhood. What passed between us was ragged and anxious, funny and forgiving, maddening and magnificent. I would not have given it up for the world.

After a few years my Donna left the nest to find her own apartment, furnished it on her own with little touches of her mom's furniture. A doll house which I had lovingly built and decorated filled with miniature furniture was a part of her living room decor. Plants and her own touch of beauty surrounded her little nest. This was located up the street and around the corner from our home and business in our hometown.

Soon after a good-looking gentlemen accompanied her while they visited our home on different occasions. He had been a resident of Easthampton as a child and had moved to Chicago. When he moved back in this area, he was introduced to Donna by a friend and one day brought his clothes and moved in with her.

Donna, at this time, was assistant manager of our bakery. One day she needed to go home for lunch and asked me to work at the bakery for her. It was a couple of hours before she returned looking rather frazzled.

While crying she said, "I just kicked my boyfriend out and he left and said in an angry voice, he'd be back." Many different incidents had happened and this was the last straw. I knew there were drugs involved and was happy to hear she had done something about it and perhaps stopped from drugs herself.

A few weeks later, on July 15, 1985, around 5:00 AM, early morning this ex-boyfriend entered her apartment and ransacked her place. Everything that was of importance to Donna he destroyed, like her television, stereo and her doll house. He had not had a job and demanded money from her, knowing she had two large checks which she had not cashed. Donna had been in a car accident and received a check for damages to her vehicle. He probably thought she had softened and might give him her checks because his father had passed away and she went to his wake. She just kept saying no way, no way.

He proceeded to beat her and threatened her with a long bread knife he had taken from her kitchen drawer. He then picked her up and banged her head enough to cause a hole in the wall. A pistol was

aimed at her, but because of his drugged condition
his aim was extremely bad and the bullet landed in
the closet door.

Finally, he tripped over the bedspread falling
to the floor. Donna grabbed her pocketbook and
partially clothed fled her apartment and ran to her
car parked in the driveway. There were three
bystanders who watched her run to her car to escape.
I was both horrified and angry that no one tried
to help her by calling the police.

She had screamed while inside, "Call the cops,
please call the cops!" No one had called the police.
As she got into her car he stood in front of the
car and she nearly ran him over. She drove her
car over to my home which was down the street and
around the corner. I called the police and brought
Donna to the hospital immediately. She was hysterical
and her head had blood dripping everywhere. Donna
was treated for a variety of injuries such as black
eyes, a piece of glass in her back and a loose tooth.
She was black and blue and swollen everywhere on
her body. Her doctor released her and suggested
she undergo counseling as a result of this incident.

The detective had been waiting outside her
apartment for a few hours. He knew in most cases
the assailant comes back to the scene of the crime.
By about 9:00 AM the assailant was taken into custody,
when a friend of his drove him back to the apartment
where the incident took place. The detective told
his friend who drove him to the apartment to drive
off immediately, or he could very well be involved.
The judge denied a request to release him without
bail. He listed no address, was charged with assault
with a dangerous weapon, assault and battery,
discharging a firearm within 500 feet of a building,
unlawfully carrying a firearm, and ordered to stay
away from the alleged victim, meaning my Donna.

Somehow Donna made it through all of the
questions asked by the detective. We helped her
clean up her apartment and she moved back home.
She feared to live alone at this time. A large hole
was made by a .38 caliber bullet shot at the window
of the front door. She shared with us some of the
awful experiences she had while he lived with her.
Such as, if she was not wearing make-up she could
not join him to watch television in the living room
of her own apartment. He told her how ugly she was,
and she began to believe him. He also kept her
isolated from her friends by not allowing them to
visit her or forbidding that she see them outside
of the home. For her birthday he gave her some dead

flowers. She feared what he might do to her after kicking him out, but tried to be brave.

At the pre-trial conference he denied the charges. His lawyer said he had an excellent work record (never had a job) had a previous conviction but never missed an appearance in court. He was ordered held in lieu of $2,000 bail.

Donna was referred to the Victim Witness Program as she was jumpy all the time and cringed when anyone hugged her. Her attacker was in jail in lieu of a $2,000 bond, but his face was still in front of her each time she closed her eyes. Nights were the hardest. Most nights she knelt under our window watching the night shadows for him to come and finish the job. Sometimes she dropped off to sleep, only to wake from a violent nightmare. Afraid to get up in the dark to even use the bathroom. Afraid to open her door for many months after. She could not wait for the ordeal to be over as there were many delays and she felt assaulted by the legal process. She was told that delays were alright as the constitution was bigger than any victim or any crook. That justice takes time.

The Victim Witness Program helped Donna through the legalities and delays. Candy, her counselor helped with everything from translating the legal terms, to getting a Kleenex. She was there for every hearing, pre-trial conference and meetings with the Assistant District Attorney.

Having to face the Grand Jury was the hardest of all for Donna. Dale, a friend of our family, accompanied her but was not allowed to go in with her. Meanwhile my husband Michel and I had reservations to go to France to be with his daughter and family. It killed me to leave her at this time, but as she was an adult and I knew this was going to be a long haul, for the court system moves slowly, also knowing her assailant was in jail made me feel better. There in the Grand Jury Donna felt victimized again. Hour after hour she sat at the podium where thirty-five strangers got to hear her story repeated several times. They were allowed to ask any and all questions they wanted. The purpose of this was to bring the case to a higher court for a longer sentence and to make certain the victim was telling the truth. Donna was forced to relive all the events over again. This reopened partially healed wounds. When it was finally over Candy was waiting with open arms and a big box of Kleenex.

It was a big relief for me when in court I heard

the Grand Jury believed my Donna and the case was
sent to Superior Court on November 22nd. He
plea-bargained and then plead guilty to assault and
battery with a two year sentence. He was granted
a "grace" period, where he was allowed one week of
freedom to attend his son's birthday before serving
his sentence.

In the Superior Court an order of full
restitution was made. As Donna had no apartment
insurance at this time, a list was made and a check
mailed out to her as restitution payment. .. two
years later. He was released on good behavior, after
only serving six months. Donna found out about his
release by running into him at the local 7-11, a
convenient store in our town. Fear set in again.

Not long after his sentence was served, his
name occurred many times along with others as being
arrested and plead innocent to charges of possession
of cocaine with intent to distribute, etc.

Donna had to learn the hard way and I believe
it helped her become responsible for her own actions
in life. As a parent my hope for my adult children
was only that their lives include people and events
to bring them joy and that they discover their own
power to generate inner happiness. If they can
generate inner happiness their happy days will last
a lifetime.

While we were living in France, Donna and Rick
decided to elope while they were on their summer
vacation in Chatham, Massachusetts. This was special
to Rick as his family and he vacationed here for
many summers. Accompanying them was Donna's best
friend Patty and Rick's friends John and Gary. They
needed to wait three days after their blood test
to acquire their marriage certificate. Meanwhile
the Reverend Water Pitman, known as Scooter,
conducted their marriage ceremony at the Walt Whitman
Band Stand a white Gazebo in the Kate Gould Park
in Chatham.

They chose to be married on June 21, 1988 the
first day of summer, the longest lasting day of the
year which was a Tuesday, at 10:00 a.m. Donna was
ten minutes fashionably late as she walked down the
long path with her maid of honor Patty by her side.
Donna was attired in a strap-less sun dress, tea
length flowing skirt which was painted of purple
iris and green leaves. This was pulled together
with a light lavender sash and a long sleeve tuxedo
type jacket which was knotted at the waist. Donna's
shoes had lace up ankle straps. She carried a bouquet
of purple iris from Chelsea Gardens in Chatham.

Standing in the gazebo overlooking the Atlantic Ocean was Rev. Pitman and Rick outfitted in white pants, shoes, mauve striped shirt and jacket waiting for his Donna. Their best man John played, "The Wedding Song" on his guitar while their friend Gary snapped many photo memories.

After the ceremony they dined at Chatham Square across the street from the gazebo. Their menu consisted of lobsters, steamed clams, corn on the cob with all the fixings and champagne. Later Donna and Rick took a plane ride to Nantucket Island off the Cape Cod Coast to see this historic island.

Michel and I received a phone call from Donna saying, "Forget the wedding plans," and in an exciting voice said, "We just eloped."

Rick grabbed the phone and said, "Hi Ma, how does that sound?" I wanted to have been there, but I was happy for them. When we returned from France, Michel and I walked the long path, stood in the empty gazebo overlooking the Atlantic Ocean, then dined at the same restaurant at Chatham Square.

Rick returned to his business as co-owner of Cernak Fuel and Donna to hers as assistant secretary of an H.& R. Block. A few years later when they conceived a baby boy, they nicknamed him Scotter after the minister who married them.

Many years passed after Donna married, had children, and the assultant still stalked her. Her home had a security system and she kept a beeper on her at all times, even when she hung her clothes. The police came and asked him to leave many times.

"Drugs Suspected In Man's Death," was a heading in the news section of our local papers about eight years after Donna's incident. The emergency workers were unable to revive this man who apparently died from a drug overdose. It was finally over for my Donna, for good.

Al-Anon

Thank God for Al-Anon, a place where I gathered to help my family by practicing the twelve steps of A A. I had seen an ad in our local newspaper listing places where these meetings were held. We decided to attend Longmeadow and Westfield meetings because we had not revealed our problem to family, co-workers and friends. Therefore we did not want to bump into anyone at these meetings who knew us. This was difficult for me to talk to my regular friends on the phone of my happiness of attending Al-Anon. The Al-Anon motto was... what you see here - what you hear here when you leave here - let it stay here.

John needed to be ready to discuss his problem of alcholism, not I. Neither did I want to discuss things happening in my home because of alcholism. I was ashamed of what took place, and I convinced myself things could change. John's self-image continued to deteriorate and his ego ebbed. Because of his wide mood swings, he was a formidable person to confront and was skillfully able to rationalize his behavior. Any attempt on my part to interrupt his drinking habits was viewed by him as meddling in his affairs.

John read my Al-Anon book, my Bible (instead of his AA book) backward and forward and each time I slipped, he reminded me. The purpose of me attending Al-Anon was to help solve my problem with alcoholism in the home. I needed help. I did not know who to turn to without hurting my spouse. I loved him dearly. I needed a chance to complain, cry, and be hugged by others who did not know me, but understood what I was going through. I needed to gather myself together for all my dreams had fallen apart. Later, I shared my experiences, strength, and hope with others in circumstances similar to mine.

I improved my own emotional health and spiritual growth. I wanted to provide a more wholesome environment for my whole family, including the alcoholic, drunk or sober . . . AA, Al-Ateen and Al-Anon usually met at the same time and place. I attended a group session of Al-Anon, the girls in Al-Ateen. They were in their early teens, and

I found that my spouse John had not attended his
AA group that evening. Many evenings I drove him
home in a stupor.

Al-Ateen was good for the girls to attend.
They learned how some children lived sometimes beaten
and perhaps had to find food on their own, due to
their parent's alcoholism? My children did not have
to cope with beatings or no food in our household.
Donna, our youngest, felt she should have known the
family secret of alcoholism well before she was told.
She knew her friend's fathers did not change jobs
as frequently as hers, did not lock themselves in
their bedroom for days, and perhaps did not have
to put up with the smell of vomit in the bathroom
day after day. I am sure she suspected something
was definitely wrong, well before her daddy and
I felt she should know.

(One Day at a Time in Al-Anon,) book, in my
opinion, should be required reading for all human
beings. This book suggested living one day at a
time, and the ways in which I might find in each
day a measure of comfort, serenity and a sense of
achievement. When I discussed with John that I needed
to attend Al-Anon he said: "You don't need Al-Anon,
you are fine."

Later he told me he was not happy knowing I
attended these meetings because he thought I
discussed his behavior. He was proven wrong, as
the program discouraged me from dwelling on past
errors and disappointments. That way I visualized
the future only as a series of new days, each a fresh
opportunity for my self-realization and growth.
I took each day as only a small manageable segment
of time in which my difficulties would not overwhelm
me. This lifted from my heart and mind the heavy
weight of both past and future. My 4 X 6 blue book
was literally falling apart. This was like a Bible
to me.

I will never forget my speech at my anniversary
meeting, shaking in my shoes, but confident in myself
to share my story of how Al-Anon changed my life.
I said, "My name is Marie - I've been a member
of Al-Anon for two years and this has changed many
things for me."

I needed to be the perfect wife and mother
and after attending Al-Anon I tried instead to create
a cheerful environment for all including my alcoholic.

Instead of saying to myself he does not go to
enough meetings, the scotch level is below the mark
I made, I accepted the fact that sometimes he tried
and allowed him to find his sobriety in his own way.

I decided to forget the bad moments and not blow them up into tragedies. I remembered a song that said, "Pick Yourself Up, Dust Yourself Off, Start All Over Again."

I knew if I remembered the kind of person I wanted to be, I would not forget myself. I knew "quiet" always set the stage for calm.

When a splinter pierced my finger, I quickly removed it: resentment could only be taken care of by being grateful. I did not want to clutter up my thoughts with this. It did not profit me, but worse it, hurt me.

I now knew, contentment came when I accepted gratefully the good that came to us, and not from rage at life. I learned not to expect much of anyone, not even myself at times.

Finally I admitted there were things I could not change. I tried putting an end to my futile struggles and freed my thoughts and energies to work on things that I could change. I stopped reliving and retelling my stories for I could not be happy and useful if I carried such a load of unpleasant emotional turmoil.

A bit of humor worked to lighten the heavy seriousness of my daily life and smoothed out the rough spots in our communications with each other.

I knew I was not being fair to John, if I allowed him to outmaneuver me at every turn. I am an individual with the right to a good life. I learned I must not look to anyone else to make a good life for me. This I must do for myself.

Watching our children was like reading a fascinating and often amusing book. I tried hard to enjoy what was good and pleasant in the world around me.

I continued to go to Al-Anon for there I learned to have a better environment by having compassion, detach with love, be grateful, share my experiences, have slips and learn from them. "Keep coming - keep coming to Al-Anon," I said. "And your life will change too. There is lots to learn and many ways to grow. A good beginning, for a better way. Don't be afraid to use the 'ASK IT' basket for questions we all have in the beginning, if not ready to verbally share with us." These questions with answers were shared with everyone at our next meeting.

With Al-Anon, the new Marie arose full of confidence, speaking eloquently and thinking independently! I have many people in my life with whom I live and love openly. I am so glad I have not hidden my feelings.

ONE DAY
AT A TIME
IN
AL-ANON

Divorce

I made the decision to seek a divorce from John; already I felt some relief. I was tired as I pretended to be happy, tired as I tried to figure out where our marriage had gone wrong, why it had gone wrong, what I could do to make it better, and I was tired of denying that I was tired. I had to let go.

The usual gnawing sense of guilt washed over me. I felt as if everything that happened was my fault. I needed to seek support, say good-by, accept what had happened, leave the blame behind, and try to help others.

As I lay down next to John, who was already fast asleep, too exhausted to sleep myself, I tried to think how I could break this news to my children. At breakfast on a Sunday morning, Dad had already left for a walk; the children and I sat at the dining room table and discussed my decision to divorce. I spoke honestly, but gently about loss, changes, and how I felt. There was nothing written in stone on how to cope with divorce. I knew my children's adjustment depended on how both of us as parents handled our divorce. Knowing children imitate our behaviors and attitudes, I wanted to put aside our anger and resentment toward each other as we tried to handle this divorce in a mature and positive way so our children could benefit and make a healthy adjustment to it.

Sleepless nights were many, as I imagined what to say when someone asked me why I did not want to live with John anymore? I dipped into my inner reserves to finally leave a difficult relationship. My worst pain of all was to tell my sister Edith. When I did she said, "I told you so," face-to-face, and behind my back she said, "It would be nice to hear his side of the story." Support was never there for me.

(Legal papers addressed to Mr. John C. LaBarge arrived. Enclosed he found a copy of Domestic Relations Summons, Motion for Temporary Orders, and Complaint for Divorce. Marie Pratt LaBarge, plaintiff vs. John Cyrus LaBarge defendant.)

Even though we discussed the possibility of a divorce to our capability at this time, John still

reacted with shock. "You finally did it. You showed
the true you," he said. He never did know how hard
this was for me to do, finally taking charge of my
own life and the lives of my teen-age girls. My
first thoughts were that this threat of divorce
would make him stop drinking, as he walked unsteadily
through the door. But little did I know about
alcoholics. I slipped from the Al-Anon program.

(The complaint for divorce went on to say that
we were lawfully married on August 8, 1959.) It
was now August 11, 1976 seventeen years later.

(The defendant be and hereby is prohibited from
imposing any restraint on my personal liberty of
plaintiff.) Sex was not an issue with John and I
was not afraid of him, even though he slept with
a knife under his pillow. He said, "This knife
protects me from the demons in my nightmares."
I was more afraid of what I would do to harm him.
I had been a gentle wife and did almost anything
to avoid a fight, but now I was aroused as never
before. One evening, when he was half naked, passed
out on the floor, and we stepped over him several
times, I took his bottle upside down and was about
to break it over his head, when I caught myself.
I could have killed him. I did not realize the anger
I still had bottled up inside me.

This was my turning point as I decided I could
not live this way much longer.

At this time, I had a full-time job working
as a computer operator for Agway Distribution Center
in Westfield and part-time catering job at Alexander's
restaurant in Northampton. Here at my part-time
job I was able to talk with my friend Winkie who
understood and supported me through what I was
experiencing. I worked two jobs, just to make ends
meet. This was no picnic and I was exhausted. With
all the confusion and pain I threw myself into my
work which gave me comfort and relief.

(The minor children, and date's of birth, of
this marriage were:
Deborah Ann LaBarge - February 18, 1960
Diane Mary LaBarge - June 29, 1961
Donna Jean LaBarge - January 24, 1963
Plaintiff shall have the care and custody of these
children and defendant be given reasonable visitation
rights.) He always had unlimited visitation access,
restricted only by being intoxicated. We maintained
a cordial relationship with each other, my home open
at all times. Long periods of time went by without
my girls receiving a visit, phone call, or even a
note from their father. From the time Donna was

thirteen to seventeen she heard from her father no more than four or five times and felt rejected. For my Donna, if her daddy had dropped a line or just called to say, "Hello" it might have made a difference during her adolence years to know that he still thought about her.

(The defendant must vacate the marital home within reasonable time.) John never left the house until months after our divorce. My divorced spouse still lived with us and I knew if I did not physically find a place for John and pay the first and last months rent, he would never leave. Still on the merry-go-round, I did precisely that. I will not forget the last time he looked at me. He was at the door with some of his clothing in one hand and his other hand on the door knob. He did not smile, was not vindictive, nor sad but just still. I knew he was waiting for me to go to him, as I had before and take him in my arms. My feet refused to carry me over to him. Before this instance I had said, "I care about you."

He said, "You sure have a funny way of showing it." I did not know what to say or do, it seemed impossible to explain. This did not seem real, he did not seem real, either. The day finally came when he was really out of my life, and I cried without him being there.

(Plaintiff certifies that no previous action for divorce, annulling or affirming marriage, separate support, desertion, living apart for justifiable cause, or custody of children has been brought by either party against the other.)

(The plaintiff demands that the court waive the 30 day requirement to grant a divorce for cruel and abusive treatment in state of Massachusetts.

Grant her custody of the above-named children Defendant pay to his spouse sum of $50.00 on each and every Friday hereafter, beginning on November 26, 1976 for support of the minor children.)

I never saw any support money for our minor children in the next eight years, because of alcholism and inadequate funds to cover the commitment. John received a monthly check from the government to support his habit and living expenses. My financial position throughout this ordeal had changed drastically. Going from full-time job to part-time job, I was exhausted. I fell asleep at the wheel when going to my second job one evening. I jumped the curb with the car on Main Street, which jolted me, for I was headed to the fence that surrounded the cemetery when I awoke.

My girls had small part-time jobs and school, sports and dance kept them busy. My bosses were not happy with me at the time, as I called home to find out who was doing what at what time. Survival was the name of this game.

(A hearing was held in Hampshire County Court House, Northampton, Mass on Wednesday August 11, 1976 at ten o'clock in the morning on all prayers for temporary relief set forth in motion.)

The day of the hearing humiliated me. John sat in the court house at the table with his head bent as he cried and cried. The judge told him how sorry he felt for him. He reprimanded me for chewing gum in court and had me get rid of my gum before he went on with the hearing. I felt like I had been attacked and was seen as the bad guy. The judge's questions were very abrupt, and I was told to only answer the questions and add nothing else. Finally the divorce was granted. I could not wait to get out of there, stopping to see my friend Janet, to talk and cry with relief.

At this time most marriages I knew were ended by the early death of one spouse, so a child's risk of family disruption had remained relatively stable in the early 70's.

My divorce stigmatized me, was a social embarrassment, but I had to have peace of mind. I felt I had not achieved a good marriage, but I would not settle for a bad one. Having no relatives who cared and no one to confide in while this was happening made this time very difficult. Sometimes I felt maybe divorce would or could shock him to stop his drinking or maybe I was not the right person for him to spend his life with. I thought our love could withstand anything, but again I cried a river that winds and winds. Divorce was the only way I could find a way out of this journey and into another. I needed to release time and to save only the good memories for the sake of my three daughters. I said over and over again to myself, I do not know how it all started. I made some wrong choices and could not imagine my life ever being right again. I tried to make the divorce better by keeping the lines of contact open between Daddy and his girls, painful as it was, this was important to me.

My divorce was a mixture of sadness as I faced reality and began a process that had a prescribed ending and therefore a day of release. Being totally responsible for my own life and that of my girls was not an easy course to travel. I thought I was down to my last teardrop, but again I cried as I

stopped at my friend's house after my day in court.
     I found in time the cause of my marriage break-up
became history   and the effects it had on us all,
became the real issue.
     Returning to the house after being at court
granting   my divorce, it did not seem like home
anymore. Despite my efforts, I could not keep up
the mortgage payments.   My eyes filled with tears
as I remembered how beautifully my fifteen rose bushes
had grown and all the memories and hard work I had
put into this wonderful house.   It had three bedrooms,
living room, den, library, kitchen, dining room,
bath and a half, screened porch, garage and a pool
in the back yard.   Located on a dead end street,
it sure was my dream house for eleven years.   This
was the first time since I sold my home I found myself
so close to it.   I was silent for a long time trying
not to cry.   I still have a mental snapshot, John
in his last months as he sat outside in the sun,
his badly sprained ankle propped up on a pillow,
his creatures nearby and his head nodded down.   Later
my friend Joy said, "When life throws you lemons,
you make lemonade!" That made me feel confident and
I went on with life.
     I received a letter from John's lawyer that
said John wanted my diamond and my dining room set
back.   These perhaps were the two most important
items I owned.   On my 15th anniversary John had given
me a round $\frac{1}{2}$ct diamond solitaire set in 14K gold,
which was to be worn with my wide wedding band of
a $\frac{1}{4}$ct diamond with six side-stoned diamonds, three
on each side.   Since this was charged to our
Mastercard, I helped pay for this with my two jobs.
I perhaps paid more money towards the Mastercard
than John,   therefore contributed more than he
towards my diamond. Our dining room set was given
to us as a house warming gift by Mr. Steiger, one
of the owners of Steigers, an outstanding department
store where John was employed at one time.   This
was an antique dining room set that the Steiger
family no longer needed.   It consisted of a very
long buffet, a large glass door china closet, and
an eighty-four inch pop-up inserted leaf table.
The eight armless chairs with sculptured backs and
two arm chairs had carved arms.   I had made fabric
cushioned seats which matched our dining room
curtains. This was close to looking like the dining
room set I grew up with and loved as a child.
     John had no room to put this dining room
furniture in his two-room apartment, so I refused
to allow him to pawn this set, nor did I want my

diamond pawned. I still wore my diamonds at that time and our dining room set fit nicely in my new apartment, which was a six room duplex. I ignored his letter and nothing further was done about this, but it sure was a scary heartbreaking time for me.

As you remember, my oldest daughter Deborah, not able to cope with the divorce, had already run away from home, stopped at a friend's house, lived there, and never had any contact with us as a family again. Deborah realized what happened was real and that her needs were not met; she felt anger. Through anger, Deborah felt an empowerment; anger was also a protective emotion. Her anger kept away her pain and sadness. She expressed her anger as she blamed me. I felt perhaps after time, tears and talking, an adjustment could take place.

This was very difficult as all three girls attended the same schools, participated in scouts and shared other activities in our small town. My other two daughters and I stuck it out together and survived it all. We grew even closer and stronger in the end. They went through their sadness with our family change. Even though the change was a relief in some way, they grieved for the loss of their dreams as a happy family.

John continued to have his slips over and over again going from one job to another, my never seeing any medical or financial help of any sort from him. John had three different jobs our first twelve years. Each time his profession was a children's ware buyer for McCallum's which later became Forbes and Wallace, Steigers, and Blakes. All of these were very expensive clothing stores; each time he bettered himself financially.

Later I was told by his secretary, he had been fired from the last two jobs, but very quickly acquired another with even better pay. At the time I had no clue he was an alcoholic, but now I realize when he said he worked overtime in the evening, because during the day the phone rang constantly and he could not accomplish anything, he really hung out at a very classy bar. When he arrived home he immediately went into the dining room and made himself a drink, therefore I could not smell liquor on him. I even had him bring some of his bookwork home and I did it for him.

When John was fired from Blakes he worked the next two years at PapaGeno's, Lowe's Cinema, as a carpenter, and an attendant at the Veterans hospital. The children loved it when he worked as a manager at PapaGeno's as pizza was one of their favorite foods. Lowe's Cinema was fun as we got to go to all the latest movies free.

I tried my best to enjoy all of these fringe benefits. Knowing John loved theatre and movies, I felt perhaps he would enjoy this job and it could help him through this difficult time. Our children seemed to be real happy as they thought their daddy had a very important job. John's carpenter job lasted two days with several of his fingernails black and blue for he was not a manual person. At this time he left the house as if he had a job and returned home when he thought the day was over. He unlocked the door with unsteady fingers and staggered into bed extremely intoxicated. After going through the rehab at the Veterans hospital, they offered him a job as an attendant. This time for sure I felt John would be fine. Back on his merry-go-round I went, calling him in sick so he would not lose his job because he was intoxicated.

Then came the last three years of our marriage, John had no job. By this time he did not care what bars he hung-out at, whether he passed out in the middle of the street, fell in the pool, or just did not get up at all for several days. On a good day he said, "Let me help you by going grocery shopping." I was thrilled he wanted to pitch in and gave him the needed amount of money to do a good amount of food shopping. That evening, after working all day, I came home and he was passed out on the floor in the middle of our family room. No grocery shopping had been done and no money had been seen either. This threw my well planned budget right out the window.

I gave him very little money, so to support his habit he threw out the bills and tore up the checks that I had made out for the electric and gas company, and make out a check for that amount to himself. Meanwhile when the utility companies called me saying I needed to make a payment or be shut off, I insisted I mailed the payment out giving them the check number I had written out. Only until I received the bank statement did I realize what he had accomplished in his mind. His famous statement was, "Don't take things so serious, lighten up!"

Years later after our divorce, our middle child, Diane sought John out, whenever he was not seen around town, to be sure he was all right. Diane was not afraid to ask for help from his non-alcoholic friends to find her father when he was not heard from for a while. She cleaned his apartment for him and started him back on his feet again. Diane

threw out the papers, bottles, and accumulation of
trash; Daddy smiled his humble, grateful smile and
told her in as many ways as he could how much he
loved her and how wonderful it was to have such a
good daughter. The girls understood their father
had a problem with alcohol and with telling the truth.
Donna did have remarkable wit which was a rallying
point for us at times when the going got rough.

I wanted to tell John myself when our grandson
was born. I knew he wanted to know. His apartment's
disorder was frightening. Scattered around the room
were boxes of cardboard. The table was loaded with
items, newspapers, and empty bottles. It was eerie
as the wrinkled potatoe's sprouting eyes looked
at me. Red wine had been spilled on the floor,
allowed to dry and it made the air in the room smell
sweet and heavy. I offered him a ride to the hospital
in the next town where Diane and Troy were, he
refused. "Don't worry I will be there," he said.
John did arrive at the hospital the next morning
to view his first grandson, afraid to hold him because
he was extremely shakey. He was so happy, tears
flowed down his cheeks.

I tried very hard to help my children understand
alcoholism and divorce, so it could be laid to rest.
I wanted them to leave the injured child behind and
emerge as a healthy adult.

Meanwhile John had a hard time as he accepted
the reality of the divorce. He had a wedding
portrait of us enlarged and at the top of the picture
in large print was;

FOR THE GOOD TIMES
and under the portrait he attached the poem:
>Don't be so sad-
>We know it's over! But life goes on,
>And this old world will keep on turning.
>
>Let's just be glad
>We had some time to spend together.
>There's no need to watch the bridges
>That we're burning!
>
>Lay your head upon my pillow.
>Hold your warm and tender body
>Close to mine.
>Hear the whisper of the raindrops
>Falling soft against the windows,
>And make believe you love me one more time!
>For the good times.

> I'll get along - you'll find another;
> And I'll be here if you should find
> You'll ever need me.
> Don't say a word about tomorrow, or forever!
> There'll be time enough for sadness
> When we're parted.
> For the good times

John
August 8th, 1959 - April 28, 1978

This he framed for me in a 16 x 20 gold frame, which was lovely and caring, I thought, until I found out he mailed a flier of this same print to all our friends. They did not know that the last few years of our life together had really been hell. For days on end he spoke only to the children, and never to me. He succeeded in hurting me, and again I forgave and forgave, allowing this to happen to me.

I had to step into a new life. I stumbled quite often, only to pick myself up, dust myself off and get on my way again. I was able to meet each crisis as it came, letting none faze me. I could not get caught up in my own grief over the end of my marriage for I had to pay heed to the needs of my children. Parents divorce each other but they do not divorce their children. I tried to feel my family was not being destroyed only altered. I tried not to show my emotions, to complain when taxiing teens around; I made light of things, gave comfort, and never admitted I was tired, for I felt I must be like a rock. I read once where it was said the harder you fall, the higher you bounce and I hoped this would happen to me. Sooner or later this all overpowered me, and I broke down crying when no one was around. I decided I had to rely on my own strength and be in control of my own life.

Leaving John was an act of bravery and love for which I had to become strong. Besides I got the divorce only to shock him into stopping his drinking, and because John said, "You will never be able to make it on your own."

He angered me, and I was determined to survive without him. I truly believed he would stop drinking and we would be together again; what a dreamer I was.

Sadness was inevitable when our family changed. Even though the change was relief, we grieved for the loss of our dream as a happy family together.

What began at our wedding ceremony, with our minister, parents, and friends, ended in a courtroom with a judge, lawyer, and strangers.

I found in my mailbox the following week a note from a friend saying, "Congratulations on your Divorce! Now you can say Home is where the heart is, instead of Home is where the old fart is!" Even if I did not feel that way, it surely made me laugh!

Dating Service

I was lucky to have some male friends with whom I could be with and feel comfortable to attend different functions, so I would not have to go to events alone. One night I had a blind date, whom a so-called friend of mine wanted me to meet. After dinner with him at a really nice restaurant, as we walked to his car, he said," I've had a vasectomy," with a leery grin on his face, and I with a grin on my face said, "Your father should have had one." He drove me directly home.

I tried very hard to be HAPPY by myself, doing things to make myself glamorous. Later I found that glamour comes from within and has to be nurtured. It takes some of us longer than others to learn this. But I tried; I took a bath accompanied by soft music and put on a soft piece of clothing that felt good against my skin. Then I cooked an elaborate meal and sat and ate it. And then I cried my heart out. Okay I said to myself, I'll go shopping, that will do it for sure, HAPPY I will be. In the large department stores, I allowed the employees to experiment with make-up and perfume; they spent a long time with me, thinking I would spend my money. What money? I barely had enough to make ends meet. I walked into an expensive dress shop, tried on everything in sight, and then walked out, depressed again. Being alone did not work for me; as I needed people around me.

In January of 1979 I went through a lonely time of my life, when a questionnaire from a local dating service asked, "What type of man would you like to date?" was before me. This was called "Introductions," a dating & counseling service out of Easthampton, Massachusetts owned and operated by Jim & Judy Yorio. My answer was, "A loving, touching, traveling, family and friendship type person is my fantasy." I paid the expensive bill with my charge card, not knowing it would be eventually paid by the man of my dreams. As a member of this club, each month I received a picture of a man along with information about him. He in turn received the same on me. If I wanted to pursue this possibility I could call him or wait for his call.

Being married before, my teen-agers rated the

men I dated, with a thumbs down or thumbs up. This Frenchman, my daughters said called several times wanting to speak to me.

I finally was home when he called again on a Saturday morning. He asked me to lunch that same day. This wonderful foreign voice sounded soo romantic on the telephone. I could not wait for lunchtime to come. I never realized a woman of my age could have this predate indigestion I experienced.

As I entered the restaurant I saw a gentlemen about my size with receding hair, blue eyes, broad shoulders, and a quick smile. While having lunch in a unique restaurant called The Goldmine, he sat back in his chair and looked directly into my eyes. He created a spark in me and made my heart pound. Michel focused his entire attention on me while I talked, and I felt more important than I had before he started to listen. I liked Michel from the minute I laid eyes on him, for great warmth radiated from his face. As I listened to my Frenchman talk and smelled the aroma of his pipe, my body became alive again. I was elated by the whole experience for it reminded me that I was still a woman with the deep feelings and longings of a woman.

We later drove to my place in his sexy little yellow car, a Renault R-17, and played UNO, the "in" card game at the time, with my teen-age daughters and their friends. Even then our feet kept the warmth of togetherness under the table. Here was when my daughters gave me the thumbs up signal. My entire past seemed to lift, lighten, shift and dissolve.

Meeting me and my daughters was a very nervous experience for Michel. He came here to America in 1973 for a short time, he thought, working for a French company based in New York City. His mom saw this advertisement in their French newspaper and thought it good for him to get away from a very difficult divorce he was going through. Between Paris and New York he had a good flight, his first on a Boeing 747. The excitement of New York City (one of the most exciting cities in the world) was fine at first. After being amongst the huge buildings and traffic jams, he longed to find a smaller community that reminded him of home in France. He took several trips to many states, longed to find the right place. In Northampton, Massachusetts, he found the community surrounded by lakes, mountains, wooded hills and streams to accommodate every outdoor activity, a community with a desire for a good way of life. He recognized that the natural beauty

was very close to the surroundings of his home-town
Grenoble, France, where the Winter Olympics were
held in 1968. He relocated here in the States and
went to work for a French Bakery in Northampton.
He told us later he saw us as a loving American family
and knew this was what he was looking for. He felt
we were responsible, hard working, loving, and caring
people.

My daughter Diane was pregnant with her first
child and it was nice to have someone like Michel
to share this wonderful experience of being a
grandparent, for the first time. Diane was living
with my daughter Donna and me, for her husband Tim
was away on duty in the Navy assigned to the USS
Philidelphia. This was one of our Navy's newest
nuclear attack submarines. I was there watching
Diane go through the fears and joys of the birth
of her first child. She delivered a beautiful baby
boy whom she and Tim named Troy.

Michel and I spent intimate time together engaged
in adventure and the enjoyment of sexual pleasures,
which fulfilled some of our fantasies. With his
sexy accent he said, "Je taime beaucoup, and Voulez
vous coucher avec moi, ce soir," I just melted.
Even though I did not know French, it was easy to
understand he loved me and wanted to take me to bed.
We decided that our life together could bring
physical pleasure, stability fulfillment and a loving
emotional relationship. We decided to get married
in June, only six months after meeting. This was
a case of saying to my children, "Do as I say - not
as I do." My Frenchman rented two rooms with a cot,
dresser, couch, chair and table all borrowed. This
was unimportant to me, as I was in love. Everyone
wanted to meet my romantic Frenchman. They could
tell he was warm and friendly after they were
introduced. He kissed their hands and smiled broadly
which melted any doubter.

The day came when we picked up Michel's parents
and daughter at Logan Airport in Boston. I was
quite nervous as I knew I had taken their son for
keeps here in the States. Michel had been ready
to return home before we met; he was very lonely
for a family. His daughter Laurence was just a
few years younger than my teen-age daughters, so
it did not take long to see them have a good time
together, despite the language barrier. His parents
were easy to be with, for they were warm and caring.
I needed to remember to turn cheeks each time we
kissed in the evening before bed and morning when
we awoke. This was their tradition in France. They

had come to our country to share the joy as we began
our new life together at a candlelight ceremony,
when we exchanged marriage vows.

At seven o'clock on a Saturday evening on June
23, 1979 at the Easthampton Congregational Church,
a double ring ceremony was performed by our pastor.
Our teen-agers started our ceremony as the usherettes
and lit the candles. I was very touched by seeing
Donna and Diane from United States and Laurence from
France taking part in our wedding. The memory of
this joyous time will always stay with us as our
friend and photographer, Connie Kodak, as we called
her, snapped that camera every moment possible to
catch all our memories.

Natalie, a friend of mine played the organ at
church for us as Sharon my former Easthampton's Junior
Miss sang for us. My friend Winkie from U S A and
Michel's friend Jean from France, were our
attendants. I wore a mauve long sleeve dress, while
Michel was attired in a tan suit with tie to match
my dress. The church altar was decorated with white
& yellow daises and roses.

After the rice was thrown, our reception where
all our family and friends gathered, was held at
the local American Legion Club in Easthampton,
Massachusetts. We had a great evening of dinner
and danced to the Melodares with Henry Turban, our
friend on the accordion. I loved Michel's body
language, if not every word of his French. Our table
was near the dance floor, and as the orchestra tuned
up, Michel said, "Madame voulez-vous danser avec
moi?" It was easy to understand he asked me to
dance.

I stood, nodded my best "Oui," and we danced
as he never stopped talking. We thanked all our
friends and relatives for all the joys they wished
us and for their presence there, bringing home all
the exciting gifts and envelopes to open together
before we retired for the evening. As a wedding
gift to each other a Hamilton grandfather clock,
a fine timepiece, entered our home with the pendulum
working one tick at a time. This tall case clock
is of solid wood, solid weight shells, brass lyre
pendulum, with Westminster Chimes. It still chimes
today, twenty years later, and I hope forever more.

Our honeymoon trip was my dream come true as
we flew to France. We fastened our seat belts and
returned our seats to the full upright position before
we deplaned, the way the stewardess said to. "Have
a good day," she said on a pleasant philosophical
note in both English and French. I had motion

sickness quite often in my life, so we asked for
seats on the right-hand side of the plane. Because
when the pilot circles he usually makes left turns,
so I would not feel the sick sensation of the
turbulent so much on the right. I wore an expandable
skirt so if my stomach expanded when we were over
5,000 feet in the air, I would not be uncomfortable.
Knowing I was to travel in the air for eight hours,
I was determined to be extremely comfortable. I
also used the airplane socks given to me, hoping
my feet would not swell up, for it could have been
awkward to stocking-foot it down the ramp when we
landed.

In Paris as we landed we viewed the Eifel Tower
- grand old lady, slender and elegant as she used
her beacon to guide us in Paris, with her 1700 steps.
What a sight. As I traveled with Michel in France
it was like being Cinderella at the ball everyday.
Since Michel was fluent in French, being his country,
and I spoke not a word of French, I clung to his
side and picked up easy phrases. I carried a
French/English dictionary in my purse.

We took an evening ride down the Seine River
to see the Cathedral of Notre-Dame de Paris, the
romantic Gothic architecture seating 9,000 people
which has seen eight centuries of history.

In Versaillas we viewed beautiful castles and
gardens, water mills and water fountains of great
statues. This was a delight for my eyes and a prime
target for my camera. We climbed the old ruins
of LePont Du Gard. When we saw LaGrande Motte,
the large city started by General Degaulle which
reminded me of a line of dominoes, very modern
indeed, so different from the rest of France. We
took a drive up to the "Paysages des French Alpes"
- this was June - where people skied in their
sweaters. I was amazed by the flowers on one side
of the road and snow on the other.

For a few days we sunbathed in the French Riviera
where women with bare breasts on the public beaches
were found. The French regard toplessness as a sacred
human right. In some of the small seaside towns
we found toplessness not only on the beach but in
shops and cafes. Lying on the dazzling white beach
was perfect for a French tan and a refreshing way
to spend a warm summer day. We ended the day as
we watched the sunset over the Mediterranean Sea
that was just breath-taking. Each day's sunset seemed
even more spectacular than the one the day before.

On to Gronoble, France, where we stayed with
Michel's parents, brothers, his daughter and extended

family. Before Michel put his key in the lock, the door was opened from within by his mother. This was his birthplace, his old home, the land he loves in a unique way. Geographically, Grenoble is 350 miles from Paris and Lyon is sixty miles away. The 1968 Winter Olympics was here in Grenoble. This city is also famous for its University with the streets and cafes filled with students, noisy, but lively. These university students disappeared on the weekends to the ski-slopes.

Driving up to the family's summer home in the Village of Meaudre, we passed pastures filled with grazing cows. We reached the house in the Alps and the field of purple flowers reminded me of Heidi on TV. Inside, our Victorian bedroom setting made me feel like I was in the movies. Michel came close to me on the bed and we touched glasses. We drank a little, he watching me all the while, and then he kissed me. Lying beside him in another country was strange and away from reality. I was happy as I discussed all my thoughts. For I did not need to pretend, did not need to look perfect for him as he accepted me as I was.

I rose early and fixed myself a cup of coffee. Seated on the veranda, I prayed for each of my children and for each of theirs. Dawn just broke over the mountain, suddenly a symphony of bird songs surrounded me. The air was filled with music, it was as if the whole creation praised God for the beginning of a new day. Who could possibly have a better honeymoon than that?

I feel today Michel and I share independently our lives together. The key word is share, rather than control each other's lives. I am strong with Michel and depend on him for love but I love my own life, for he gives me extra confidence to succeed in my own way.

Our Bakery

We both wanted to own our own business, and now the perfect opportunity came our way. In 1979 with Michel's baking experience in France and here in the United States as well and my experience as a secretary-bookkeeper, we purchased from the Romanowski's a garlic bread company and expanded it into a French Bakery business.

Everett Street in Easthampton, was like any other small town residential street, until you pulled up in front of our bakery. One did not have to leave one's car to smell the aroma of fresh baked goods that drifted out to greet everyone.

I do not think people realized all we did. When people entered the front of the store, some thought we were a grocery store, others a small neighborhood bakery, even though the sign read, "Everett Street Bakery - Frosan Foods Specialties." (Yes, it's FROSAN, which stood for the three Romanowski's we bought the bakery from. F for Frank - ROS for Rose - and AN for Anne.)

I listened to people speak about our bakery and I got a chuckle. They did not realize we shipped our frozen "Rose's Garlic Bread" and "Michel's Croissants" all over New England. Near-by colleges like Smith, Amherst, Holyoke Community, Mount Holyoke, and the University of Massachusetts received our rolls, grinders and breads. Many of the area's finest restaurants were serviced by us, from local subway shops for grinder rolls, to the Goldmine gourmet restaurant for our Croissants, to the Marriott Hotel for mouth-watering Brioche.

When one walked past our establishment on the corner of Franklin and Everett Street in Easthampton, it was hard to imagine that such large volumes of bread, rolls, and pastries were baked and packaged there. This was possible running three shifts as we never closed our doors, except for Xmas day. Available behind the counter was other assorted pastries and breads, fresh out of the oven.

"Rose's Garlic Bread" and "Michel's Croissants," two frozen products, were sold all over New England and as far north as Canada. It was fun to walk into a supermarket and see which garlic bread people picked up, and we said, "Allright" with thumbs up, when

it   happened to be ours!   Even neater was to stop
in a little store in Vermont and see our very own
garlic bread and croissants on display in the freezer
section, for people to pick up.

Our broker Manny, from Northeast Food Brokers
had us deliver to such distributors as Sweetlife
Foods, Allied Grocers, Lady B's, Bozzuto's, and
C & S Grocers. We delivered refrigerated truckloads
to distribution centers, and they in turn delivered
to their assigned stores.

Our "Rose's Garlic Bread" was mixed, baked,
sliced, buttered, wrapped in foil and then packaged
12-7oz boxes packed to a case.   Carton dimensions
were 14$\frac{1}{4}$ by 9$\frac{1}{4}$ by 7$\frac{1}{2}$ with a minimum order for delivery
of 100 cases.   Truck loads of 430 cases and at least
one week notice was expected before delivery.

When we first started billing and sometimes
needed to call our distributors to remind them of
overdue bills, they said "The check is in the mail."
Towards the end of our owning the business, the answer
became, "The computer is down."

A cash register sat on a small counter just
to the right of the front door of the store.   Four
or five shelves of canned and convenience goods,
plus dairy products were maintained to serve the
needs of the immediate neighborhood.   Our sales
clerk took just a few minutes to get some items on
a grocery list brought in by children.   Usually they
had a quarter to spend of their own money. My sales
clerk told them, "This is your mom's money and that's
your change," as they bought some gum or candies
for themselves.

Twelve ovens sat against one wall behind two
long work tables.   While one baker mixed and shaped
pastries, another fed dough for dinner rolls through
a roller and put them in bread pans to rise.   Diane
and Donna, two of our daughters involved in the
business, took large, delicious-smelling rolls of
French and Italian bread out of the oven.   Then they
remove un-baked loaves from the proof cabinets and
put them in the ovens.   When customers asked, "Where
does all this bread go?"   The girls used to say "Don't
worry, it all goes so fast, there is no inventory."
We walked around in circles trying to find a place
to put the finished products until the trucks
returned.

We mixed about 120 pounds of garlic butter and
spread it on the loaves after each had been through
a bread slicer.   Diane and Donna said, "The only
baked goods we pick up and eat all the time is the
garlic bread."   However they admitted that an apple

turnover, hot out of the oven, had passed their lips earlier in the day.

A typical letter to us many times read as follows: "Just a note to tell you how much we love 'Roses Garlic Bread.' We have tried many others, but like the way this is seasoned and cut. It's really good. Thank You for making it."

We ventured into making Croissants un-baked to be finished by our restaurants in (three easy steps.) These directions we had printed up for the in-store bakers to follow; 1. Put on sheet pan the number of croissants you desire, having them in the refrigerator over night. 2. Proof them until they rise. 3. When ready, bake them at 375 degrees for 12 to 15 min. If any problem arises please call us and we would be happy to assist you. Michel went to the stores to assist the in-store employees (bakers) in baking these croissants. The aroma of the croissants was the best advertisement any store could have. Many of our restaurants used these for brunches they were serving, on Sunday's especially with the aroma filling the air.

For those who did not have a taste for garlic or croissants and who did not need to worry about their waistlines, we had available to purchase in our bakery: Bear Paws, Napoleons, Eclairs, Almond Horseshoes, Cream Puffs, Brioche, Danish, Palmiers, Tuiles, Petit Fours, Chocolate Meringue, and of course, Brownies.

A typical workday for Michel began at four a.m. He and our associates baked about 200 dozen (2,400 loaves) a day of garlic bread and dinner rolls, grinder rolls, finger rolls, salt free breads, as well as French, Italian, Rye and Pumpernickel. To do this they needed about 60 100-pound bags of flour a week, plus pastry supplies. When we started our business, we used only five 100-pound bags a week.

A WHMP am-fm radio commercial sounded something like this; Picture yourself picking up a warm glazed danish. It's so fresh that your fingers sink into the dough. The aroma of cinnamon fills your space, you take a big bite, the glaze sweetens your lips and satisfaction fills your senses.

Experience the flavor, the freshness, and the satisfaction...at The Everett Street Bakery in Easthampton. Finally, A bakery that caters to fine taste without additives or preservatives...ever. The Everett Street Bakery features delicious pastries and baked goods from fine European recipes. Tasty breads and pastries are baked to order...and also available for restaurants and pizza shops.

Everything is baked with tender loving care right
on the premises. Need a special occasion cake for
a birthday, wedding or anniversary...The Everett
Street Bakery knows how to fuss. Experience a good
bakery...The Everett Street Bakery, at the corner
of Everett and Franklin Streets, Easthampton. Open
every day and, yes, Everett Street Bakery has Sunday
papers too.

Michel believed customers recognized a better
product when they tasted it. Too many additives
and preservatives spoiled the character of French
bakery foods.

My husband's French buttercream was made using
a two-stage process. Sugar and water were boiled
together, while egg whites were whipped. The
sugar/water solution was added to the whipping egg
whites to make meringue. Then he whipped up butter,
to which the meringue was added. The results was
a light, not-too-sweet buttercream that melts in
the mouth without overpowering the cakes. Cake layers
were brushed with simple syrup sometimes flavored
with liqueurs. This way the flavor of the cake was
enhanced and the syrup helped to retain moisture
during storage.

Chocolate Mousse cake, which consisted of layers
of chocolate cake with the chocolate mousse between
was also popular. To make this, Michel whipped egg
whites with sugar and at the same time whipped
whipping cream. Then he folded the whipped cream
into the meringue adding chocolate. He then did
a gentle folding action so as not to knock the air
from the meringue.

So a cake commercial on WHMP radio sounded like
this; Birthday music started it and then they said,
"When someone's having a birthday..light a cake!
Make sure it's a beautiful and delicious birthday
cake from Everett Street Bakery in Easthampton.
They have cakes for all occasions...with a frosting
message right on top..for that personal touch."

Then wedding music started and they said,
"Everett Street Bakery designs and fusses with
beautiful wedding cakes...picture perfect and priced
just right. For years to come...ask Everett Street
Bakery about Anniversary cakes...A Delicious yet
beautiful way to remember."

"New babies, new homes, graduations, parties...
when someones having a celebration light a cake from
the Everett Street Bakery. It's located at the corner
of Everett and Franklin Streets in Easthampton.
Open daily...Where good things are always baking."

All kinds of cakes were available such as Black

Forest, Carrot, White, Chocolate and Marble with
such frosting as buttercream, whip cream, raspberry,
vanilla and chocolate.

Yule Logs were popular as a Christmas Item,
decorated with Santa, Christmas trees and other
holiday symbols.

"Galette des Rois" was a Twelfth Night
celebration cake, usually ordered for New Year
celebrations at Franco-American clubs, especially
in New York. We called this the cake of the kings
in honor of the three kings who visited the Christ
child. This cake consisted of a thin dough with
an almond paste filling inside. Each cake had a
gold crown made of thin cardboard and a petite
figurine placed inside it. Whoever received the
piece of cake with the figurine became the queen
or king for the evening wearing of the crown. You
were the ruler of the party and everyone must do
what you did. Funny thing most of the time the
children found the figurine.

The French also celebrate their special holidays
with Croquembouche, which are small and medium
sized petite cream puffs filled with pastry cream
and dipped in melted sugar and corn syrup. These
were stacked in a large cone shape like a tree.
In the Christmas season the bakers added red and
green candied cherries to represent ornaments.

Michel and our pastry men's skills included
many things like working with sugar, marzipan, and
chocolate. All cakes and pastries were made with
fresh eggs and all-scratch formulas. Pure whipped
cream, pure chocolate, real butter, fresh fruits
and real liqueurs added to the product cost.

Sometimes customers felt uncomfortable asking
about prices, so signs above our pastry cases gave
them prices plus described our French pastries,
as some were unfamiliar to them. Michel priced most
of our products by multiplying the ingredient cost
by three.

Baskets of bread and rolls graced the windows
of our store attracting attention to different
approaching holidays. Signs in the front window of
our bakery read like this; "Bring some treats to
a friend--have a nice holiday...and may it be
homemade, healthy and happy from our Everett Street
Bakery."

When Michel made his appearance in the front
of the bakery, his French accent assured the customer
that his products were subjected to scrupulous French
culinary standards. Even American products acquired
a continental flavor when Michel spoke of them.

Many a time classes of young school children came and observe us baking our goodies. A small cookie in hand before leaving our bake shop was not unusual.

The farmers' markets were great fun for me, as I went different days of the week, in my Winnebago, filled with pastries and breads. We attended them in Springfield, Holyoke, Westfield, Northampton, and of course our home town of Easthampton. I displayed my items along with the vegetables and fruits of the season that the farmers were selling. It was quite an enjoyable day being able to be out of doors. This was a great way to advertise our bakery.

Michel and some of our associates took part in judging the pie contests in our home town of Easthampton as well as The Three County Fair, which is a yearly event in Northampton, Massachusetts.

We enjoyed putting on French dinners at our Easthampton Congregational Church, where we were members. We decorated with wall posters, flags of France and America as centerpieces and of course a French dinner with French pastries.

As members of The International Food Service Executives Association we spoke pertaining to our bakery at one of their meetings. In addition I spoke at Mother's Club, Woman's Club and Business & Professional Women's Club of which I was a member.

A friend of ours, Bernie helped us as Santa Claus pass out gifts for our little ones at our employee's Christmas party held in our home each year. We always sent a Christmas letter to our associates which read something like this: "As we approach the end of another year and enter the holiday season, we want to take a few moments to reflect on the past year. In many ways it has been a frustrating and yet exciting year for us as a family, and for you as our associates. Trying to increase business as well as putting a new product on the market has sure been a challenge. But, with all our frustrations and disappointments together we have weathered the storm. You have helped roll with the punches, and as a result helped FROSAN FOOD SPECIALTIES be competitive on the market, for our retail and wholesale customers. Don't forget - Success is doing what you like to do and doing it well enough that someone recognizes you for doing it. We have appreciated all you have done. For just a few figures, you have made 201,876 'Michel's Croissants' and 95,988 'Rose's Garlic Bread' plus thousands of pastries and breads. We wanted to take this opportunity to thank each and everyone of you for making our company a successful part of this business world. You can be proud that you have been a vital link in the successes which FROSAN FOODS SPECIALTIES & EVERETT STREET BAKERY has achieved during the last twelve months. My husband, daughters and I want to wish you and yours a safe, joyous and happy holiday season and a new year filled with good health, happiness and success." Bakingly yours, Michel, Marie, Donna, and Diane.

Getting letters from such places as Holyoke Community College thanking us for assisting them in starting their retail store was an honor to us. They said they gained invaluable experience in the operation of working with us. We worked with Business majors, who were training to be in the business world.

We had many great experiences running this business, though sometimes we were disappointed because we had to drop items that we had fun making, but that did not return enough profit because they were too time consuming. Supermarket IN STORE BAKERIES cut deeply into small shops like ours, as customers no longer had the time and energy at the end of a week to stop at specialty shops like they did a generation ago. The meat - vegetable - pastry specialty shops can no longer survive. Supermarkets, with convenience and the aroma of bakery items in the oven on the premises, have the advantage in reaching the busy consumers.

Although our business was exciting, we looked forward to the weekends when we packed up our Winnebago and got away for some much-needed rest. Our daughter Donna, who became manager, was very capable of running the business while we were away.

Finally after years of working day and night, we placed an ad in the newspaper; "Thriving wholesale bakery business is a fantastic opportunity for the industrious person. Sale includes equipment, inventory and building plus a charming 6 room, 3 bedroom, $1\frac{1}{2}$ bath, 2-story home adjacent to the business. Price $265,000."

Eight months later, I typed a letter to all our business customers wishing them a Happy New Year and said, "All of us at Frosan Food Specialties and Everett Street Bakery thank them for making our company a successful part of the business world. We took this opportunity to inform them that our daughter and son-in-law, Diane and Timothy Chilson, who had been working with us for the past few years had purchased the bakery from us. The transition

would take place the first week in January and our
good service and prices would remain the same."
Saying "May 1988 bring you good health, wealth and
happiness and the time to enjoy them all." Bakingly
Yours, Marie & Michel Fiat.

This phase in our lives was over. The long
hours, the financial juggling, the incredible
responsibility of being in charge were over. We
looked forward now to new adventures.

One did not even have to leave their car
to smell the aromas of fresh baked goods
me - Michel - Donna

1987 speech on "The Changing American Family" nets trip to Hawaii as chosen one from Mass

Business and Professional Women

In 1982 I became an active member of Hampshire County Business and Professional Woman's Club.

My speech netted a trip to Hawaii as our business women's local honed their skills by offering an Individual Development Program. I was the winner, when four finalists spoke at the state convention held at the Sheraton in Hyannis. I began this winning streak in Northampton, when I was chosen best speaker locally of our Individual Development Course. This course helped me acquire more poise, self-confidence and more-effective speaking skills. After having a daughter leave home and going through a divorce, getting my self-esteem back took time.

With two feathers in my hat, in 1987 I went on to represent the state of Massachusetts in Honolulu, at our National Convention. I was excited and a little awed by my success. Noting the educational accomplishments of the other contestants (most of them having graduate degrees,) I just smiled, clearly enunciated my words, and gazed at my audience.

We contestants, from Massachusetts spoke in Hyannis on the topic of "The Changing American Family." I really enjoyed speaking on this subject.

July 1987 found my friend Connie and I flying clear across the continental U.S.A. and five more hours over the Pacific to reach Hawaii. Our captain on the intercom thanked us for the pleasure of our company and I wanted to thank him for the pleasure of his. He had been informative about pointing out the important sights including Los Angeles. It was not his fault that the sightings were generally on the other side of the plane.

"MAHALO NUI LOA" means in Hawaii, thank you very much for choosing me to represent Massachusetts IDP in a Focus Forum. My message to Hampshire County BPW brought back from Hawaii was that we needed to successfully balance the demands of work and family, for balancing has become increasingly important to us women today. Six of us from all over the United States participated in this Focus Forum.

After Hampshire County BPW supported me in this great experience I felt I should give them my time in the position of serving as President of our club in 1990 - 1991. This meant a great deal to me knowing

I was recognized by my peers as being competent enough to lead, through sharing my friendship, knowledge and experience with a membership of 130 local business and professional women. I had worked my way up as member of the board of directors, serving as secretary, first vice president, president elect and then president.

Circle of Friendship was my theme, as I welcomed everyone. I, as HCBPW president, presented our new state president, Laura the 6th from our local, with a gift of a Silver Brick, with her name engraved on it, to be used in the renovation of our BPW building in Washington DC, where we attended the "1990 Issues Symposium" sponsored by the late U.S. Representative, Silvio Conte.

At our National Convention held in North Carolina we signed a banner which read: "BPW/USA Supports A Kinder Gentler Supreme Court." This banner was taken to Washington and presented to President Bush on Lobby Day, the day in which the delegation of senators and representatives were presented BPW'S issues. We felt the empowered experience of meeting professional high powered women who came together for a week to brainstorm, energize and create change for us and our future children and grandchildren.

A great year of monthly programs were planned getting back to basics and concentrating on the two V words, Vision & Value. We read through Lifestyle Seminar Manual which guided us toward our goal.

We gave out scholarships, honored a local outstanding woman who started a support group for cancer patients and their families called, "Celebration of Life." The afternoon tea celebrating Calvin Coolidge was attended by us as well as getting involved in the Literacy Program of our city.

Our Young Career Woman went on to win the state level as well as two of our members were chosen to represent us as member of the year. We celebrated our sixty-fifth anniversary as we honored our eldest member Margaret, thanking her for 39 years of service and dedication to our local BPW.

As I stated to my officers committees and members in my presidents speech in May of 1990 - "You are the hands on earth - thanks for using them in a positive way, using the tools BPW offered and getting involved in the BPW experience. This has been my education and I thank all of you for the wonderful memories I have had of this past year."

Time Out

In 1988 we sold our business & home, stored our furniture and moved to France. We called this departure " Time Out". Our idea was to spend time with the Fiat family, our daughter Laurence and her family, traveling the country. Michel found a job in a great French bakery called, "Aperis Dor," working three days a week, which allowed us to fit some restful and enjoyable trips into our schedule. Here he baked the finest French breads and pastries.

I worked two days a week in the office of The Rotary Club. My typical working day began with a petit dejeuner (breakfast) of croissant and demi-tasse of coffee. I rode to the office with my sister-in-law Anne, never forgetting to stop at the tiny one room boulangerie (bake shop) to pick up the freshly baked French bread for our evening meal. If we forgot to stop early in the morning, it was not possible to stop for bread at lunch time because all stores closed for a two hour lunch. Sometimes there was no French bread left after getting out of work. Bread needed to picked up daily, as French bread, in France, has no preservatives and becomes very hard the next day. The daily trip to the boulangerie is still an important part of everyday life in France.

Then we entered a thirty story building, heading for the elevator and stopping on the sixth floor. Since my French was not so good, I typed, folded letters, put addresses on envelopes, photo copied, and made trips to the post office and bank.

In Grenoble, very typical of France, our small shops and offices took a long midi, closing for two hours. We sat on the sidewalk cafe having our lunch while we amusedly watched Frenchmen being rejected when they tried to join young women at their tables, or students arguing politics or singing. I found myself peering into the main dining room of restaurants to view the decor and setting that so many great people have enjoyed in the past. Sometimes at midi, after lunch we walked around the city viewing the beautiful landscaped parks of flowers and trees. Groups of elderly men gathered lazily as they played boules and spoke politics.

Incredibly, French wage-earners secured for themselves the longest annual paid leave in Europe,

five weeks, unheard of in America. The French are
the first to have made holidays (a national
institution). It was fun working in a French office
with a wonderful view of the city of Grenoble from
the 6th floor.

In the evening a dinner of many courses was
prepared by family, Michel, or myself. Anne, my
sister-in-law said: "The first course which stimulates
the appetite should be a light soup, pate, or
escargots."

"Our main course should be just enough to
satisfy our appetite, but not so heavy that we feel
uncomfortably full," Mother Fiat always said. Meals
such as meat, poultry, game, fish were many times
cooked in great sauces. I loved the smell of garlic,
being the most important ingredient of French
cookery. I have never seen a kitchen in France
without a string of garlic hanging on the wall.

Carmin, another sister-in-law, said: "After
the main course we serve the vegetables, such as
asparagus, green beans, cauliflower, artichoke,
tomatoes, lentils, carrots, and potatoes, adding
a color and freshness of their own to our evening
meal." A platter of French cheeses was then served,
followed by salad with walnuts and fresh herbs, at
the end of our meal to cleanse our palates.

Michel being a baker chose the bread, and along
with his brothers Gerard and Andre counceau of wines
said: "We will visit the family wine cellar, choosing
the best wines to accompany our meal." France is
ideally the place for the enjoyment of good wines
with the Beaujolais to the north and the Rhone to
the south.

"The dessert is the 'finale' to our evening
meal, enjoying the cakes, pastries, truffles, caramel
& chocolate mousse, puddings, and fruits in red
wines," Laurence said.

Michel bought himself a Raleigh Mountain bike.
He biked up a storm, such as the twenty-five miles
to our family place in Meadre, which is up mountain
and down all the way. One afternoon I was passing
him up the mountain in our car and he looked exhausted
- so he hung onto the door handle as I helped him
up the twists and turns. He would never have given
up and put the mountain bike in our car.

Geographically Grenoble is 350 miles from Paris.
Grenoble University is there, and 1968 Winter Olympics
were held there. The Grenobiois called Grenoble,
"Little Los Angeles in the Alps."

Grenoble became a legend in the 60's because
of their industrial and scientific boom and their

innovative search for a new open society. In two
years a permanent modern structure was built that
otherwise would have been spread over twenty years
of construction. This was the 1968 Winter Olympics.
Grenoble acquired an Olympic village with a mile-long
central walkway curving gently, which gave access
to the flats that towered above. One side is a fifty
acre park and beyond rise the snowy Alps with traffic
outside the central pedestrian area. Readied for
the Olympics, the committee had constructed a huge
new ice-rink, airport, roadways, railway-station,
post-office and Olympic village to house 4,000 people.
     Living in Grenoble, a good size city, I took
advantage of all the opportunities available to me.
I started going to aerobics once a week with Carmin,
my sister-in-law and also to silk painting classes
where I painted silk flowers, castles, etc., on
pillows.
     When I joined an English speaking club at
Cleminceau Center I was able to be among English
speaking people with an English library available
to me. These clubs were fun to attend since we spoke
of our families and friends back home. Most of these
women's husbands were servicemen, professor's,
one was an American nanny, and several similar to
myself, married a Frenchman.
     My doctor in the U.S.A. was concerned about
me. He wanted me to have a hysterectomy. I had
cancerous cells. I felt I needed another opinion
so I visited a doctor in France. The doctor's
office reminded me of the family doctor's office
I had for my children in the sixties. Not like the
health centers of today. This doctor also recommended
the hysterectomy and refilled my prescriptions. He
wanted me to be checked every four months to keep
close tabs on my situation. I did this for a year
and later returned to the states to have the
hysterectomy.
     We put our hard-topped, pop-up camper for the
season at Pont de Manne in Royans, a village an
hour from the city, a short but pleasant ride. That
way Laurence, Michel's daughter and her fiance Terry
could go to the countryside when we felt we wanted
to relax. So could Michel and I. On a stroll through
the grounds we were able to enjoy the quiet and
seclusion that this campground offered. There were
facilities for camping in shaded, flat and level
sites. This campsite was located by a small lake
and our relatives and friends kept their campers
nearby. After dinner the Mountain air grew chilly
and we made a campfire, wearing our shawls to keep

us   warm   as   music   invaded   the   still   air.
Our   visit   with   Andre   and   Annie,   Michel's
brother   and   friend   was   such   a   treat   in   a   small
village   outside   of   Grenoble   called   Claix.   Here   the
perennial   flower   gardens   were   perfectly   groomed   and
mountains   surrounding   were   so   serene.   Annie's   home
is   a   huge   mansion   with   eleven   rooms   and   are
artistically   decorated   with   famous   paintings.   French
doors   and   windows,   with   their   shutters   and   draperies
hung   in   the   living   room   from   ceiling   to   floor   along
with   several   fireplaces.   In   the   kitchen   were   hidden
modern   appliances,   which   allowed   for   the   kitchen
to   keep   it's   old   look,   but   pleasant   to   work   from.
Outside   we   climbed   cherry   trees   to   make   our   dessert
for   dinner   that   evening.
On   to   Mercury   Village   for   the   weekend   we   went,
which   is   near   Albertville   and   Courchville,   in   the
southeastern   Alps   where   they   were   constructing   new
highways,   getting   ready   for   the   Winter   Olympics   of
1992.   We   stopped   for   dinner   at   our   friends,   Louis
and   Gisele   Gross,   who   showed   us   around.
We   spent   a   weekend   in   Meadre,   where   the   fertile
farms   blanketed   the   surrounding   valleys   with   the
mountains   making   a   scenic   backdrop.   At   the   family
home   we   hiked,   picked   mushrooms   to   be   fried   for
the   evening   meal,   and   picked   a   bouquet   of
pussywillows   to   place   in   a   vase   on   the   dining   room
table.   Michel   and   his   brothers   told   us   stories   about
how   when   they   were   kids   they   hid   in   these   forests
away   from   the   enemies   during   World   War   II.   It   is
hard   to   believe   there   was   war   in   these   beautiful
mountains.   We   had   such   a   breathtaking   early   morning
view   from   our   bedroom   window   when   we   opened   our
shutters   and   looked   out   over   the   fields   of   cows.
The   cowbells   were   like   music   to   our   ears.
The   following   winter   we   cross-country   skied
in   this   valley,   and   my   sister-in-law   Carmin   said:
"If   you   can   walk,   you   can   learn   to   cross   country
ski,   because   you   can   set   your   pace   and   don't   have
to   go   any   faster   than   a   walk."   Her   technique   was
like   walking   and   performed   in   a   series   of   kick-glide
movement   that   occurred   as   her   body   weight   shifted
from   ski   to   ski   with   the   aid   of   poles.   My   goal   was
to   improve   my   technique   to   form   a   succession   of
graceful   flowing   actions,   which   never   seemed   to   happen
for   me.   I   preferred   sitting   myself   near   the
fireplace   and   gazing   out   the   window   as   everyone   else
exhausted   themselves   out   in   the   bitter   cold.
We   went   with   Anne   and   Andre   for   Easter   Holiday
to   LaFaviere,   which   is   on   the   Riviera   by   the
Mediterranean   Sea.   We   visited   villages   and   cities

like Bormes, Marocco, Nice, Cannes, Napoule and Toulon
with its beautiful port for ships and sailboats.
Here in the south is where you see the sundials
attached to the outside of the homes. They have
an optimistic motto, which reads: " I will mark for
you the sign of fine days only."

In the town of Lavandou we went to dinner at
"Chez Zete" which specializes in Bouillabaisse, a
fish soup that is a grand terrain of all kinds of
cooked fish, a delightful and filling dinner, an
awful mess, but delicious!

Verdon des Gorges was next, which is a smaller
version of our Grand Canyon. They call it, "The
God of The Green Waters." "Now a brook now a torrent,
secret and mysterious water comes from far away
through the mountains," my sister-in-law Anne said.
While I looked at this great wonder I could only
think of Genesis in the Bible: "At the beginning
God created the sky and earth, blue sky sun of honey,
moon and stars for the shepherds. He dug oceans,
rivers, torrents and planted Olive trees as peace
branches, colored and sweet smelling flowers. The
fish, birds, and rain to quench our thirst and wind
to sweep away the clouds. At last he created us
who cling to the earth get food and start like the
river our long journey through life." This gorge
is a sportif place with kayaks, canoes, rope climbers
and hikers like us.

The village of "Ste Marie" came next, with an
iron star shining in the blue sky that hung from
cliff to cliff. This star weighs about 36 lbs, is
4 feet in diameter and the chain connecting the cliffs
is 600 feet long. Strolling through the cobble
streets I saw the shopkeepers and their creations
of blue plates, vases and crockery. I smelled the
lavender fragrances everywhere we passed. Michel
insisted our Aunt Marie and I (Marie) have our photo
taken under "Ste Marie" the saints we are!

Michel and I climbed the Bastile mountain, which
is like a three hour hike that overlooks all of
Grenoble. It was a breathtaking site which gave
you an overall feeling of where you were.

Off we went on a holiday week to see Luciene,
Marie and their son John Coulon, our cousins in
Toulouse, France. As we sat at the sidewalk cafe
in the evening, it was magical as we viewed the
narrow streets and little squares of the old town
with the rose-pink medieval church and palaces as
they glowed under discreet floodlights. The
Toulousains called their city, "The gateway to Spain,"
even though Spain lies across the high Pyrenees

Mountains. Certainly a better tunnel is needed
under the Pyrenees Mountains to get to Spain. When
traveling in France, I could not escape being
surrounded by history. European history, when I
attended school, bored me because I never expected
to see Europe, not knowing what the future could
bring.

As a spectacular treat we stood atop Rocamadour,
which is as Luciene said: "The houses above the stream
- the churches above the houses - the rock above
the churches - and the castle above the rocks."
It is amazing to me that fifteen thousand years before
Christ, man was already here in the caves of the
valley of the Alzou. The medieval streets and the
palace dates from the Renaissance period. The big
stairs and seven square Chapels cling to the
cliff-side which protects them. In the Chapel of
Our Lady, the 12th century Black Virgin turned towards
the rising sun. I had read about this and now able
to see for myself. A shady lane made its way to
the "Way Of The Cross." The wrought iron bell hanging
from the ceiling vault is said to be miraculous,
because it seems that it rang all by itself to
announce some miracles. The history of Roc-Amadour
is the history of man's life in this region and his
need for holiness. Jacques Cartier was one of those
miraculously saved, as he has said in many of his
writings.

In Toulouse we walked the city and saw its
beautiful statues and capital buildings. Then on
to Albi City where the Cathadral Ste Cecile, beautiful
to see. We saw the Port-Lauragais Canals and in
the building a permanent exhibition of how the canals
really work. The canals are located between the
Atlantic Ocean and the Mediterranean Sea and called
the motor-way of the two seas. We found the
exhibition very amusing. They allowed the children
(Michel included) to play with the exhibit of the
canals with small boats. Michel could not wait to
stop at The Green Windmill Restaurant, where they
served a specialty of beans and sausages, called
Cassoulet, famous in that area of France.

In south-western France is the City of Art called
Cordes, which is built on rocks, and due to the
strength of its fortification, was never attacked
at war time. Gates, monuments, houses and of course
churches make up the city of Cordes. At the top
of the town stands a magnificent pink sandstone church
of the fourteenth century, called St. Michel. In
the chapel the marble and gold gilded interior is
unreal. As we wandered through town I found painters,

sculptors, glass blowers, and other artisans at work. We viewed and purchased their creations in an adjacent gallery to give as gifts to family and friends in U.S.A. This display provided us with the opportunity to meet the artists and to see where and how the pieces were created.

On to Lourdes (the seven marvels) museums, cinema, lake, forts, station of cross, holy water, candles, etc. Michel and I waited in line for over an hour (Michel never waits in line for anything) to touch the rocks where the Virgin Mary had stood. At night they used candles to illuminate around the church area which gave me such a feeling of holiness. Marching in the sign of the cross were healed people, for to me, the religious power is something else, letting you breath on faith. These people could hardly move and now were actually marching. We were extremely lucky to be there at this time (as this only happens at certain times of the year.)

With Michel's brother Andre and friend Anne we visited the Six Valleys of France, which are Ferrand, Veneon, Legnarre, Eau d'Olle, Sarenne, and Romanche, part of the Alps. We drove our car through snow tunnels in (mid summer). Pastures with cows waited patiently to be milked at the portable milking stations in the middle of a steep field. Michel's French sense of humor said, "The cows and goats here have two hoofs shorter than the other two and when you whistle they fall down the mountain!"

La Salette, a very moving place which is the village in the Alps where in September of 1846 Maximin Giraud about eleven years old and Melanie Calvat fifteen years old, two very poor children (who did not know each other) saw a great light and a beautiful lady spoke with them as she wept and said, "Come near my children be not afraid - I am here to tell you great news." Her last words were, "Well, my children, you will make this well known to all my people." Things that the beautiful lady spoke of were true and had happened in the children's lives. So they truly believed.

Mont Blanc, in Chamonix the "Aiguille du Midi Cablecar" the highest cablecar in the world and the longest ski descent in Europe is sure a technical achievement. This idea originated from the Romans. Fifteen thousand people live in Chamonix and 500,000 persons per year use the telepherique. Only the hardy mountaineers climb the 16,000 foot peaks to dig for quartz crystals. In June on a sunny summer day we were advised to dress real warm. When we reached the snow topped summit the temperature was

under 0° C. and our winter coats were welcome. The
sun's radiance and reflection on the snow of the
glaciers was so strong we were glad we had brought
our sun glasses.

Between Switzerland and Italy we passed through
the Alps to the Great Saint Bernard extremely cold
temperature and covered by snow. I was so excited
to be there. I hardly felt the cold. This is 8,110
feet above sea level, and rarely in summer
temperatures reaches more than 68 degrees. Snowfall
averages 65 feet deep and the lake is always frozen.
The pass has been used by travelers as far back as
800 BC. Monks accompanied by the Saint Bernard dogs
carried food and blankets to those in need, whom
they met on their way. About 80 Monks still reside
at "The Great Saint Bernard." We visited the
monastery and outside playing joyfully in the snow
were about 40 Saint Bernard dogs.

During the week after work Michel, Annie's dog,
Star, our dog Dutchess and I climbed Cole de Larc,
which is quite the smaller mountain to climb near
Claix in France, where we lived. Star is a large
shepherd and our Dutchess is a toy poodle.

Star led the way as he kept coming back to be
sure we were following him and little Dutchess quietly
stayed by our side as if she might get lost. It
was fun watching them together doing their own thing.

On Sunday we went to a car race not far from
Grenoble, a town called Vereen that Andre, Michel's
brother, was in charge of. Andre had a very fast
driving car called, Lancia, which placed him among
the best drivers. Everyone was given a road map
to follow and many games were played as their car
trophies were given out.

Later we had a lamb roast for about 80 people
with whom he raced. It was held in Meadre at Andre's
place. This lamb was roasted in an open pit, with
it rotating until the aroma told us it was done.
Salads, vegetables, desert, and beer & wine
accompanied all.

Tour de France, an annual madness as French
people call it in France, passes through Grenoble
and Meaudre. The names of those who race their
bikes through are written in paint on the roadway.
This is a 2,000 mile whirlwind race that spins around
France in three breath-squeezing weeks in July.
The route, raced in daily stages, climbs over France's
toughest mountains. At the end of each stage the
leader carries off a yellow jersey. The Tour winner,
the rider with the best time over the entire course,
gets THE JERSEY. But he pays, day by punishing day.

Fatigue abrades his mind and body. When his legs
and spirit start to wobble, the thought sweeps through
"It is the TOUR de FRANCE," so he learns to suffer.
Because they must finish in three weeks, cyclers
bridge several stretches by rail, plane, and car.
Nearly 500,000 fans line this Alpine route.

In 1988 we shouted Allez, Allez! Such a long
wait for so brief a moment, a blur of spokes, a flash
of jersey . . . an empty road. Virtually everything
happened on the run. They were handed a sandwich
or fruit to eat on the run, drink on the run and
urinate on the run. Why did they bear the unbearable,
and stay indentured to a featherweight frame with
cobweb wheels, we asked? Money, and of course, to
sweep through the Arc de Triomphe on the last day
and be able to say they finished the TOUR de FRANCE.

In Lyon, France we stayed with our friends
Christian and Christane Bador and their son Romain.
They gave us a walking tour through the alleys to
see the old houses and buildings that had been
transformed into shops and studios. During the rush
hour in Lyon we saw executives in their neat suits,
all clutching the black briefcases, as they caught
the new high-speed express train linking Lyon to
Paris, a two hour journey, which before the high-speed
express train was five hours long.

We went to the city of Perouges, which was built
in the Renaissance period with the pebbles from the
river Ain. The climb was a little stiff with the
pebbled streets so uneven making it hard to walk
on. We saw rustic arts, and the statue of the patron
saint of Perouges was extremely worn with people
touching it and over wear. It showed the tear of
time and weather. It almost seemed unreal that
Perouges was still there with its gates, towers,
prison, churches, markets, sun-dials, stables, homes
and ruins, since it was of the Renaissance period.

There are ten thousand castles in France. We
have seen quite a few and I will try to give you
an example of what they were like to see. Vizille
Castle and Chenonceau Castle are the last two castles
we visited. Most of the castles have either an
English speaking guide or a brochure that explains
in English everything you see. I personally like
to have the guide tell us about the history and
be able to ask questions as we go along. Most
castles have round towers in each corner. These
are reflected in a mirror of waters, as they are
built near the rivers as a stronghold, fortification
and defense for the towns. Many were built by the
order of the kings. Queens had private chapels of

Gothic-Style with stained glass. Numerous marble inscriptions can be seen on the walls, which in most cases now are under glass shields to preserve them. Many a large fireplace can be seen and most have wonderful portraits hanging above them of people who were very special in their time. Beautiful tapestries hang on the walls and some of the tapestry colors are extremely rare. Some of the original greens have acquired a blue tint with age. Large hand-painted canvases hang on some walls, as well as some made of leather which are worn with age.

I looked up and was awed at the extremely high ceilings with exposed beams of decoration. Some had inlaid work.   As I strolled down some halls they contained the most unusual arches, with door panels decorated with human figures as well as fruits and flowers.   The tiles laid in the hall floors were so nicely decorated. Rope-like railings, grand staircases, and some octagonal stairways, made for remarkable pieces of architecture. I felt like I wanted to climb them slowly, savoring the Renaissance times. We passed chests from the Gothic and Renaissance period, some done with leather and finely worked nails. Furniture was inlaid with pen, ivory, or mother of pearl included armchairs upholstered in leather or tapestry. I saw picture frames that were beautifully carved along with the statues. When I passed by large beds with canopy or tapestries directly behind them, I wanted to rest there. French Gardens at the castles were planted for lovers of the kings and named after the ladies of the time. Some of the gardens were the loveliest part of these estates and many a time actual rooms were added for the king's lovers. Their waxwork museums worked wonders in bringing life to the marvelous times of the story book history of France.

We pitched a tent near The Rocks, a small town and the Abbey that made "Mont Saint-Michel," a very famous site to tour with an English speaking guide. With a circumference of 2,952 feet we found among the steep and narrow cobblestone streets, old fishermen's houses, ships, hostelries and taverns. In the church we viewed the gold statue of Saint-Michel built in the 11th century. He was armored, crowned and fierce looking. Medieval Abbots were the ones who made the best use of this natural site, as a pilgrimage of its time. In the evening after our nap we returned on our bikes and walked around the ramparts and we enjoyed the bird's eye view of the high seas, which was isolated from the coast by a tidal wave.   Sheep grazed the

salt-saturated grasses. The flat landscape made
the pyramidal even more magnificent, the pyramidal
construction which is 492 feet high was like a peril
from the sea. We waited for hours with camera in
hand to see and take a photo of the sunset behind
this magnificent Mont Saint-Michel, as did many a
professional photographer. The sunset was
breathtaking when reflected off the water. The wait
was sure worth while, the best place to end my day.

"D Day" - June 6, 1944 became history when
Winston Churchill declared that, in order for allied
forces to set foot on French soil, engineering corp
of the navy needed to construct an artificial port.
Twelve days after the allies had landed, the port
was in full operation. One hundred fifteen enormous
blocks of reinforced cement were submerged under
water, and together with sixty sunken warships of
varying tonnage, formed a giant demi circular
breakwater, measuring 12km. The breakwater extended
the length of the nearby communities. Michel and
I tried to imagine four floating piers, measuring
a total length of 5,700km positioned in the center
of the port and joined to the mainland, completing
this gigantic fleet of military ingenuity. When
we visited the war museums along the beach, we felt
we relived those sorrowful and tragic hours of the
Allied Landings.

The Normandy American Cemetery site in Trevieres,
France was chosen because of its historical location
on top of a cliff overlooking the famous Omaha Beach,
which was the scene of the greatest amphibious troop
landing in history. The cemetery site covers 172
acres owned by the United States of America.
Conflicting emotions nudged me while I re-created
this battle in my mind. I felt sorrow over the deaths
of good soldiers obeying orders. Emotions nudged
me again as I wondered, after seeing listed the
Westcott name, if this was a relative of mine. We
saw 9,386 crosses of American War Dead buried there.
Three hundred seven of the headstones marked the
graves of "Unknowns." The remains of approximately
14,000 others originally buried in this region were
returned home at the request of their next of kin.
The memorial consists of a semi-circular column of
pillars with arches at each end. On the platform
is a 22 foot bronze statue, the "Spirit of American
Youth," a tribute to those who gave their lives in
these operations. Around its base is the inscription,
"MINE EYES HAVE SEEN THE GLORY OF THE COMING OF THE
LORD." While eating a dinner of mussels and shrimp

Normandy provides, Michel and I spoke of the sandy beaches, the flowering fields, and the green woodlands here in Normandy, evoking once more the true sweetness of living in freedom.

While visiting in this area on an evening of rain we took the opportunity of a farm bed and breakfast experience here in France, which was delightful! The owners of this B & B took us into their home with open arms as family. We toured their farm with the milking cows, horses and other farm animals. We enjoyed a home cooked meal of duck with the tasty extras of the meal. Well into the early morning we had great conversation with their guests, family and friends who spoke of their homes, children, life, and travels.

We visited for an entirely different experience with many of Michel's friends, reminisced and one long weekend in particular will be remembered forever. Five couples gathered as we drank, feasted, and jeeped in the mountains of Calixte's home.

We went riding in three old USA army jeeps, here in France, through the granite cliff and ridges, rivers and streams up mountains and down again. Sometimes we were not sure what was on the other side of the hill, when climbing it in the jeep. Michel got out of the jeep to look over the cliff to see if we could continue. Trees got in our way, our jeep stalled, so we cut the tree down (this US army jeep would not reverse) and we continued on our merry way. Once three of us had to get on one side of the jeep to balance it so we would not fall off the cliff. One time (I of course in that jeep) while going through the ridges we tipped to the side and I fell right on top of the driver who was a friend of ours. Bruised, skinned, black and blue, swollen and scared stiff, I survived.

A few weeks later we woke before dawn to climb another mountain. This time Michel and I joined our cousins Luciene and Marie at a campsite on the Mountains of Molard which is part of the National Parks of La Vanoise, France. Since it was a National Park, with no dogs allowed, I carried Dutchess our poodle in my knapsack, where she was just so comfortably warm and content, actually snoring in the stillness of the mountains. At certain times of the day I saw her shadow on my side, but when the mountain air got colder her whole body and little nose was also in the knapsack. We brought with us hooded sweat-shirts, special glasses for the snow which was real bright high in the Alps, our walking canes, hatchets, ropes, iron spikes for

our hiking boots and of course wine, cheese and French
bread. We saw cascades, avalanches, snowed cliffs,
beautiful Alp flowers, blue skies, and in the pastures
Chamois (goats) Mamottes (little creatures in the
Alps) along with flocks of sheep which they use for
meat, milk, skins, wool and manure. One day we climbed
for eight hours and I thought I might never make
it to the next refuge camp, I was soo exhausted.
While camping in the village of Biasins we met Madam
Darnis. She told us of a special restaurant called
LaBergerte in the area. So in the evening we had
raclette, melted cheeses on ham and potatoes which
you melt yourself, and Braserade, which was beef
you cooked yourself on a small stove placed in front
of you with all kinds of sauces to dip into. These
Val d'Isere Alps are a paradise of natural beauty
that everyone must see. The snowcapped mountains,
beautiful valleys, sparkling streams, and occasional
glimpses of wild life were amongst our memories.
This cannot be described for this must be seen to
be thoroughly enjoyed. I can only say these
exhausting trips, hikes in France, left me refreshed
and filled with wonder.

Snowcapped Mts-beautiful valleys
sparkling streams & occasional
glimpses of wild life
me in center where food is

GRENOBLE "Little Los Angeles" in the Alps

Grandthoughts

As a grandparent of nine, I have a major role in shaping my grandchildren's lives. Becoming a grandparent for me is the continuation of my life. My grandchildren are the dots that connect the lines from one generation to another. I am a holder of family history. I can help shape their sense of themselves, and feel I have a very important role.

My daughter, Diane gave birth to Troy Eric, December 16, 1978, he weighed 6lbs. 11oz. Trinity Marie was born, May, 28, 1981, weighed in at 7lbs. 1oz. using my name as her middle name. Trisha Lynn was born, September 20, 1984, weighing in at 4lbs.11oz., and claims she was born around noon while her daddy was eating her mom's lunch. Each of Diane's children were born 3 years apart.

Deborah gave birth to Stephanie and Daniel while living in Pennsylvania. I have yet to meet either of these grandchildren. Hopefully some day I will.

Donna gave birth to Richard Scott on April 2, 1989 weighing 6lbs. 4oz., naming him after his father and Jacob John on October 31, 1991 weighing 7lbs. 6oz., named after his maternal grandfather. This daughter kept the holidays for having her babies. Imagine calling your mother on April fools day to tell her you're going to the hospital. The next child she decided to have on Halloween. By the way, the babies' daddy Richard Scott decided to come into this world on Friday the thirteenth.

My step-daughter from France, Laurence gave birth to Romain Michel, Nov 1, 1989 weighing 7lbs. 1oz., naming him after his great grandfather and grandfather. Jordan Christian was born November 6, 1996 weighing in at 6lbs. 12oz., naming him after her grandmother.

I was filled with joy each time my daughters gave birth to my grandchildren. I knew hearing their first cries, that we would bond quickly. My grandbabies remind me of flowers. Their skin are like lilies, eyes like forget-me-nots, lips like tulips. Pink roses for cheeks, morning glories for ears and pollen for the hair. Daisies made their fingers & toes and a snowdrop for their nose.

Baptism brought tears to my eyes. Our friend

Ruth sang, "The Slumber of The Infant Jesus." Then
our whole church family sang to the tune of "Morning
Has Broken" (using my grandchildren's names)

_____ we name you and with thanksgiving
Offer our prayers and sing you this song.
We are the church, your spiritual family
Sing we our praises to Christ the Lord.
Then our minister Rev. Ed carried our grandchild
down the aisle so our spiritual family could see
this wonderful bundle of joy.

We encouraged ideas about how things work. It
seemed to start with the rattles, giving hand-eye
coordination to Jacob, my youngest grandchild at
this time. Then came the measuring cups and spoons
for him, which made my kitchen a great place to
play. Playing peek-a-boo with my Romain, quickly
brought pleasure to me as I lowered the blanket to
reveal my hair and forehead and he exploded in
delight. The very first time I heard him break out
in a belly laugh was while he watched my poodle
dog, Dutchess. My grandchildren's love of, and
rapport with animals has deepened which satisfied
me, to see that I have passed on this gift of
understanding animals.

When a new sister or brother arrived in their
homes the siblings imitated Mom, as they cuddled
their dolls or bears and fed them. Their toys are
arranged on low shelves and in lower drawers that
are easy for them to locate, reach and return. For
two of my grandchildren, as I helped them to put
their toys away was not easy for me, as I did not
know where "away" was. They certainly had a place
for each toy, while other grandchildren just picked
them up and put them anywhere.

Their backyards are filled with the old tires,
climbing frames, swings, and rocking toys, which
seem to challenge my grandchild's balance. I loved
to watch them with wide smiles going from one toy
to another, hopefully using up all that energy.

The finger-play songs like, "Itsy Bitsy Spider"
got such belly laughs from my grandson Scott. He
learned very early to turn the pages of the bright
picture books as I read about the animals, and
recited to him the nursery rhymes I remembered so
well from so long ago.

As Scott worked with his lego's and building
sets, I saw him get more and more coordinated. Their
sandbox brings them hours of pleasure as they pour,
measure, and combine them, using water. These were
actual learning tools, for they like to stir, pound,
poke and soon learn to pour without spilling.

My toddler grandson, Jacob grasped a marker and was delighted by the motion of scribbling. Diane called this payback - when she gave her nephew's art material such as fingerpaints and watercolors since they are a bit messy. Her sister Donna gave the messy arts when Diane's kids were younger. "Paybacks a bitch, huh," she said.

Tell Grandma about your picture, I heard my daughter say. She knew her kids learned the most and gain confidence when their art is all on their own. I cherish their art-work. It's all so magical, placing it on my refrigerator and later in a special scrapbook in my attic.

My children tried to bolster the self-confidence of my grandchildren as they praised their successes, saying: "You did a beautiful job of hanging up your coat." Then a few minutes later my grandchild will hit his sibling.

My daughter stops the physical contact and then tries calmly saying, "You may not hit the baby. People are not for hitting," she says. If my grandchild continues, he must go to the corner. You need an attitude adjustment, my daughter said.

Once, when I was on the phone with my daughter, one of my grandchildren wanted to go in the babies room to wake him. My daughter yelled, "I cannot let you wake the baby. If you need company come and play in the kitchen with me." They sure like to test our limits.

If I am at my grandchildren's home at bedtime some of them needed a night light, and some needed Mom to playfully chase around the room, to rid the room monsters. Then they spoke quietly about plans for the next day so the children could look forward to them. To prepare my grandchildren for medical visits and other potentially frightening situations, Mom talked, read about, or best of all acted out what might happen.

When my grandchildren stole Mom's pocketbook and wanted to dump everything out, Mom said, "My pocketbook has some important papers and I need to keep it with me. Please bring it back." They knew nothing about stealing, they do not yet know about, "yours", only, "mine."

My grandson Jacob, a toddler is curious and wants to be independent. He says things like, "I can do it myself!" My daughter gave him a short handled spoon for self-feeding, a plastic spreader for the peanut butter and she made sure they had a sponge handy to use for clean up. Offering choices like, "Would you like to wear your red or blue sweater, or would you like to ride your tricycle or pull the wagon?" These helped my grandchildren make their own choices.

My grandchild Scott waited to speak. The doctor said he would not talk until he could do it perfectly. He needed time to understand what he was saying. He was very proud when he learned to tell me his name and how old he was. He held up two chubby fingers when I asked him his age.

One, two, buckle my shoe and three, four, shut the door reminds me of the times when numbers became important to my grandchildren. Mom tells them it's three days until Christmas, putting another X on the calendar. Tomorrow is Wednesday and we will go to the library then. When they become older they are $4\frac{1}{2}$ not just 4. Inches were important, you can go down the water slide when you are as tall as the clown, measuring the 48" needed to attend that ride at the amusement park. I heard my daughter say, "You already weigh twenty pounds. I can hardly lift such a big boy." Making pounds important. Scott has learned the number and name of his street and his phone number.

Sometimes at the end of a trying day Donna would scream: "H E L P", which meant, she said, "Handling Energetic Little People, is not easy." I must agree with her.

My grandson Scott loves to make home repairs. As Mom hammered a nail in the wall to hang a picture, Scott hammered away down below, turned the dining room chair upside down. Then he found the screwdriver and unscrewed the seat part of the chair. What a home repairman Scott is going to be.

The young ones like to receive checks for their birthday, as they saw Mom and Dad write checks out for their new shoes, or groceries for the home. Money they like as well, for it can be touched, counted, sorted, saved and of course spent. As my grandchildren got older they learned the value of money by having allowances, knowing the money does not come from the plastic card at the bank, but by working. They also know how much the tooth fairy money can buy.

There were many relatives, on my adopted side whom I would have liked to have known much better. One, Aunt Edith Bader Brouilette, my mother's sister, I did get to know after my sister Edith and her grandson David had passed away. Sister Edith took Aunt Edith out to eat and shop many times a week. After she passed away in 1981, David, her grandson, helped her in every way he could, until he passed

away in 1983. She suffered a tremendous sense of
loss and seemed to go down hill shortly after her
two best buddies had left her side. I felt this was
about to happen and tried desperately to help her
as much as my busy life allowed me. Edith was the
5th child of my adopted mother's family and was born
June 5th of 1892 in Southampton, Massachusetts.
She had blue eyes, white hair, was a very composed,
passionate and eloquent woman. Her voice was low
and reverent, her face radiated a beautiful joy,
and I listened. Each time I saw her she had earrings
on, hair always done and very well dressed.

She married Albert Joseph, born in 1887 in
Brighton, Illinois and he died in 1962 in Easthampton.
Together they owned a school bus company in
Easthampton. We loved Abbe, for he was a heavy-set
man and quite jolly, loving all of us kids. Edith
and Abbe had three children, two boys and one girl.
Clarence Bader was born in 1910, Eileen Harriet
born in 1913, and Richmond Douglas born in 1923.
Her three children, who did not live nearby or were
unable to care for her, hired a home-care worker
and knew I stopped by daily to be sure she ate
properly. I prepared dinner for Michel and I, then
brought the left-overs each day carefully prepared
on a plate covered with love wrappings.

She was so grateful to see me and was thankful
for every little thing I did. She loved to peek
child-like at what I brought for her. Aunt Edith
had a lively brightness and amusing crinkles of time.
She was the opposite of my adopted mother, whom I
stood on my head to try and please. My aunt Edith
always told me my adopted mother, her sister, was
an unhappy person even as a child.

After picking up my grandchildren from
kindergarten, we went over Aunt Edith's home and
brought her a plate of food. She loved spaghetti
and I came in and said, "I have some spaghetti, if
you want to get up."

"Oh I would love spaghetti, but I'm wet and
it's so much trouble," she said.

"Nah," I said, helped her into a diaper, a dry
nightgown, and changed her bed. She pulled the
chair she liked best up to the kitchen table and
savored every mouthful, like a child who has just
discovered a favorite food. Sometimes she dangled
a strand of her spaghetti in the air and leaned her
head back, dripping it into her mouth.

"My, that was good," she said, as she wiped
her mouth with the back of her hand like a child.
Many a time she looked across the table with a sweet

sad smile and said, "You're so good to me and I love you."

The daily activities in the neighborhood fascinated her, as she watched endlessly out the window of her bedroom. She loved my dog Dutchess who sat by her all the while we were there.

She loved life and was like a child when it snowed or the seasons changed. "I have never seen anything so beautiful," she said.

Sometimes when I went to see her I tiptoed in thought she was asleep and she woke and said: "Hi, how was your day?"

My friends asked me, "How are you doing all this along with managing your own business?" I thought the love for her I had in me, made it manageable.

The time did come when it became unmanageable. She really needed to wear diapers, but wanted to be so clean she washed by hand, her smelly panties, and dried them over her kitchen gas stove, which obviously had an open flame. This frightened me to death. The many times she had fallen frightened me as well. I found her one time, she had fallen in her own urine and laid there for hours. After this a walker was given to her and finally, the last time she fell and hurt herself enough to be taken to the hospital the decision, which had to be made by her children, was to go into a nursing home.

They called nursing home after nursing home knowing that finding a home with an available bed on any given day was strictly a matter of chance, not choice. As I saw her in the nursing home for the first time, it was hard for me. I wished I had more time at home to care for her. She was scared, but sharp enough to know her life was no longer under her control. I hated to leave her, but she said over and over again, "It's just temporary." I did not answer, I kissed her each time goodbye.

Meanwhile an auctioneer went to her home to buy off all her belongings. This was a sad day for me, as she talked very lovingly about her piano, grandfather clock, special pieces of glassware, and many gatherings held in her home. Over and over again, I thought of my adopted mother and how lucky she had been to be taken care of, in her own home by her daughter Edith, but how she had never showed any appreciation even until the day she died.

The nursing home they chose, "Poets Seat" in Greenfield, was twenty-five miles away, and it became harder for me to see her. I managed weekly visits and I brought jelly beans. (She picked out the black ones and shared the other colors with anyone who came around.) Stuffed toys were brought when my grandchildren and poodle dog, Dutchess accompanied me. The nurses loved Aunt Edith dearly. She was such a delightful person. Men passed her by and she said, "Did you see him look at me?" This cracked us up, for at this time she was in her late nineties.

Edith reminisced about her long and eventful life, savoring her extraordinary moments. Her voice was low and reverent, her face radiated a beautiful joy, and I listened, admired, and appreciated her precious memories, she passed down her wisdom and traditions from generation to generation. Sometimes I heard the same stories over and over again, but it was easy to divert her as I expressed my interest in other stories she might have, or by asking her questions. She was the kind of person I longed for my mother to be, loving, caring and just wonderful. My aunt Edith, age 98, passed away January 6, 1990, and is buried in the Brookside Cemetery in Easthampton, along with my mother and the rest of her family.

My granddaughter Trisha, started writing at a very early age. Her teacher felt she needed more time on her school work than she was getting. She seemed to love writing as early as second grade and did a great job. The following are some of her works.

SCHOOL LUNCHES

She says, "This book is dedicated to my sister and to my brother, who have to eat school lunches too."

Our schools serve some very interesting lunches. Did you ever eat one? After you read this, you may never want to!

Do you know the hamburg sundae they serve once a month? Well, what I want to know is this; is it really hamburg in there or is it chunks of sponges covered with brown paint?

Are the potato puffs really made from potatoes, or are they pieces of rope stuffed with old used tissues?

Is the pizza with cheese really pizza with cheese or is it slices from trees covered with melted yellow crayons?

Is the meatball grinder really meatballs and bread or is it marbles and soft red wax on sponges?

Is the taco shell really a taco shell or is it curved and toasted cardboard?

Is the baked macaroni really pasta noodles or is it our old milk straws cut into little pieces?

Is the french toast really bread drenched in syrup

or is it bread shaped pieces of soggy styrofoam?
Is the beef and bacon burger sandwich really beef
or is it fried dog food?
Is the spaghetti with a meatball really spaghetti
with a meatball or is it boiled strings with rubber
bouncy balls?

If you don't know the difference in your foods,
you can eat a school lunch anytime. However, if
you like good food, BRING YOUR OWN LUNCH EVERYDAY!

In the back of this book she has a page for
Reader's Comments: Her teacher Ms. Dushane writes
- You poor child, having to eat those disgusting
school lunches! How did you ever manage to survive
first grade and all those lunches? You've written
a very creative story about our lunches! Her friend
writes - I really liked your book!

Each page is accompanied by a little sketch
and bound by a colored jacket.

When in third grade she wrote:

MY GRANDMA

My grandma is different because of a lot of things,
here they are;
She was adopted and the way in which she brushes
her teeth. (false)
My grandma is very special to me!
Her house is always tidy.
She has funny sayings - all over everywhere in
her house.
When I'm sad, she always makes me happy.
She tells me my favorite stories or poems when
I ask.
She always takes the time in whatever she does.
My grandmother wears neat little Mary Poppin shoes.
She always plays games with me, round the world
with basketball as well.
My grandma is not the smartest or richest but,
I still love her whether she is or not!

Then she wrote:

GRANDMOTHER OF MANY NAMES

My grandmother Marie Westcott, my mother's mother
was born May 3,1939 in Boston, Massachusetts.
She has a double heritage. She was born with a
mother Mary Westcott and a father Alfred Westcott.
She had fourteen brothers and sisters. Then her
father died one year after she was born.
Her mother couldn't take care of all of those
children. So they were all put into foster homes.
When my grandmother was seven years old, she was
adopted.
First they wrote her name in the newspaper, MARIE
EUNICE WESTCOTT to see if anyone disagreed. Then,

she walked up a long flight of stairs to the courthouse in Northampton, Massachusetts. Inside the courthouse there was a lot of files and bookcases.

They gave her a paper that was signed by the judge with a big gold seal on it.

Now her name became MARIE SHIRLEY PRATT. She spent her childhood in Easthampton, Massachusetts.

When she was twenty years old, she married John C. LaBarge, (my pepe.) Then her name became MARIE PRATT LABARGE. After seventeen years, she divorced.

Then four years later, she got married again to Michel R. Fiat (my grandpa.) Now her name became MARIE PRATT FIAT.

All my grandmothers names together now are:
MARIE EUNICE SHIRLEY WESTCOTT PRATT LABARGE FIAT

My granddaughters collect some adorable memory dolls. Authentic doll collections made of genuine hand-painted porcelain bisque face, hands and feet. The lips are hand-painted as are the finger nails and eye lashes. Their arms have wire in them that permits adjustment to form a real life pose. Detail is given in the selection of each dolls clothing and is emphasized in the quality, design, and handwork. The hair and eyes are life-like, adding natural beauty.

Troy, my oldest grandson, plays center position in basketball. Sometimes my older grandchildren and I play "Around The World" and I (Grandma) beat their butts each time. This game is played by marking out seven evenly spaced circles in a row on the ground. If you make the first basket you try for each after and so on around the world until a miss. Whoever goes around the world, making all the baskets, and back again first is the winner. Troy also plays soccer: His position is full-back. He plays on the Suburban Team, which is the traveling team, and has won many trophies.

Listening to Rock music and good team spirit gets Troy psyched to swim the butterfly, back, breast and free strokes. In 200 (individual medley) Troy does 2 laps of each stroke with his best being the breast stroke. His room is filled with plaques and gold medals for different swim meets. The Bay State Games (Junior Olympics) have given him many gold medals. Troy swam, ran, and biked for the Annual Triathalon each year.

At the Easthampton Summer camp, Trinity received awards for such things as friendliest camper during

the four weeks, most cooperative camper, most
talkative camper, and won first place in the Queen
Contest.

Trinity played softball in the Junior Olympics
American Softball Association in which her team
did not lose or tie a game. In basketball she
received an achievement award. She placed in a
lot of events receiving many ribbons swimming for
Easthampton Barracudas, Pioneer Valley and Western
Massachusetts leagues doing freestyle, butterfly
and backstroke. She received an Amateur Athletic
Union of the U.S.A. certificate of attainment,
certifying that Trin has achieved the attainment
level of performance for her group in the physical
fitness program. This was awarded for the dedication
to attain the personal fitness goals, and was signed
by the physical fitness and amateur athletic union
personnel.

At the Hackworth School of Performing Arts,
the schools 60th year students danced for love, danced
for joy, and danced for dreams. They also danced
to bring smiles and happiness, striving for
excellence. Trinity's achievement is due to strong
legs, learning the skills of ballet, gymnastics and
jazz. She likes ballet the best, but is told she
is better in jazz. She says, "I guess because jazz
gets me in a good mood." She wants to go on to do
a Lyrical (ballet and Jazz) solo, soon. Trinity
is part of a company which performs in opening
and closing the recital. I asked her what she thought
of before she performed. "I run my routine through
my head and the part I don't know to the max, I
practice in the hallway while I wait to go on stage,"
she said. Trinity has placed in the Star Systems
National Talent Competition, received ballet and
jazz achievement awards and silver medals at American
Dance Spectrum. Hackworth Studio of Performing Arts
is the same school her mom attended for years and
Jackie, the owner, is one of my very best friends.

Trisha received a certificate of congratulations
reaching the road across the U.S.A. Read-A-Thon.
They say she did a royal reading job. She is my
little writer, the grandchild who wrote the story
of me.

At the Western Massachusetts Summer Swim League
and the Easthampton Baracudas Trisha won ribbons
and the Easthampton Youth Soccer Team watched her
play her best.

Trisha learns the word of God at Awana Clubs
International. Each week she competes in Awana games,
hears challenging messages finding her needs being

met in the Chums Program, the second rank called Princess. Along with Bible study the club has crafts such as baking, sewing, writing stories and they receive points for accomplishing each of these phases of Awana. I attended her Christmas party with her and met many of her little friends while having our ice cream and cake. Trisha received ribbons for being in a Bible quiz.

My daughter gave me a plate to put on my car that says, "If we had known grandchildren were so much fun, we would have had them first." How true that is. Some of the "momlies" used by my children just crack me up to hear. They sometimes said, "I'm the mommy and that's why. I can do ten things but eleven is really too much. I waited my whole life to be boss."

The memories of hugs I shared with my daughter, Deborah are so pervasive in my thoughts that each knock on the door around the holidays renews an undying hope that a hug will be shared with two grandchildren whom I have never seen. What a dreamer I am.

In the 90's my girls tried to raise their sons so that they know their wife is not their mother or their maid, but their partner and friend. They want them to share not just help with parenting and household responsibilities.

If I were to write up some notes for my grandchildren I would look at my small treasures and want them to know it is OK to learn from their mistakes, explore and be interested in life. For my older grandchildren I hope they will not wait around for someone to direct them to do what they are able to figure out and do for themselves.

There is a happy glow - a growing excitement when your kids come to visit. They will only understand this when their children grow up, leave, and come home again. I am delighted to be in the role of grandmother. Giggling with my grandchildren and suddenly I bend down to hug them or stand on my tip-toes to hug them (the child of my child) and want that moment to last maybe forever and ever.

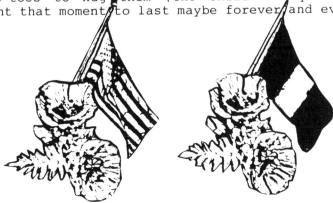

Jacob & Scott   Jordan & Romain
     USA   France

Troy - Trinity - Trisha
       U   S   A

Deaths

My mother was an invalid for many of her last years of life and my sister Edith constantly cared for her in her own home. I often wanted to relieve Edith, but Mother never wanted me to care for her for any length of time, until her dying days in Cooley-Dickinson hospital in Northampton. Just before passing away mother said to my sister Edith: "Get out of here and I never want to see your face again." Mother, before this statement looked weak and dead. She almost jumped up and said these awful words and after she said her prayers. I was teary eyed and felt bad for my sister. She never deserved that in a million years. My sister Edith and Linda, one of the latest girls living with us when I was a child, left the room and I followed wanting to hug Edith to release the pain. At that moment Mother beckoned to me to come close to her. "Marie help me say the twenty-third psalm," she said. I did, and she quietly passed away on October 25, 1968. I wanted to believe Mother did not want the person closest to her near when she decided to die or that the white uniforms Edith and Linda wore scared her. They had come straight from working at the State Hospital.

Her private funeral was held at the Edmund B. Mitchell & Son funeral home, 21 Center Street. Edmund and David were relatives of ours. They placed her in an extravagant mahogany casket with her favorite color blue liner. I could not help but almost hear her say, "What's this shit, just throw me in the ground." The Rev. Roettger pastor of the Providence Methodist Church officiated and the organist played Mother's favorite, "The Old Rugged Cross." I could almost hear her playing this song on her harmonica. Her internment was at the Bader Family burial lot in Brookside Cemetery situated near our Nashewannuck pond in Easthampton.

Beautiful flowers arrived from our relatives and friends. I placed a heart shaped pillow of pink roses and baby breath from Deborah, Diane, and Donna our three young children, her youngest grandchildren.

Our relatives, most of whom I had not remembered or never met, came from Kentucky, Vermont, Connecticut, and Massachusetts. Mother, at the age of 82, outlived three of her children, leaving Edith

and I. In 1979 I was not listed as an adopted
daughter of Lillian Bader Pratt in their
Historiography of the Bader family, although the
next generation of adopted children was mentioned.
I am sure this was not done to hurt me. Perhaps my
relatives did not want the hassle of calling Mother
for information needed on me. Mother was not a
very cooperative person. In 1995 I updated this
historiography including my name, births, and deaths
since 1979.

My home filled with conversation after the
funeral of my mother as we lingered over a buffet.
One of my aunts said, "Their mother used to say,
where did we get Lily?" Others said, "They were
afraid to come and visit her in her home because
if they said anything disturbing to my mother, she
became very violent." Confusion was in most
conversations, probably because everything about
her life, present and past, was in a jumble.

I had never spoken to any of my adopted
relatives about the abuse before this, and I didn't
after either. It took me fifty years to want to
discuss my childhood. Linda, one of the girls living
with me in my childhood and her husband Jimmy seemed
to have some sort of relationship with my Mother
but did not want to discuss it. I feel Linda blocked
out most of her childhood to cope with everyday life.
Linda's sister Carol was like me, having very little
contact with Mother.

In our home years passed between my relatives'
visits and we were forbidden to speak with our
relatives when they did visit us. Reminiscing with
my relatives in my home was a pleasure for my husband
and children. They had never met most of my
relatives. We tried to speak of good times (sister
Edith was amongst us) trying to get an understanding
of her life before me. All ended as each said
they were certain that she loved me in her own way
and loved me very much.

I had hoped to have more contact with my adopted
relatives after this funeral. We went on with our
busy lives and never gathered again until the next
funeral.

For my mother, the pain of death was past, labor
ceased, life's long warfare was closed, and hopefully
she found peace. In my mind I felt life had ended
for mother...but begun for my sister Edith at age
fifty-eight.

Many years passed, I stood at Mother's grave
with tears in my eyes, thanking her for the good
things she passed on to me.

Thirteen years later my sister Edith passed away at seventy-one in the Holyoke Hospital. Michel, my husband and I had been vacationing in Florida returning very late in the evening. I phoned the hospital and asked if they would allow me to take a run in to see my sister Edith that evening. She was a diabetic, suffered from arthritic pain and had her gall bladder removed. There answer was, "Sure, that will be fine." Tired as we were after our long drive, Michel and I drove to the hospital and visited for a short period of time in the intensive care unit. She looked very tired to me and the nurse said, "Edith came through the operation very well and was doing fine, soon to be taken upstairs to the regular floor." Michel and I returned home and in the early morning I received a call from the hospital saying, "Edith had departed from this life." I was rather stunned. My mother was in her eighties when she passed away and I assumed Edith had another ten years to enjoy life since she was only seventy-one. I was glad I had a chance to visit with her for even a few minutes the evening before.

Edith Mable Pratt, my sister, one of five children, was born September 2, 1910 and passed away October 28, 1981. She attended Easthampton High School, leaving school at age sixteen when her father died, to work as a packer at the Hamden Mills and later retired from the Northampton State Hospital. Edith was on the heavy side, towered over me, very quick spoken, and her face untouched by make-up. She never married, and after my mother's death Linda and Jimmy moved in with her in the old homestead.

Again we entrusted our relatives at The Mitchell Funeral Home. This time only David, (his dad had passed away) was there to help us through these times. He helped me as a grief therapist, relieved me of every detail, made our loved ones look like a beautiful memory. He did everything in his power to make the funeral pleasant for everybody concerned. David's mom Eileen was always available and his sister Donna, an excellent teacher in our Easthampton's school system, taught my children and later my grandchildren.

We placed a small cross of pompoms from Rodney, who was her youngest nephew, and a pillow of pink roses and baby's breath from toddler Troy and infant Trin, her great nephew and niece, my grandchildren. My children Diane and Donna, then in their twenties, sent a lovely bouquet of flowers later placed in our home. Edith's homemaker, Linda sent a pink

carnations and white pompons in a formation of a
cat. Edith loved cats. Our funeral director and
our relative David placed a large white cross of
carnations, and our church deaconess and friend,
Shirley Mullaly brought a single yellow rose with
love.

Our pastor Ed, from our Congregational Church
officiated with our organist playing selections Edith
loved such as "The Old Rugged Cross," "In The Garden,"
and "How Great Thou Art." Edith's final resting
place was Brookside Cemetery in the Bader family
burial plot.

Again we had a grand buffet. Michel and I
invited all our relatives to join us. We reminisced,
socialized, and commented on Edith's strong will
and her sharp and humorous comments. She did get
a chance to live again after Mother's death, was
able to associate and become good friends with my
Aunt Edith. The two Edith's were able to enjoy lunch
at some exclusive places. Someone in our family
helped financially to make this possible.

Edith was treasurer of the Friendly Club at
Sunrise Manor where she presided her last few years
of her life, after selling the homestead. Years
later, when she was unable to drive her own car,
I picked Edith up to join me at our church, drove
her to her doctor appointments, and helped her
grocery shop. Linda helped Edith more than I, and
spent lots of time with her. Linda never conceived
any children, joining my family on most of the
holidays.

Edith continued to do crafts and my children
enjoyed the Raggedy Ann and Andy dolls she made for
them. Edith spent many holiday dinners with us,
but I never felt closeness to her and she never
wanted to become close to my children either. She
baby-sat for Carol's son Rodney while Carol worked
or went out in the evening. Carol was a single mom.

Edith loved cats and while working at the
Northampton State Hospital, as an attendant, she
and her friend Lois shared ownership of a cat named
Patches. Her friend Lois Wheeler wrote a book on
cats mentioning Edith's name in it.

Later I received notes and letters from my
relatives and friends who said they enjoyed our
hospitality, socializing, and getting acquainted
with my new husband Michel. They said, "My sister
Edith would have been very proud and happy about
the way I handled everything."

Among Edith's belongings was a post card still
in her mailbox, I had mailed from my vacation in

Florida, she did not get a chance to read, as she never returned home. I found a poem amongst her papers which fit her to a tee.

> "The Housewife's Eulogy"
> Here lies an old woman who was tired.
> She lived in a house where help was not hired.
> Her last words on earth were, "Dear friends, I am going.
> Where washing ain't done, nor sweeping, nor sewing.
> But everything there is exact to my wishes.
> For where they don't eat there's no washing of dishes.
> I'll be where glad anthems forever are ringing.
> But having no voice, I'll be clear of the singing.
> Don't mourn for me now, don't morn for me never.
> I'm going to do nothing forever and ever."

When I called Edith on the telephone to see how she was doing, she said, "Fine, except Author is here still bothering me," meaning her (author-ritics) was paining her that day. Her famous saying was, "That's that" - and her sharp and humorous comments hurt and each time I tried again to get to really know her, imaginary, real, or creating my own problem, I hurt again.

It was difficult to piece together a kind of history, but I am not sure how much of the unhappiness happened before or after we children were living there. No way to sort the past from the present.

My two sisters still living nearby were some of the last to leave my home after the funeral. One was gay, and good humored this night. There was a side I had never seen before as she sat silent unable to eat the good food, drinking too much liquid, smiling at the wrong places in a complicated story, shaking her head when she should have laughed. My other sister as she sat across from me, her upper body seemed to sink in toward the back of the chair. Her hands were clenched together in the cavity of her lap. One leg was wrapped tightly about the other. She appeared closed in. It is clear to me at the start that their childhood was not something they were able to talk about with ease.

I hope in the future there is comfort for each of us dealing in our own way.

David Engley was a twin born October 22, 1938 his twin is Donna, and nephew is Jeffery. His maternal grandmother was Edith, mother was Eileen and the late Edmund was his father.

David attended Wiliston Academy and graduated from Easthampton High School in 1957. In 1959 graduated from the New England Institute of Mortuary Science. He married Anne of Florida December 24, 1967 and they conceived in October 3, 1972 a daughter Kendra who was ten years old at the time of her father's death.

David was my cousin, church and school mate, and a good friend. He belonged and participated in many clubs and churches in our hometown. On Saturday morning, many times, friends and I gathered at Norm's Coffee Shop where David generally gathered to have breakfast. He was a handsome gentleman, witty, good sense of humor, and we reminisced and just had a great time talking before my friends and I shopped for the day.

The House of Mitchell, as our townspeople called his funeral home, was started three generations ago with Vivan E., Edmund B., and David E. The Mitchell's Funeral Home and The Mitchell Company of Monuments was located on Union Street and later on Center Street in Easthampton.

David was president of Mitchell's Funeral Home for thirteen years and worked with his father from a very young age, therefore he knew the business inside and out. Once I asked David what actually did take place after a person died. He proceeded to tell me after they picked up the body, they brought it in the preparation room of the funeral parlor and in a very short period of time embalming and restorative art was performed on the corpse. He did a good job making the body presentable for viewing. David was loved by many in our town. He entrusted many sacred obligations, served many in a manner which lightened their burden of sorrow, comforting the bereaved families for many years.

David was stricken with a heart attack while attending a function on a Saturday evening at the University of Massachusetts, located about ten miles from his home. He was forty-four.

He passed away March 13, 1982 with his wake held at his funeral parlor. Four hundred people stood in line half way around the block in the cold night air to pay their respects. Flowers were placed everywhere possible and cards of all types for many reasons were left.

The following day our Easthampton Congregational Church overflowed with hundreds of mourners as Rev. Dibble, our pastor officiated and was assisted by Rev. Barnett, chaplain of Williston-Northampton Academy, and the Rev. Berthiaune, assistant pastor

of Notre Dame Church. Many more pastors of area
churches, our church boards, delegations from
Massachusetts funeral directors Assoc, Easthampton
officials, The Grange, Eastern Star, Farmers Club,
Ionic Lodge of Masons, VFW Pitch Club, relatives,
and friends attended. A private burial service was
held in the Brookside Cemetery with our Rev Dibble
conducting the committal prayer, at the Mitchell
burial lot.

I felt like I had lost a buddy, a friend, and
a relative and I knew beyond that gate, David would
find happiness and rest.

Aunt Edith was born in Southampton,
Massachusetts, June 5, 1892 one of eight children
of Casper and Johanna, my mother's sister. She
attended Easthampton schools and she and her husband
owned a school bus business in our town. She was
a long-time member of the Easthampton Grange.

She married Albert and conceived three children.
Eileen Harriet and Clarance Bader passed away in
the eighties, son Richmond Douglas spends the winters
in Florida, falls and springs on a farm in Virginia,
and his summers here at Norwich Lake in Huntington,
Massachusetts. Edith outlived all seven of her
brothers and sisters and one grandson, David. She
had six grandchildren, eleven great-grandchildren,
and several nieces and nephews.

Edith lived in Easthampton most of her life
and passed away January 6, 1990 at the Poets Seat
Nursing Home in Greenfield. She was ninety-seven,
not quite making it to one-hundred years old. Edith
had already picked out her pink dress to be laid
out in, and asked me to keep it for her. I hung
it in the back of my closet and when the phone rang
telling me of her passing, I brought it to the funeral
home. With the family in the funeral business she
had been prepared. The funeral was held at another
Mitchell Funeral home (not her daughter's or
grandson's place.) They had passed away before she.
This funeral parlor belonged to her son-in-law's
brother, Walter. A reverend from the Providence
Methodist Church officiated.

Private burial with the family was in Brookside
Cemetery, where her mother, father, brothers, and
sisters laid to rest. After the burial our immediate
family gathered at Norm's back room for a brunch.

Edith had blue eyes, white hair, was very
composed, passionate and elegant. She radiated a
beautiful joy, and I listened, admired, and

appreciated her precious memories. I miss her loving
smile, her gentle face, and I feel no one can take
her place.

My first husband John, father of my three girls,
was born August 25, 1933. He was one of eight
children, the first to pass away, born to Marguerite
and Cyrus of Leeds, Massachusetts. His siblings
names are Elmer, Edith, Virginia, Lorraine, Dorothy,
Richard, and youngest is Kathleen. He had three
children Deborah Anne, Diane Mary, and Donna Jean.
His seven grandchildren according to age are: Troy
Erik - Trinity Marie, Trisha Lynn, Stephanie Lynn,
Daniel, Richard Scott, Jacob John, his latest
grandchild named after him.
John was robust, gegarious, broad-shouldered,
quick-smiled, self-confident, soft spoken, sensitive,
and chose his words carefully. John graduated from
St. Michael's High in Northampton, and American
Academy of Dramatic Arts in New York City. He served
in the United States Army's Special Services of Drama.
John worked at McCallum's, Forbes and Wallace,
Steigers, Blakes, Lowe's Cinema, Papageno's, Veterans
Hospital, and in his last few years at The Northampton
Nursing Home.
John, Michel, and I were able to enjoy a
relationship with our children and grandchildren,
getting together for birthdays and holidays. I have
a snapshot of John smiling in his last months in
the kitchen (without Jack Daniels by his side,) doing
his fun thing cooking dinner for us, his ex-wife
- my husband our children + our grandchildren. Our
family life is built around such emotional experiences
and our grandchildren are quick to sense a change
in our emotions. Each of my daughters is unique
and has different personal feelings about death.
I give credit to my girls who handled their
father's death with love and care. Their reaction
brought tears to my eyes over and over again. My
husband, Michel was by my side daily to help me
help my girls through this exhausting time of grief.
Donna, mother of one year old Jacob, knew that
a child lives only in the present, but is aware
of emotional changes around him. The only thing
she could do was to hold him in her arms and talk
gently to him about her sadness. Her other son three
year old Scott, could not realize that death is
natural and final. To him, she supposed, death was
like sleep; you are dead, then you are alive again

or like a trip you go on and then you come back again.
Trying to convince him their "Pepe" was dead, a final
thing, not sleeping or away, was a painful task for
Donna.

Diane's eight year old Trisha had enough
religious training to have some idea of a soul, which
helped to comfort her through her grieving. Trisha
told her mom: "God needed 'Pepe' now more than us,
to make everyone in heaven happy."

The mystery of death can be added to the other
mysteries of life, and Trisha understood that not
all questions about death could be definitively
answered. Eleven year old Trinity recognized that
death was inevitable for all persons including
herself. She had a mature idea of what death meant
physically and emotionally. Thirteen year old Troy,
who is physically fit and aware of bodily needs,
emphasized the need for good judgment and care of
one's self. He understands that the body eventually
grows old and wears out and can no longer do its
work, especially if not taken care of. Troy knew
his Pepe was an alcoholic who had not cared properly
for his body, therefore passed away at a young age.

My daughter Deborah, who had not had anything
to do with our family since the family breakup, was
called when her father was seriously ill in the
hospital. When told of his condition, "Thanks for
calling," she replied. When contacted again, to be
told of his death, "Take care of yourself," she
replied. Diane, my caretaker-middle child, was hurt
deeply by these remarks. No flowers, letters, or
cards arrived or phone call later, to see how everyone
was doing. I have not been with Deborah for many
years now and have never seen my two grandchildren,
who are being brought up in Pennsylvania.

My girls had to decide who was ready to attend
the funeral. They felt that as long as the children
were mature enough to have strong feelings about
wanting to attend, they should be allowed to do so.
This grief in their lives had great meaning, the
experience of shared loss and was a part of the
family circle at such a trying and traumatic time.

John had taken vacation time from work. He
called his children and told them he was going to
be on vacation with his sisters on a bus trip,
meanwhile told his sisters he was going to be with
his children on his vacation. I feel he must have
known he was not well and needed time to be alone.

He was barely alive when the ambulance brought
him into the hospital. He had called one of his
sisters, because he had been bleeding internally

and externally. He was in intensive care and when
they let me in to see him, he gasped for every
breath he took. The girls were by his side every
moment they could, but in spite of loving care, we
could see no improvement. The doctors held no hope.
In the intensive care unit there was neither night
nor day. There were only bright lights and the
humming of machines, the pumping of respirators and
the occasional whine of a computer, the sound of
gasps   for   air   and   the   smell   of   blood.

His heart was still pumping, and the nurses
had him on the respirator, but there were no brain
waves. "I feel the fight is over," the doctor said.
He was legally dead, but technically, with artificial
help, he was still breathing, but with difficulty.
The doctor told the girls they could keep him on
the machine as long as they liked, but there really
was no point. It was up to them now. Both of my
girls were in tears, but the truth was that the daddy
they both loved had died a while ago. John had
been working in recent years as a nurse attendant
and had often expressed the belief that he felt
people should not have to suffer. My children felt
he was exhausted from fighting that bottle daily
and let him go, knowing he needed to be free.

During the final stage in their dad's life they
spent twenty-four hours a day with him doing as many
things for him as possible. No one else could have
given more tender and loving care. They understood
both positions wanting to be with their father but
knowing if they became exhausted and their resistance
was low they would be unable to be of any help to
their children. Being willing to call on me to help
was a sign of strength, not weakness.

My girls believed that the last of the senses
to fail was hearing, when a person was dying. So
even when their dad was unresponsive, they spoke
to him as they shared words of love and respected
the feelings he might have had. I watched my girls
as they rubbed his back and said, "It's all right,
we will miss you, never forget you and we will
eventually be okay."

John's brothers, sisters and two of his nieces
were also at the hospital continuously. Other nieces,
nephews, friends, and coworkers came and went in
a constant blur. He was much loved and respected.
In his sober years he was able to help several others
find the path to sobriety.

When the neurologist came to the Intensive
Care Unit waiting room to confirm that John was
indeed brain dead, the fate of his body rested in

the hands of my girls. They asked the family for
their thoughts and feelings and were very much
relieved to know everyone was in agreement.

The time had come to allow his body to go, so
his soul could rest in peace. With heavy hearts,
the girls signed the papers allowing the medical
staff to remove all life support, leaving only comfort
measures like oxygen and I.V. Since there were many
loved ones who wanted to be with him, he was moved
out of Intensive Care Unit to a large room where
we could all be together. All day long people came
and went as they said their special good-bye.

Finally, late in the evening Donna, Diane, and
I were alone with him. For a long moment my girls
held their dad's hands, kissed him, touched his
cheek for a lingering moment, and walked outside
blinded by tears. They knew if they turned away,
he would leave this earth. He never wanted them
around when things were not right for him. In the
far distance were the sounds of a fireworks display,
giving us a chuckle as they needed at this time
knowing he left with a bang. The fireworks was
a sign and symbol for us all, of the departure of
one who had made a significant impact on all of our
lives. He passed away October 11, 1992 at the age
of fifty nine. Detailed arrangements, such as hospital
papers and funeral arrangements had to be made,
as well as a cemetery plot. Aunts and uncles of
the girls helped immensely in funeral and cemetery
arrangements. There were many differences of opinion
and some friction amongst them, but since his sisters
and brothers felt strongly about a Catholic funeral
and a specific church, the girls gave in. Death
puts a great strain on all and the need for love
and support of one another allowed them to not let
the differences of opinion drive a wedge between
any of them.

Funeral arrangements were made at the Czelusniak
Funeral Home, with one evening and one afternoon
for his wake. His pallbearers were his nephews.
Two hundred twenty-five people gathered to pay their
respects, for he was known and loved by many. Over
one-hundred relatives and friends gathered at The
American Legion Hall in Northampton for a luncheon
which followed the service. He had rooms filled
with flowers, thirty Mass cards, and many
contributions made to the local chapter of Alcoholics
Anonymous. John was buried in the Ryan's family
plot, at St. Catherine's Cemetery in Leeds,
Massachusetts.

Father Vincent O'Connor, from St. Catherine's

Church in Leeds, gave the Eulogy and said John's life was like a play with a opening, middle and closing scene. He played different roles; opening scene showed him born a son, middle being a brother, husband, father, grandfather, love as an actor, director, and AA sponsor. His funeral was his final act. The organist was Susan Anderson who played his favorite song, "Oh What A Beautiful Morning," this brought tears to my eyes as John loved the early morning and sang this song often to his children.

A flat marker was all that could be used in the cemetery plot, so the girls decided to have a bench dedicated in his memory at Look Park in Northampton, where he went daily to feed the ducks and read his book. This bench, for the tune of $700.00 is located in such a beautiful place, where his sisters walk, his daughters bring their children to play, where we used to picnic as a family, and where John and I as children picnicked, making three generations. Inscribed on his bench is, "In Loving Memory of - John LaBarge - August 25, 1933 to October 11, 1992." Relatives, friends, and acquaintances remembered this area where he sat to read his book and smoke his pipe - maybe never knew his name - But Remember.

I know that death brings sorrow and grief, but that this grief work is necessary. My grieved girls felt loneliness, anxiety, emptiness, guilt, anger, self-pity and depression. They talked and talked, cried and cried and even lost control for a while screaming throughout their homes. I listened as they talked about their dad again and again. They mourned not only for the loss of their dad but mourned too the loss of their dreams and fantasies and expectations. It seems that grief is like a spiral, starting with you, at you, and draws a circle around you, holding you tightly in its grip. Then it loosens its hold on you, yet comes back again to touch you at moments of good memories such as Memorial Day, with its ritualization of the spiral of grief. One day one of my girls felt angry and unhappy and decided this feeling was not right. After driving back from Dad's gravesite she felt a griefing relief.

Throughout all of this my girls' relationship grew into a wonderful new bond of sisters and friends.

John was the first child of eight to leave this earth. He was the third person in my life close to me that passed away in October. The first was my mother Lillian Pratt, second was my sister Edith Pratt. We carry the dead generation within us and pass them on to the future through our children.

This keeps the people of the past alive long after we have taken them to the churchyard.

The feelings that swept over me as I grieved were uncomfortable and strange as we had been divorced for seventeen years. We had many good years together and I like remembering the good times. Death gave me value to my life. I feel to live life well I must work when I'm energetic, sleep when I'm tired, take a walk when I'm restless, and to hug my spouse or a friend when I need to be touched.

Mother & favorite Aunt

I became more excited as time got closer & closer
to touching & seeing someone who looked like me
standing: Gladys - Roger - Lillian - George - Hermina
Muriel - Alfred
seated: Anne - Marie (me) - Walter
unborn: Pearl - no name twins - Mary
searching: Mary or Patricia

Today Reunites Yesterday

For years my adoptive parent discouraged me from searching for my birth-family. Their was a common misconception in my adopted family. If I said I wanted to search, they presumed I was ungrateful and hated the family I grew up with.

If I did not want to search then I was grateful and loved the family that I grew up with. I spoke of search only once while I lived with my adopted parent. Mother said in a very angry voice: "Why would you want to search for someone who never wanted you." I had no answer for her. I could see she was upset with my asking.

Over and over again I was told I was a chosen one and that my adoptive mother took the place of my birthmother. I really did not believe people were that interchangeable. As time went on I felt I was nothing like my adopted mother or sister. My adoptive parent was intimidated by my desire to know about my past. I felt search had a lot to do with my wanting, not ungratefulness. I wanted desperately to be like other people to have a father, brothers, and sisters. People I spoke to never could understand why I wanted to try to have a relationship with a generation that had nothing to do with my conception. As I matured I all the more wanted to have a somewhat completed view of myself in terms of my history and heritage. It is hard not to know the person you are born to. I silently kept a life-long desire to find my birth family. Half of myself wanted to do what I was told and half wanted to search. In deference to my adopted mother and sister, I waited for 45 years to start my search. By this time my adopted mother and sister had passed away, my children were married, and I was more than ready to start.

Surviving the intensity of my search was hard, even though my husband and adult children, as well as friends, were as excited as I, as time got closer and closer to touch and see someone who looked like me. Fantasies I had. That was a way to deal with pain and to relieve something unfinished. I very often looked at people and said to myself, "Who are they, are they someone I know." I searched to be able to fill in the gaps, record my family tree,

and to reconnect my genetic genes. My search took
a great deal of strength and was a commitment for
me to get on with my life.

Twice I went to Probate Court to ask the judge
to open my files and twice the request was denied.
I had to decide. Did I want justice or just to forget
the whole mess? Beating the adoption game was not
easy because the records were sealed and filed away
according to law. Most birth certificates were
amended at the time I was legally adopted. (My
certificate was not amended because I was adopted
in 1943, by a widow and therefore a father could
not be listed.) I needed to obtain a court order,
which was a difficult task. The records were sealed
for many reasons. The most important reason was
to protect the rights of those involved, such as
birth-parents and adoptive parents, since these
records contain names and background of those
involved. Few of the laws were specific, therefore
most were subject to the individual judge's
interpretation. Good cause, such as need for genetic
information, was accepted but curiosity was not
considered sufficient cause.

Curiosity should have been reason enough when
I was in my forties. This was extremely emotionally
upsetting to me. In 1982 I saw in the newspaper
an advertisement of an organization called Adoptee
Search Connection located in Connecticut. I called
and made an appointment to go and register with this
group. I spoke to a very nice woman, spilled out
my heart to her. There I registered with the I S
R R (International Soundex Reunion Registry) located
in Carson City, Nevada. In 1984 I read in a Dear
Abby column, to write and sign up with an organization
called A L M A (Adoptees' Liberty Movement
Association) located in New York, New York. Having
my own business during these years took up a lot
of my time and I put my search aside at this time.

In 1988 my search took over a major part of
my life. I was between jobs and about to have a
hysterectomy. Search was time consuming and expensive.
My needs accumulated and multiplied until the
compulsion to search was overwhelming and unstoppable.
The third time I went to Probate Court to petition
the court for permission to examine my adoption
records in 1988, the judge wanted to know why after
50 years I needed to know about my past. I was
upset and disgusted that he asked me such a question,
and responded, "Do you have siblings and aren't you
glad you know them and know how they are?"
The court officer came over to me and took my arm,

quietly said, "Be careful what you are saying."
    "I need to know my family history for medical
reasons," I then said.
    The judge's answer was, "I will respond to this
request in writing at a later date." All I thought
of this situation was, "another dead end."
    I ran to the rest room as soon as I could, only
to weep some more. Weeping because I was embarrassed
of the way I acted in the court room and mad because
I did not get the answer I had come for. As I stood
there wiping tears from my eyes, I heard someone
walk into the ladies' room. Not looking, I dodged
into the toilet stall. Whoever came in wrote on
a piece of toilet paper a telephone number for me
to call, and shoved it under my stall. By the time
I came out of the stall, that person was gone. She
must have seen the condition I was in while in the
courtroom and wanted to help. I thank this person
over and over again.
    While driving home I memorized that number,
but scared as I was, I could not get myself to call.
I guess I just did not want rejection again that
day, and not knowing who might be at the other end
of the phone, I was scared. We had just moved back
to the states after living in France. Since I was
not working at this time, I had several job interviews
lined up that week, and that alone was frustrating
and emotional. My hysterectomy decision was in the
back of my mind and the uncertainty of not knowing
whether or not I had cancer.
    The following Friday I received a letter in
the mail from the court that said, "the request to
open my file was granted." The courts learned the
law of sealed files in Massachusetts did not go into
effect until 1950 and I was adopted in 1947. The
telephone number I was to call was the same one I
had memorized. My enthusiasm just turned the sparks
into flames again. Immediately, I ran to the phone,
dialed this wonderful number. It was Friday afternoon
and all the lines were busy and by the time I dialed
again there was no answer. They were closed.
    First thing on Monday morning, I dialed and
spoke to the receptionist at the courthouse. "My
name is Marie Fiat and I wanted to make an
appointment to sign a request for release of my
adoption information," I said.
    "In order to locate your records, you need to
fill in the section that said adoptee requestors,
answer all the questions and specify the nature of
information you have requested," she told me. After
I filled out the questioner with general information

wrote my name, address, phone number, date of birth, and social security number I proceeded to fill in my;

Adoptive name: Marie Shirley Pratt
Adoptive parent (s): Lillian Bader Pratt (only)
Birth name: Marie Eunice Westcott
Nature of information requested: Needed to find birth siblings under Westcott or Wescott
Birth mother: Mary Hambelin Westcott
Birth father: Alfred Westcott

A copy of my driver's license, as verification of my identity, I also enclosed. I signed where it said, signature of requestor, and the clerk mailed this to the Department of Social Services in Boston, Massachusetts. This request for release of adoption information needed to be reviewed and approved before I could meet with someone to hear my file and receive any information to help me find my parents or siblings.

Meanwhile, I was referred to Ann Henry, a search consultant and co-founder of TRY (Today Reunites Yesterday.) This is a nonprofit organization supporting adoptees (a word not found in most dictionaries, including my word processor) adoptive parents, birth parents, significant others, and all people in search. Their research team is connected with many other groups who support and search across the United States. I met Ann at The Maple Leaf restaurant in Westfield, in October of 1988 and joined her support group. Soon in the Try Newsletter under TO CONNECT read; "Ad'ee born MARIE EUNICE WESTCOTT DOB 5/3/39 in Boston, MA b'm MARY ESTELLA (HAMBLEN) WESTCOTT b'f ALFRED WESTCOTT OR WESCOTT DOM 9/14/19 looking for siblings called Roger or Richard Westcott." They were names I thought I had heard in my childhood. I registered again, with International Soundex Reunion Registry, and was given a great list of books, tapes, and questions to think about before our search began. Ann shared with me why she decided to start this organization they named TRY (Today Reunites Yesterday). She had searched for her son after she gave him up for adoption many years ago. Ann felt an organization was needed to help with search and as a support group, for those in search.

At this meeting Ann had asked me several questions like: Was my family supportive? Did I have the time to search along with all my other responsibilities? Did I had a logical, not emotional need for my search? Would I be able to cope with the search if I found out I had cancer at the time

of my hysterectomy? The answer to all four of these
questions was "yes."

She asked me, "How do you feel about adoption
in general and my case in particular, inquiring about
my life experiences." (I quickly gave her an idea
of what my childhood was like, my first marriage,
my children, the divorce I endured, and how life
at this time was great with my new husband and my
adult children's lives.) "You had better prepare
yourself for a negative response from authority
figures, including rudeness, scorn and guilt trips.
Be prepared to argue, cite regulation or law, and
to appeal decisions." Ann continued to say, "Start
a search diary, list all your questions so you can
add your answers as you find them. (Since I am a
list maker, this was right up my alley.) When you
find the people you looked for, are you prepared
for possible rejection or acceptance?" (I felt by
this time, something was better than nothing.) "Are
you willing to balance your needs with theirs, and
maybe acknowledge holidays and birthdays, and even
write an occasional letter to keep in touch?"

Writing was something I have always loved, so
I believed this would be easy. "What if you do not
like what you find, or what if they do not like,
you?"

Since I had not expected to find kings or queens,
I felt I could be happy just to know, hug someone
who looked like me, and it would be up to them, to
decide how they felt about me.

After I discovered my rights and what my
limitations were, Ann, as my search buddy, understood,
listened, encouraged, and helped me all along the
way. My search began with a letter to Brightside
for Families and Children. I hoped to find a family
member I thought was in Brightside at one time.
My adopted mother often said to me, "If you are not
a good girl, I will put you with your brother at
Brightside." I later found out that this was a common
threat for children in this area of western
Massachusetts when they misbehaved, especially
state wards. I, as you can tell, took this statement
seriously and kept that threat in my mind for years.
I was convinced that a brother of mine had been
there. I was disappointed with Brightside's answer.
They said in their letter, "No one by the name of
Westcott was found in their records." I was furious
that my Mother said such a thing to me, leading me
to believe another one of her lies.

I went through all the local phone books, called
many a Westcott name, hoping to find a brother at

the other end. Everyone was quite friendly and helpful. They took my phone number or sent me their Westcott genealogy or family trees. No luck was had by telephone.

Boston Department of Social Services mailed my files to the Springfield Department of Social Services and in Springfield (under agency guidelines) he read my files to me. You can not understand what it felt like, to sit across the desk from a strange social worker, who sat back in his chair and asked me: "Why do you need to know?" He read the records of my life and pulled out little tidbits that he decided he wanted to let me taste. I was so angry inside, but I kept my cool. That file was my life. Who had a better right, to that record than I? My birth certificate, newspaper clippings in the Daily record of Boston, many letters, photos and my adoption decree, were all in my file. While my records detailed some background information, they offered no hint of present whereabouts of my birth-parents or siblings.

Meanwhile we traveled the 100 miles to the Boston Bureau of Vital Statistics, where Ann, my search buddy from Try, and I looked up births of anyone we felt might be a sibling. The Boston Bureau of Vital Statistics was open for search on Mondays and Fridays from 2:00pm to 4:30pm and on Tuesdays and Thursdays from 9:00am to 11:30am. Those two and a half hours flew by, especially when we had to wait in line for the employees to slowly seek a particular volume. This was extremely annoying for me to travel 100 miles for such a short period of time to search. Their policy was as follows: I signed in first at the desk, stated my name, address and what agency I was with. I was then given a checkpad and went to the aisle of the year I wanted to search, and if I was lucky enough to find a familiar name, I then wrote this name on the checkpad and stated whether I wanted birth, marriage, or death.

Knowing I was born in 1939 Ann, my search buddy guided me to look up in the large volumes years before and after 1939. It was especially difficult, because sometimes my birth name was spelled with one "t" instead of two, or a "t" left out in the middle of our name. Westcott was my birth name, spelled Westcott or Wescott on some certificates. Therefore, I had to be sure the mother's name was Mary and the father's name was Alfred. The large volume which I found told the year, volume number, and page where the original record might be found. After I wrote

this information on the checkpad, I then stood in
line, for only the employed persons from the Bureau
of Vital Statistics, could find these volumes for
me. When the volume was indeed found, they inserted
my little piece of checkpad in the correct page
and I was instructed to read only that page. I took
my time reading that page and turned to the next
page, not thinking. I was quickly reprimanded as
I turned to the next page, by an officer on duty.
He slammed the book shut and took it from me, but
he did not realize why I had turned the page and
he did not allow me to explain. At this time I was
intimidated by this officer. The brother I had found
on the page given to me had a twin listed on the
next page, I was sure.

Being extremely annoyed, I timidly glanced around
to be sure this officer was not watching me and
proceeded to get in line again, asked for the next
page on my little checkpad, and was given the same
volume again, only my checkpad this time was on the
next page. Standing in line I watched as the
government employee was not able to find the volume
where it was supposed to be filed. I very much
wanted to say, it is right there, because I just
had it in my hands. Finally he found it not filed
away as yet and handed it to me. Quickly I grabbed
it. There was the twin's name on his birth
certificate, for I was indeed right. Ann had warned
me there might be times like this.

Many days later I returned to Boston as I looked
for more information. I searched large volumes which
told me the year, volume number, and page where the
original record could be found. After I stood in
line, I received from these employees the volume
with my little piece of checkpad in that page. This
time I found and read silently baby NO-NAME with
date of birth and death the same day. This page
was the only reminder of my mother's still-born
children. Name was not known, only they were each
one of fifteen children. Later as we drove home
to western Massachusetts I thought to myself, I will
never know how my mother expressed her grief at the
loss of her still-borns.

Knowing most of these birth-siblings were born
in the Boston area, Ann and I went to the Boston
Library where I scribbled phone numbers on paper,
called and waited for a voice at the other end, but
was not discouraged by their dead end answers. We
ended that day at the Norwood Library where I found
a street of a sister after going page by page, until
the 93rd page, gave me an address to go by. I had

found my sister's marriage certificate and a George
Cooper was listed as her husband. Here was a glimmer
of hope. We felt we had found one sister and a
brother-in-law, finally.

We ran to my car and proceeded to drive there.
It was a housing project for the elderly. After
I rang the bell to the main door several times,
a man answered, asked who was there and I said,
"It's Marie Westcott, and I think I'm Gladys' sister."
"No-no I don't want to see you, Gladys," he
responded. I realized he did not hear correctly what
I had said, so I repeated, "No, I am Marie Westcott,
not Gladys. I think I am Gladys' sister."

He said, "Oh - oh," and unlocked the main door
so Ann and I could enter the hallway. George lead
us to his apartment, which was spotless, and offered
us a cup of tea. While we drank our tea we
reminisced, as he and my sister had separated twenty
years ago. He had no idea where she might be at
this time, as they had not kept in touch, but perhaps
she was still in the Boston area. Another dead end.

At this point I got desperate, so close and
yet so far. I went home again, continued to call
many more Westcotts listed in and around the Boston
area. I had great conversations with all, but found
no more clues to my own family's whereabouts.

On the next trip to the Boston area, Ann and
I drove to the Cambridge Library, where a wonderfully
helpful lady told us they did not have any new
directories, only a "77-78" directory. It seemed
like only a slim chance of this not being another
dead end, since this was now 1988, ten years later.
There was my brother's name, GEORGE, leading to the
jackpot, his home address was not listed in this
directory but it did list where he worked in those
years, at Harvard University, Boston. Ten years
ago, but I took my chances. As I looked up, I saw
a pay phone right down the hall there in front of
me, and dialed that number. The answer was, "George
does work here, but is in another building at this
time." I asked them to please give him a message
that Marie Westcott had called, and to have George
call me back at my phone number in my home.

Meanwhile, Ann and I rushed to my car parked
in the library lot, and drove home to Agawam, as
soon as we could, because I wanted to be there to
answer my phone when George returned my call. He
ignored my call. The next day came and still no
response. Later in the day I called the same phone
number again and he was there this time. I was
nervous when I heard the phone ring, I did not know

what to say, I felt awkward. What was I going to
say to someone I had not seen in fifty years? We
had an answering machine so my husband, who was as
excited as I, taped my brother's reaction. When
I said to him, "I believe I am your sister Marie,
Marie Eunice Westcott was my birthname." "Oh My God,
I can't believe it, Shirley Temple - Shirley Temple,"
he said.

That apparently was my childhood nickname.
When I was home with them, I sang and danced mimicking
Shirley Temple.   I had the ringlets and all.   My
brother George became incredibly excited, as he knew
it had to be me, a middle name like Eunice was not
very common. His associates who worked in the dining
hall with him became very excited for him, as fifty
years had passed us by. They could not believe their
ears.

George said, "The reason I never returned your
call was that a woman by the last name of Westcott
worked at Harvard, borrowed items from me and never
returned them." He thought I was she, calling to
borrow again.

Once I found my brother George, the excitement
really began, because he knew addresses and telephone
numbers of most of my siblings. I never dreamed,
fifty years later, I would discover I had fourteen
siblings. My search found that seven of my siblings
have been in contact with each other, four passed
away at birth, two died later in life, one I have
not found yet, and myself which made fifteen children
my mother gave birth to. She had four sets of twins.
Unbelievable to me. The childhood longing that gnawed
at me throughout my adult life was finally fulfilled
after several years of frustrated efforts to tie
together separated bloodlines.

After this phone call, I spoke on the phone
to each of my other brothers and sisters. I was
incredibly excited and it felt good to know I
accomplished finding my siblings. I was amazed at
the things they remembered about me, being together
but a short time. It was at this time my hysterectomy
was scheduled and I needed to wait to meet my new
found family, until after my surgery. For a very
brief moment I thought, "People do die of surgery
- maybe this is it - since I have accomplished finding
my family." At the same time while recuperating
in the recovery room the thought never entered my
mind that I might have cancer. I was therefore shocked
when I received good news from my smiling doctor
that their was no cancer found. I then made
arrangements to meet with my siblings. All kinds

of questions entered my head. What was it really
like for each of them as they grew up without our
mom? Where did they live? What type of schools,
churches, or work did they do? What were their
experiences of marriage and motherhood?
We all had unique stories to tell and each one
was important to me as we pieced the puzzle together.
They were the only persons who could share this with
me. While we cried and laughed about our lives,
you had better believe my pencil and pad was kept
very busy, as there was so much to remember about
each sibling.

Today, my surviving siblings range in age from
48 - 70 years old. Each encounter we had became
an adventure, each person was a lesson in life.
All were as full of dreams and doubts as I. Each
of us had stories to tell, and I had the time to
listen and the ears to hear.

I often wondered if the man who rung up my
groceries was my brother, or the woman who passed
me on the sidewalk was my sister and now I know.
My mirror is not needed anymore.

Except - I still have one more sister to find
- On my checkpad I had written yr 1940 - vol 28
- pg 165. Again I stood in line and when they found
me the volume and I found her birth certificate and
I had them make me a copy of it, and this became
part of my files. After, I looked up her marriage
certificate, or death certificate occurring after
these years, to no avail. I am still searching.
Later on after speaking to the Department of Social
Services, one of the letters in my file said her
name might have been changed to Patricia. At one
time my records said Mary was living with a service
family. Meanwhile after finding all my other
birthsiblings, they never knew of anyone being born
after me and my twin. Perhaps, she was taken away
from my mother directly from the hospital.

Meanwhile, I have again asked to hear my files,
wondering if I missed hearing something that could
help in my search for Mary.

In such associations as the International Soundex
Reunion Registry, Adoptees' Liberty Movement
Association, and Today Reunites Yesterday it still
reads: F-Ad'ee searching for F-sibling
            NAB   Mary Westcott
            POB   Boston
            DOB   9/27/40
   Mother: Mary Estella (Hamblen) Westcott
   Father: Alfred Westcott
         Contact   me   if   found.

Reunion

In November 1988 attired in a navy pant outfit
as I did not know what to wear to meet my oldest
sister <u>Anne Marie</u> and my brother in law Nicholas
for the first time) my husband and I boarded the
airplane to Florida. Just before landing, I felt
nervous excitement that made my skin tingle for Michel
and I were to spend time celebrating their 50th
wedding anniversary and our reunion after fifty years.
We were very emotional as we cried, hugged, studied
each other's faces, seeing a resemblance to one
another. <u>Pearl Mary</u> was Anne's twin and Anne said,
"If I didn't know any better I would think you were
my twin who died at birth." Anne was 4ft 11in, fair
skinned, and very soft spoken.

As we looked in the mirror standing side by
side, Anne kept saying, "We look alike! I can't
believe it. I'm shocked you found us!"

After fifteen years of marriage Anne and Nick
waited to adopt Gregory Joseph and Nicole Anne, later
becoming grandparents of four.

I will always treasure a metal based Pyrex glass
domed 9" Elgin anniversary clock which strikes hourly
Westminster chimes which I surprisingly received
from them shortly after my search for my family.

<u>Gladys Cora</u> is taller than most of us and seems
to be the caretaker. When we met we cried, hugged
and just kept hugging.

Gladys married George and conceived a girl she
named Judith Anne and later became a grandmother
of two.

My sister has mastered the art of embroidery
and made me a pillow embellished with a raccoon who
is surrounded by a butterfly and flowers.

Gladys and my sister Hermina spent their
childhood together and now, without husbands, they
are sharing their lives together again.

<u>Hermina Marion</u> rather short and chubby with
a loud voice enjoys her sister caring for her. As
we met she nervously smoked up a storm as she cried
and cried of happiness. She married my sister Muriel
Estella's husband's brother. Therefore two sisters
married two brothers. Muriel passed away before I
found my family.

In Hermina and Walter's twenty-fifth year of
happily married life, Walter passed away of a heart

attack. Shortly after she and my sister Gladys joined
to share a smoke-free apartment together. They roam
around downtown, sit in the park and speak in
friendliness to all who pass them by.

Hermina shaded and contrasted different colors
into a pillow of cross-stitch for me to enjoy.

<u>Alfred Raymond</u> was born a twin named after
our father. He was drafted in the army serving under
General George Patton in Europe. Just eighteen years
old he died as he served in combat in 1944. Buried
in the American cemetery in France, Mom later had
his body shipped home and buried in Mt. Hope Cemetery
in the Hyde Park section of Boston.

Among his possessions was a picture of me at
age three and a picture of Shirley Temple with my
name written across the picture. Now, I have in my
possession not only those pictures but his 5 X $9\frac{1}{2}$
foot burial flag with its 48 stars. This was used
during Alfred's burial service, as a token of sympathy
and appreciation from our grateful nation.

<u>Walter George</u> named after one of our uncles
was Alfred Raymond's twin. Neither twins married.
Walter never made the service because of his medical
condition. Most of his life he was very skinny and
frail. He never marched in the infantry, rode in
the cavalry, shot in the artillery, never flew over
the enemy, but he is in the Lord's army now, yes
sir, he is in the Lord's army now!

He was an artist with most of his works of
landscapes of country and ocean scenes, perhaps he
wished he was there.

People who knew he lived in a little yellow
Volkswagon underneath the stadium of Fenway park
sometimes gave him money. He had to decide whether
to buy a quart of milk or a bottle of port.

I wonder if or how many times I might have just
seen my brother as he slept on a park bench or a
sidewalk grate, or huddled in a doorway in the city,
and I unknowingly passed him by.

Though I only knew him for two brief years,
I sensed a great loss in his passing. At his funeral
was sung The Old Rugged Cross a favorite of the
Salvation Army as well as Walter's favorite song.

As we visited his grave-site, George said, "Poor
Walter, no-one really understood him."

<u>George Wesley</u> was named after my Uncle George
Hamblen. He is robust, gregarious, broad-shouldered,
with a quick-smile, soft spoken, sensitive, and he
chose his words carefully.

While growing up, a foster home was found for
George. At seventeen George left this home to strike

out on his own to find new adventure in New York
City. Here he became a "Hoofer" dancer that is in
"Look Ma I'm Dancing," "High Button Shoes,"
"Oklahoma," "Bloomer Girls," and "Student Prince."
He said, "Dancing was the most immediate and
accessible of the arts, for me because it involved
my own body. It's the art of time and space, and
that is what our universe is about."

George joined the paratroopers and after serving
his time decided to be a cook and went to the Culinary
Institute of America in Hyde Park, New York. He
retired from Harvard in food management and it is
there I found him.

My husband and I drove to Everett to visit with
my brother for the first time. We held each other
for a long time and found it hard to believe we were
together again.

Once George accompanied us on a visit to Paris,
France. On our flight home to the United States he
expressed again how he never, never expected to see
the arts in the Louvre. This was the fulfillment
of a dream he thought could never be fulfilled.
After this trip George gave me a one foot high statue
of Victory of Samothrace, which is my Business and
Professional Woman's Club symbol. I will treasure
this wonderful gift from my newly-found brother for
years to come.

George resides in a lovely home with his backyard
filled with perennials, the result of much time he
spends as he cultivates and weeds; his garden rarely
has a weed. This garden is both physical and healing
to him, providing a sanctuary of strength and beauty,
better than any vitamins could ever provide.

<u>Lillian Blanche</u> is blond, cheerful, easy going
and shy. When I contacted her for the first time
she responded, "I knew my baby sister would find
us, I knew my baby sister would find us." As we
looked in the mirror side by side she touched my
hair and said, "When you were a child I combed your
hair into ringlets, and put bows in your hair, making
you look like little Shirley Temple."

Today after married for over 35 years Lillian
and Robert have four children, Barbara Anne, Donna
Marie, named after me, Robert Ethan III, and Richard
Alfred. Lillian and I in the early 60's both named
one of our children, Donna. They have six beautiful
grandchildren.

Lillian has given me a treasure - our
birthmother's mothers ring of 14K gold with five
stones around it. Despite giving birth to fifteen
children my birthmother never used all of the months

of the year.

"Why did it take you so long to find us?" Then
a little laugh follows, almost like a chuckle. She
wished I had found her sooner.

No name twins followed. I wondered were the
minutes time enough for Mother to hold them, hear
them cry, or press them to her breast to quiet them?
We babies were born in a time when newborn loss was
not acknowledged as the tragedy it really is.

Roger Williams was named after the founder of
Rhode Island who was a distant relative of ours.
We re-united with hugs and tears, after 50 years
of separation. When I phoned Roger awkward pauses
and laughter interrupted our conversation. Roger
is of thin build, blue eyes, fast moving, and somewhat
shy.

When I was four and Roger was nine we were driven
by the social workers to the western part of
Massachusetts. Roger was dropped off on a farm in
Amherst and I to an apartment house in Easthampton.
Roger said, "You cried during the trip wanting to
stay with me when I was dropped off."

On Roger's way to work with the clinky clink
of the streetcar he met his sweetheart Patricia,
a licensed practical nurse at a nearby hospital.
They married and conceived Roger David, David Charles,
and John Albert.

Their latest son John Albert was born retarded.
He needed more care then they could possibly provide,
they sent him to a special school in the Berkshires,
picking him up on weekends to be home with them.
John was found dead, and his loving and caring parents
Roger and Pat, were deeply hurt by this.

We caught up on the past fifty years of our
lives aboard America's most entertaining harbor cruise
ship called, The Spirit of Boston. Here we had a
wonderful clambake lunch, live band played songs
from the 40's to the present, and a rousing Salute-
to-Broadway revue.

Roger and Pat gave us a lovely marble-based
desk pen set with our names inscribed on it. I will
treasure this gift forever.

And then there was me, Marie Eunice, my twin
Mary Unite who died at birth and Mary Patricia to
be found.

I was an adoptee in constant reunion. They
kept hugging, feeding, telling, showing and giving
me memories and special items for me to treasure.
Finding my siblings at the peak of the Holiday Season,
was one of the best gifts I could have been given
in my lifetime.

Birthparents

My birth-father, Alfred Westcott was born in 1891 in Bohemia, Germany. Sometimes my birth name was spelled with one "t" instead of two, or a "t" left out in the middle of our name. Westcott which means Western Cottage, was my birth name, spelled Westcott or Wescott on some birth certificates of my siblings. On my birth parents' certificate of marriage, on September 14, 1919, my father's name reads Alfred Wescott. He was 30 years old at the time of his marriage and lived in Cambridge. This was his first marriage, and at that time he was a sheet-metal worker.

His father Anton Westcott (Wasa - Waska - Wosca) and his mother Wilkelmina Shoenauer were born in Germany.

Making a trip to Ellis Island, I looked out at the Atlantic and realized, my grandfather and his family were able to make the ocean crossing in a steam powered ship which replaced the sailing vessels, cutting the time from three months to two weeks. His voyage was taken some time after 1891. This cut in time had to have been wonderful because they slept in long narrow compartments jammed with metal-framed berths, three bunks high. The air ranked with heavy odor of spoiled food, sea sickness, and unwashed bodies.

Awed, I entered the French Renaissance exterior of brick and limestone. The main building of Ellis Island with the glass canopy was a grand gesture, not intimidating emotions my grandfather might have felt when he arrived with his family on the American shores. Ellis Island was an Isle of Hope, a brief stopping point on the way to a better life. To an unfortunate few, it became an Isle of Tears.

After my grandfather's trans Atlantic journey from the steamship to a ferry, to an inspection line amongst the thousands of immigrants that day, he climbed the steep slate stairs to the great 56 foot high ceiling registry room, the principal way-station for all immigrants. His name was passed from a steamship manifest to an inspector's record book at Ellis Island. In my research I found most German names were derived from occupations, colors or locations. Names were spelled differently hundreds of years ago, because of language changes, carelessness and a high degree of illiteracy. Fortunately my grandfather, as an immigrant, convinced the legal inspectors that he was strong, intelligent, and resourceful enough to find work easily.

After inspection my grandfather descended from the Registry Room, down the Stairs of Separation, so called because they marked the parting of the way for many family and friends with different destinations. I hope my grandfather, bound for Manhattan, met relatives or friends at the "kissing post," where many joyous and tearful reunions occurred. At some point later my father made his journey to Boston, Massachusetts.

It seemed our father was in and out of our life often. On each and everyone of our birth certificates, our same mom and dad names appeared. My father's occupations in an eighteen year span, were listed on our birth certificates in order, as follows, as each baby was born: Chemical Engineer for Boston Rubber Hose, machinist, laborer, foreman, rubber worker, Woven Hose Employee, and a cabinetmaker. My brothers and sisters did not have any kind of relationship with him.

In my court files it states that my father died of a heart attack in 1939 (the year I was born). He was 48. At time of death he was living on 52nd - Broadway, New York City. I contacted New York City to have a copy of his death certificate. They said there was none. Another story was that it was war time and since he was not a citizen he might have gone underground, so as not to be sent back to Germany. If I found my father at this time, he would have been ninety-seven years old. That is why I started my search for my siblings, first.

My birth-mother, Mary Estella Hamblen, was born on February 24, 1901 in Pawtucket, Rhode Island. She married at age eighteen to Alfred Westcott, who was 10 years older. Birth-siblings of mine say Mom was about 4' 11" had dark brown hair, hazel eyes, friendly, loving, great sense of humor, slow moving, but she had a temper. Her discipline consisted of wacking and hitting. She never went to bars or drank but was a chain smoker. My birth-siblings spoke well of my mom. She worked in a paper box factory before marrying and later as a housemaid at the Statler Hotel in Boston Park Square, where Park Plaza is now.

Fifteen of us were born, ten girls and five boys, four sets of twins, including several who did not survive infancy. Mom had sixteen grandchildren. She was a widow, single mom, who had little money,

few skills and many mouths to feed. She became
worn-out by the struggle.

Many thoughts entered my mind, such as, she
knew how to conceive but not care for her off-spring.
Maybe the physicians who delivered these babies
should have given guidance to her. Maybe he did
and she did not hear.

When interviewing my siblings I was told life
was not easy while they were growing up. Each time
my mom became pregnant, one could hardly tell she
was bearing a child. Each newborn suffered from
our mom's self-deprivation. Bed rest and proper
nutrition were impossible as she carried luggage
and toddlers from place to place. My siblings said:
"When the landlords did not want our family living
in their apartments anymore they started harassing,
saying vulgar things to us kids. Sometimes we acted
back calling the landlord names like witch and bitch.
Packing began again taking our most valuable things
with us, and one time, the next morning we went
back to get our bunk beds and the door was locked.
The landlord broke items of ours, that were still
there. We knocked on the door and the landlord cursed
at us, and dialed the police, so we just got out
of there in a hurry."

"They never knew when my mom was pregnant,"
they said, "she carried babies well. It seemed each
time a baby was born, it was time to move again.
Money was an issue, our rent was low and the landlord
brought it up higher. We could not pay it and we
asked the landlord, 'To lower our rent' and he angrily
said, 'No, you gotta pay what the rent says.' We
became scared and thought he might hurt us because
he was so angry, so we left."

Our source of income was bad and Ma did not
know what to do. Sometimes the welfare case was closed
and had to be re-opened. Ma was not always capable
of filling those papers in again and again. Perhaps
she was illiterate, sick, or depressed.

My siblings story of moving as each new baby
was to arrive, proved to be right in my search, as
our birth certificates listed place of residence
as follows:

```
Anne     Marie    twins         28  Decantor Street
Pearl                                            Mary
Gladys   Cora                     47  Portland  Street
Muriel       Estella             75  Washington Street
Hermina  Marion                  13  Washington Street
Alfred   Raymond      twins       42  Portland  Street
Walter       George
```

George	Wesley			242	Broadway	Street
Lillian	Blanche			650	Concord	Avenue
no	name	twins		47	Portland	Street
Roger	Williams				Woodlawn	Street
Marie	Eunice	twins	me	350	Armory	Street
Mary						Unite
Mary	Patricia			43	Fort	Avenue

I was Ma's 13th child.

One memory I have of where I lived is when I was asked in school to draw a picture of the house I was born in. I drew a house with six peaks, four doors and lots of windows. My teacher wrote: "This is not a house," across the top of my picture. When I got home my adopted mother was furious with me and I received a punishment. She did not want me to remember my past. Years later when I took a ride with my brother George to view the apartments I had lived in, it was in a very poor Boston neighborhood, a row of apartments. This was my creativeness as a child, drawing my own vision of truth.

On the day I was adopted at eight years of age, a memory in which I saw for the first and last time my birth-mother, who seemed very stout to me, head down, slowly walking away. I remember none of my siblings, I was only four years old when I became a ward of the state.

In 1943 the day came when our mom sat us all down and told us what had to be done. We would be put in the hands of the state of Massachusetts, until she could find us an apartment with heat and hot water and a place to rest our heads. "It would be best for all of us," she said.

My siblings remember the day, as the Prevention of Children took our portrait and it was put on a poster and placed on a billboard at the post office in Boston, Massachusetts. They thought the portrait came out pretty good despite all the tears and movement of all of us children.

In the same year I was adopted, Mom remarried a man by the name of John Blakely in November 1947. Everyone says he was wonderful to her and he and my mom took most of us back home to live with them. Not I, as I had been adopted. Our stepfather was a roofer and after only a few years he fell off a roof and died. My mother and siblings were devastated. They had grown to love him very much.

My birth-mother's father, Fred A. Hamblen, was born in 1875. A Yankee, of Indian blood, very tall and thin, he was an artist and a sheet metal worker. Her mother, Annie Williams, was born the same year,

in Yorkshire, England. She was a very short, stout
woman. She was related to Roger Williams, who founded
Rhode Island. Fred and Annie had six children:
Walter, George, Muriel, Cora, Gladys, and Mary,
my birthmother. They had many grandchildren and
great grandchildren.

It seemed my mother loved her family, since
she named her first child after her mother, and each
child after was named, after one of our relatives.
I was told Aunt Cora and Muriel tried to help us,
but they had their own families to take care of.
Grandma Hamblen, our mom's mother, lived close by
most of the time and seemed to hold us together.
When Grandma passed away in 1935, Ma gave up and
had increasing difficulty coping with her grief.
Grandpa Hamblen must have passed away while most
of my siblings were very young, because they do not
remember much about him.

Aunt Cora was born July 3, 1904 our only living
aunt at my time of search in 1988. She married Joseph
on June 28, 1927 and had one child, named Virginia.
At age 85 when I first spoke with her, she did not
want to re-live the past, rekindling unpleasant and
distressful memories of my family. At first Aunt
Cora did not want to see me, but when I persisted,
my husband and I visited her in her lovely home.
She gave us big hugs, not hugs like someone not
wanting to see us. I was extremely happy with her
greeting. Aunt Cora had a lively brightness and
amazing crinkles as she spoke lovingly of my uncle
Joseph and reminiscing about her long and eventful
life. She savored the extraordinary moments of raising
her daughter Jennie and now enjoying her granddaughter
Marianne.

She was moving into another house with her
daughter Jennie and was in the process of going
through her old pictures. She had in her possession,
and gave to me, the picture of me at age three, which
was sent home from Europe after my brother was killed
in action. My brother Alfred had this picture of
me in his wallet and my aunt thought I might like
it, especially knowing that he carried it with him
in the service.

Aunt Cora was sharp enough to know she needed
care and did not want to burden her daughter Jenny.
She entered a nursing home five miles away from
her daughter's home.

Our mom became very sick in 1974 and went to
live with my brother Roger and his wife Pat.
Eventually they had to put our mom in the Faulker
Hospital. She had cancer of the lymph nodes. She

asked Roger and Pat not to let her suffer and soon
after the oxygen and I.V. was not enough, she passed
away   January 23, 1976 at age 75. (This was the
same year I divorced my first husband, twelve years
before finding my siblings.)   She is buried at Mt.
Hope cemetery in Roxbury, Massachusetts.

My birth-siblings and I reminisced about our
mother and they most willingly shared photos of
earlier times in their lives. They gave me our
Mother's mothers ring which consists of five stones.
She had fifteen children using only the months of
February, May, June, August and October. This was
nice to be able to touch and wear something belonging
to my birth-mother, helping me strengthen the lost
tie and easing the pain.

My brother Roger and I visited her grave.
I cried out my feelings, mourning the relationship
that never was and now could never be. You may not
be able to understand why I mourned a stranger.
She was a birth-mother to me, not a stranger, so
I hurt and regret forever that I did not begin my
search twelve years earlier.

The following poem gives you an example of what
was handed down from my ancestors.

THE LEGACY OF AN ADOPTED CHILD
        Once there were two women
        Who never knew each other.
        One you do not remember,
        The other you call Mother.

        Two different lives
          shaped to make yours one;
        One became your guiding star,
        The other became your sun.

        The first gave you Life,
        The second taught you to live in it.
        The first gave you a need for love,
        The second was there to give it.

        One gave you a nationality,
        The other gave you a name.
        One gave you the seed of talent,
        The other gave you an aim.

        One gave you emotions,
        The other calmed your fears.
        One saw your first sweet smile,
        The other dried your tears.

        One gave you up;

It was all that she could do.
The other prayed for a child,
And God led her straight to you.

And now you ask me through your tears,
  The age-old questions through the years;
Heredity or environment...which are you
  the product of?

Neither, my darling, neither;
  just two different kinds of love.

Author unknown

Finding my siblings at the peak of the holiday season of 1988 was the best gift I had ever been given. When I walk down the street in my small town with one of my siblings, I see someone I know and I say, "This is my real, sibling." Those that do not know me and overhear, look at me like I am crazy, but I was never able to say that before. It feels so good.

I found that all my siblings have an enormous capacity for life, and I gained immediate acceptance from all. My birth brothers and sisters and I, have a lot of catching up to do, piecing together memories, getting to know one another, and I believe God played a big part in our reunion. HE truly does work in mysterious ways. I feel we are just starting history. We have laughed, cried and hugged, knowing deep in our hearts we will never be separated again.

Mother   Mom
Once there were 2 woman who never knew each other

I visited Mom's grave - cried out my feelings
mourning the relationship that never was
and now could never be

Rusty Knife

Christmas of 1994 Laurence, my step-daughter, gave Michel a beautiful ivory handled French knife called Laguiole-Arealete, as a present. This French knife is used by the head of a French household, so it has a special meaning between father and daughter. The following summer when Laurence came from France on a visit, Michel showed her his new knife which, somehow had changed color, with an almost rusty look. Michel asked Laurence to exchange the knife, knowing the cutlery shop always stood behind their product. He knew it was a very expensive knife and a warranty would be there.

When we arrived in France, Laurence had not yet exchanged the knife. She felt intimidated to do so since she is a young woman. Michel was to ski with his brother the following day and said, "On my way home from skiing I will exchange my knife." After skiing all day, he met some of his friends and it became too late to exchange his knife that evening.

The following day Michel said, "Lets go shopping today at the mall and I can exchange my knife at the same time." Into the cutlery shop we went to exchange his knife. While Michel was discussing the knife problem with the manager, a salesman was standing nearby waiting to finish his sales presentation with the manager. While he was waiting he kept glancing at me and smiling. Finally I smiled back and he started to walk towards me.

As he came closer he said, "Pardon me for staring, but you look so much like my wife, Pat." At that time Michel turned to see who I was speaking to. Michel was wearing a cap imprinted with Massachusetts. The salesman said "Boston, Massachusetts?"

I said, "No Easthampton," and he exclaimed, "Oh, my God my wife Pat is from Northampton, (only five miles away) she won't believe this!" Grabbing my arm he said, "Come, come with me, there is a phone in McDonalds, and I will call my Pat immediately."

Hurriedly we went to the phone around the corner. He dialed his phone number and unbelievably, he handed me the phone. I said, "Hello, I'm Marie from USA - Easthampton, Mass and have met your husband here at the Mall while we were shopping."

She was so excited, stating it was wonderful to hear someone speaking her language and especially someone from a neighboring town. "Let's have dinner together this evening," she exclaimed.

We delightedly agreed and phoned Laurence to tell her not to expect us for dinner. We explained why and she said, "Leave it to my father to find someone on the street and join them for dinner."

Excitedly, we continued to shop and met Constant and Pat at a nearby Chinese restaurant in the mall.

We met with great hugs and kisses on each cheek (as is the custom in France) already feeling close. Pat and I were wearing the same blue colored (our favorite color) long sweaters and black stretch pants. Our height and weight, hair color and length the same. We were both wearing black and gold rimmed eye glasses and we each wore pearl earrings. Our husbands are both of French descent, and we woman are both Americans.

Constant keep saying, "This is incredible, see - see I told you Michel, my Pat looks like your Marie, their mannerism and smile is totally incredible! I can't believe this, I just can't."

"We have been traveling to France for sixteen years and never met anyone from New England, let alone Western Massachusetts," Michel said.

In between bites of dinner, which I ate very little of, I found myself glancing, peeping, and staring at Pat. She shared her middle name with me: Marie. My mother used Mary and Marie many times when naming us children.

All of a sudden my mind began to wonder and it took me a little while to realize that Pat could be the sister I was searching for. I glanced at Michel sitting beside me and I said to Pat, "What's your name again? Patricia Marie? Were you adopted? Are you sure your not my sister?"

"I wondered when you would start wondering," Michel said.

Pat started to laugh and said, "I don't believe I was adopted, but now I surely will ask some questions of my family."

The reason I was having a difficult time finding my last sister, Mary Westcott (whose first name was changed to Patricia according to my state file), was the family she was living with as a child, were armed service people who were transferred from state to state. Pat's father was Colonel LaValley, from Northampton. However her birthdate was not September 27, 1940 and she was not born in Roxbury,

Massachusetts.

A few days later, Constants and Pat invited us to their home for Rocklette, a French specialty of melted cheeses. Barking at us as we entered her home was her white poodle. My white poodle died a few years earlier.

Meanwhile, Pat called her relatives in the U S A and asked if she might possibly have been adopted. (In the forties adoption was kept very secret.) The answer from her family in U S A was, I do not believe anyone one of us were adopted. Although her mother and father were both remarried with children on both sides joined together to make a blended family. Both of Pat's parents are deceased. Pat's dad Col. LaValley has an army post and a street named after him in Northampton, Massachusetts.

Pat searched for her St. Michaels high school year book and we found friends and acquaintances I had in my grade school were the same friends and acquaintances Pat had in her high school years. Also, my former husband graduated from St. Michaels, a few years before Pat. (Back then grade school children, when wanting to attend a Catholic High School, needed to go to St. Michaels in Northampton.) Therefore Pat and I had never met because I attended public Easthampton High School.

We found we were married in the same church by the same Father Crowley. Both of us divorced an American husband. Also, my former husband John LaBarge and Pat's LaValley family are related by marriage.

What were the odds of something like this happening? If Michel's daughter had returned the knife or he and his brother returned the knife after skiing, we never would have met.

A knife usually means violence, in my case friendship! Pat and I both remember and speak of our good findings to our relatives and friends who become astonished hearing of the eighteen similar happenings in our lives, and we know we will always be special friends.

I was disappointed not finding Pat to be my sister. We formed a bond together that was real special, and look forward to seeing each other every six months when Michel and I return to France.

My sister - ?
Our friends in France
Constant - Michel - Me - Pat

Me and my Dutchess Daisy
of Dover clinbing the Alps

Epiloque

Reviewing my life is valuable in that it helps me to maintain my self esteem and gives me a sense of identity. I gained by reminiscing and writing my personal history, which puts a sense of perspective on my life. Remembering and recreating my main events helped me to put my story into a meaningful framework. Starting my book with my Mother and ending with my Mom.

Everybody's life is a story filled with facts, feelings and issues, but mine is a double heritage, born to one set of parents, given up for adoption in the year of 1947, and raised by a widow.

My household was like an earthquake quivering and shaking without warning. I lived a dramatic life piecing together details of abuse that no one should ever experience.

Child abuse, does not only occur where poverty and ignorance are factors. These adults were perceived by the community as ones who served the public by taking in state wards.

I knew I was helpless and powerless, but I also knew Mother loved me. Being adopted (the chosen one) was not an easy task. I lived and breathed to please my adopted mother and sister, but most often not successful.

I never wanted to give up on my adopted family. I tried to stay in touch, talked on the telephone, tried not to judge. I wanted to connect as one adult to another, not as a child to a parent. Confusion set in, probably because everything about their life, present and past, was a jumble to me. Throughout my life this gave me discomfort.

In the sixties I conceived three lovely daughters within four years. I loved them before I knew how they would love me, who they would become, and even what they might do to hurt me as they grew up.

As they took off 8-9-10 steps to the wide world beyond, I captured the belly-laughs of my toddlers knowing that the magical vision of a child was discovered in me.

My occupation, hobby, and vocation was motherhood. I was determined that my girls have everything physically and emotionally, making up for what, as a child, I did not have.

My first husband was threatened by an addiction. A disease he tried desperately to deny deep inside him. He chose the bottle and I chose life.

With teen girls the entire house was filled with adornment, I thought, until my first born ran away.

Issues going on in my life at this time brought me to AlAnon. My tattered AL-Anon book, should be required reading for all human beings, as it provides a guide for everyday living, a wholesome environment for the whole family including the alcoholic.

At the time of my divorce, taking charge of my own life and my teen-agers was tough financially and emotionally. In time, the cause of the break-up became history and the effects it has on everyone became the real issue. Eventually my children saw they could love their father and still love me.

I applied the very expensive dating service bill with my charge card, not knowing it would be eventually paid by Michel, the man of my dreams.

Michel and I had many great experiences running our own bakery. One did not even have to leave their car to smell the aromas of fresh baked goods that drifted out to greet them.

B P W stands for Business and Professional Women's Club where I was president of a local chapter. Using BPW's tools in a positive way and getting involved in BPW was an education for me.

Living and working in another country for a short period of time, fitting in exhausting trips and hikes, leaves me exhilarated and filled with wonder.

Grandchildren are the dots that connect the lines from generation to generation and I as a grandparent can help shape their sense of themselves.

Coping with death of our loved ones was emotional experiences, as we each are unique and have different personal feelings about what's to come.

Surviving the intensity of the search of my birth-siblings, I became more excited as time got closer and closer to touching and mirroring someone who looked like me.

All my joys and sorrows within the range of my human emotions characterized the reunion experience for me as an adoptee. I looked for missing pieces, looked for feelings that seemed impossible to describe.

When my brother Roger and I visited Mom's grave, I cried out my feelings, mourning the relationship that never was and now could never be.

Exchanging a rusty knife formed a bond that

was real special, even if it was another dead-end
to finding my latest sister Mary (Patricia) Westcott.

Let me speculate on my future beyond my story.
My daughters and I most certainly desire a
reunion with our Deborah. My grieving goes on and
on with all kinds of feelings. Sometimes I am not
sure what my feelings are. I do know that she was
conceived and raised out of love. We hope sometime
this will be possible and probable, when and under
what circumstances is still a mystery. As we often
say, maybe we have to wait until she is ready to
want to be amongst us.
It would be great to have a knock at the door
renewing an undying hope that a hug will be shared
with a daughter and two grandchildren whom I have
never seen.
My happiness is a direct result of positive
emotional attachment to others. Now that I am older
I begin by looking over my shoulder, down my arms,
into my own hands at what I am holding and what I
know can be passed on. Letting my children and their
children know they will make mistakes along the way,
but try never to stop trusting your intuitions.
My mature grandchildren know there are many ways,
many solutions, and many conclusions. Just remember,
imagine, wish, wonder and want. Remembering to give
to others the best of yourself and it will return
in three folds. What is going on inside us is
revealed by what we are showing outside. Whatever
the complexities of my life, I can achieve a joyous
and loving bond with my children, my children's
children and in all probability the experience and
pleasure of great-grandchildren ahead of me.
In finding my birth family, I know now, I did
not need to feel ashamed of my feelings or desire
to know my identity, not excepting being cut off
from any part of myself. It is too bad my mother
did not have a choice and had open adoption, because
she could have used some comfort, care, respect,
and peace of mind. She must have suffered a lot,
alone in her seventy-five years of life. I balance
my needs with my siblings, visit them, acknowledge
holidays and birthdays and write an occasional letter
to keep in touch. Hopefully I have helped develop
relationships which will fasten the feelings of
extended family - never to be as separated as we
were when we were children.
I feel I have taken the best from each female
parent. The Mom I did not remember, and the one
I called Mother.

As a member of TRY (Today Reunites Yesterday) a support and educational group for birthparents, adoptees and adoptive parents, in the future my experience gives me the impetus to see what I can do to help others who "need to know" and have a "right to search, promoting open adoption."

I am a needleworker, stitching 20 X 24 pieces and smaller sizes on canvas artistically creating beautiful needlework designs with an easy yet fascinating stitch. Elsa Williams created beautiful Bargello designs which I have used for potholders, footstools, pillows and ects. I hated the endless nights I needed to learn, with Mother and her angry face at my side, Erica Wilson's crewel embroidery. It sure was (crewel) to me at this time. Thank God I learned all the wide choices of stitches, from simplest ones to split, buttonhole, braid, rope, couching, rosette, zigzag, herringbone and fishbone. I really enjoy the teachings of my mother now in my life. I hope to pass on this talent to my children, grandchildren and great grandchildren. I was delighted to find I have a brother with the same hand-skills as mine.

One year I was employed by Intercultural Friendships, one of the largest student exchange organizations, as a coordinator. I found host families, special people, to open their homes to French students to share their cultures and way of life. I organized trips to Boston and New York City as well as day trips here in Western Mass. On the last weekend we organized a camping trip in Vermont, hiking and tubing down the river. Our teens in U S and France gathered around the camp fire reminiscing about their fulfilled dream of coming to America.

Having my own business, I utilized all my skills learned in my past business experiences.

I then went on to work for a mobile National Pictorial Church Directory Publisher. This directory was used as a ministry tool for churches of all denominations. As a Portrait Consultant I show the parishioners their family portrait on a Video Image moments after being photographed. Different finishes and special pricing options was available to them, handling around twenty customers a day. After being on the road servicing the New England area for many years, I decided to work in a portrait studio nearby. I became manager and a certified professional photographer, playing-teasing, having fun with children and babies to create the best portrait for the mom and dad.

My newest career challenge is as a certified
DOULA (doolah). Bet you don't know what that is?
Don't bother to look it up in the dictionary or your
word processor for it is not listed as yet. A doula
is a woman experienced in childbirth who provides
continuous physical, emotional and informational
support to the mother and family before, during and
after childbirth and during the first week at home
with the new baby. This service is provided by some
H M O's.

The birth of a woman's first child has an
enormous lifelong impact on her, and her mental health
or psychological transformation to motherhood. We
aim to have women remember their birth experiences
with joy, pride and a sense of accomplishment.

As a prenatal doula I am able to provide
childbirth education in your home when bedrest is
required of the mom, or when you are unable to attend
traditional childbirth classes.

As a certified labor support doula, trained
in non-medical labor assistance, I bring the couple
closer by making sure the couples' needs are met.
I allow the couple to participate at their comfort
level suggesting simple but useful tasks. I ensure
them that their birth plan is acknowledged and
followed as close as possible, especially when labor
is intense and things are happening rapidly. I help
with decision making by asking questions that will
ensure the right information is given to all of us.
I am there solely for the emotional well-being of
the woman. Nurses, doctors, midwives have other
patients, clinical responsibilities, hospital
policies to follow and will be in and out of your
birthroom. As your doula I am continuously present
where you can see, feel, and hear me. The combined
contributions of partner, doula, along with
competent considerate and caring staff gives the
woman the best chance for the birth experience to
be as rewarding and satisfying as possible.

As a postpartum doula I provide emotional
support, nurturing and practical help with your baby,
your home and your adjustment to a new life. In
your home we will discuss your birth experience,
help you bond with your newborn and answer any
questions you might have. We will want to be sure
you are getting enough rest, liquids, nourishment
and suggest ways to avoid feelings of isolation.
Suggest different ways of breastfeeding, being sure
baby is wetting enough and taking enough nourishment.
Demonstrate bathing and message of infant. Calm infant
so mom can take a long shower or nap. We go grocery

shopping or prepare meals for the next few days.

This is a perfect gift for a person whom you love - a helping hand from a doula service. This giving of myself as my newest career I know will be extremely rewarding.

Hanging out with my teen grandchildren in their bedroom, they had a vision. Troy a physiotherapist, Sports Physical Therapist. Trin a masseuse, Massage Therapist. Grandma a mothering support, certified doula. Mom accountant, examining our accounts. Trisha, giving advice, a lawyer pulling us all together in one big complex!

My family, faith, health, personal strengths of being organized and patient have helped me through life. My self education has led me to a fantasy of someday receiving a college degree.

Adaptability, survival, search for self, educational drive and that old fashioned American dream, "I bet I could do that" brings me to be a published author writing you, my autobiography.

Putting my feelings on display, I hope can help others.

My calendar will remain full of activities. Michel and I have a happy relationship because we respect and accept our differences. Together we enjoy our flower garden, hikes in the mountains, and every chance to travel in both countries.

As we approach the millennium, a period of peace and happiness, I am not worried for I am married to a wonderful man, my friend, have my happiness, self respect, and I believe the future is whatever I want it to be.

About the Author

Marie Eunice Shirley Westcott Pratt LaBarge Fiat

born in Boston, Massachusetts
grew up, married and raised three daughters
in Easthampton, Massachusetts

Still reside in this "cupcake valley"
with my husband Michel.

I'm SIXTY.

ORDER   FORM

Please complete and
mail this form with
    payment to:

Cupcake Valley Press
    P O Box 634
Easthampton MA 01027

        Title
   DOUBLE HERITAGE
My Life In Two Worlds

     224 Pages
   20 Photographs

     $14.95
3 or more $12.95

Shipping & handling
 $3.00 first book
50¢ each additional

Payment Enclosed:
_____Check
_____Money Order

Ship to:
Name_____

Address_____

City_____

State_____Zip_____

Phone_____

Thanks in advance
 for your order